D1598914

# No Monopoly on Suffering

# No Monopoly on Suffering

## Blacks and Jews in Crown Heights (And Elsewhere)

### Reverend
### Herbert D. Daughtry, Sr.

## Africa World Press, Inc.

P.O. Box 1892

Trenton, NJ 08607

P.O. Box 48

Asmara, ERITREA

# Africa World Press, Inc.

P.O. Box 1892
Trenton, NJ 08607

P.O. Box 48
Asmara, ERITREA

Copyright © 1997 Herbert D. Daughtry, Sr.

First Printing 1997

Book and Cover design: Jonathan Gullery

**Library of Congress Cataloging-in-Publication Data**

Daughtry, Herbert.
    No monopoly on suffering : Blacks and Jews in Crown Heights and elsewhere / by Herbert D. Daughtry, Sr.
        p.    cm.
    Includes bibliographical references (p.    ) and index.
    ISBN 0-86543-586-3
    1. Crown Heights (New York, N.Y.)--Race relations.  2. New York (N.Y.)--Race relations.  3. Riots--New York (State)--New York--History--20th century.  4. Afro-Americans--New York (State)--New York--Social conditions.  5. Jews--New York (State)--New York--Social conditions.  6. Afro-Americans--New York (State)--New York--Relations with Jews.  7. Antisemitism--New York (State)--New York--History--20th century.  8. Daughtry, Herbert.  I. Title.
    F128.68.C76D38   1997
    305.8'0097471--dc21                                                  97-7987
                                                                              CIP

# DEDICATION

Dedicated to our fathers and mothers upon whose shoulders
we stand and move forward. And to my grandson, Lorenzo,
symbolic of our future hope, with the prayer that he will carry
on the family tradition of service to the people and struggle
with and for the people.

# Contents

## PART II

### INSIDE THE STORM
### MY ROLE IN CROWN HEIGHTS
### AUGUST 19-26, 1991

## APPENDICES

# Acknowledgements

In this, my first publication by a major publishing house, there are so many people who deserve my deepest gratitude. This book grew out of a movement in which innumerable people were involved; another volume would be required to list them all. I have confined myself to a few, but I know that I have failed to mention someone; I ask their pardon—attribute it to my human frailties and the limitation of space. But the Cosmic Law doesn't forget nor is it confined to space; no good deed, no sacrifice, will go unrewarded.

Where shall I start? First and foremost, I am eternally grateful to Jesus Christ, my Lord and Savior, who picked me up out of the "muck and mire," cleaned me up, and entrusted me with a special mission.

Then, to my family: During the times discussed in this book, much of my time, energy, and concern were given to the struggle; so much time was spent away from home, so many threats on our lives, so many inconveniences, so many demands. Yet they all managed, somehow, to handle it extraordinarily well. They completed their education, and are pursuing their chosen professions; they remain dedicated to the church and to the community.

To Leah, Dartmouth College Class of 1984, without her editorial expertise, mediation skills, computer wizardry, and research experience, this book would not have seen the light of day.

To Sharon, Dartmouth College Class of 1987, for her exuberance and encouragement.

To Dawn, Syracuse University Class of 1989, for her typing and helping others to decipher and interpret my scribbling.

To Herb Jr., University of Chicago Class of 1991, Georgetown Law School Class of 1995, for his wise counsel.

To my wife of thirty-five years, Karen Smith Daughtry, D.Min., for her love, patience, wisdom, advice, endless typing and obsession with detail.

To my only grandchild, Lorenzo Alexander Daughtry-Chambers, "you're the boss, apple sauce," "you're supreme, jelly bean," "you're the most, brown toast," "you're way ahead, rye bread," and "you're the top, apricot."

If, at the beginning of my marriage, I had written the script, it would not have been much better. To God be the glory!

There are no words to express my gratitude to the parishioners of my church, The House of the Lord, "The House," who have allowed me to serve as their pastor for thirty-nine years. Without their unparalleled support I would have known no achievement and therefore there would have been no book. In particular, I want to thank the faithful foursome: Dorothy Isaac, Alicia Jerriho, Robin Renaud, and LaVerne Walker for their tireless typing; Jeffrey Horton, Jean Taylor, and Pearlie Tripp for their research help. Sharman Blake for her word processing and public relations skills, and a super special thanks to Toni Banks who arranged my meeting with Kassahun Checole, Publisher of Africa World Press.

Then, for their love, support and loyalty, I want to thank my community, particularly the members of the African Peoples Christian Organization and the National Black United Front, who gave me great affection and unstinting support during my years as chairperson. Especially I'd like to thank the veterans of the Pan-African, nationalist, radical, revolutionary wing of our struggle who always showed me, a Christian preacher—a profession not highly regarded in their circle—great respect and who were always there to help.

More specifically in that number, I want to thank Sababa Akili, Atchudta Bakr, Safiya Bandele, Amiri Baraka, Dr. Jacob Carruthers, Maulana Karenga, Chokwe Lumumba, Haki

Madhubuti, Jamala Rogers, Segun Shabaka, Michael Simanga, Kwame Ture, Ebora Turner, Dr. B. Wright, and of course the other members of the NBUF gang of five: Ron Herndon, Oba T'Shaka, Jitu Weusi, and Conrad Worrill.

I am forever indebted to William "Bill" Banks who stood beside me and protected me when I took the mic from Mayor-Elect Ed Koch.

I am also grateful to my editor, Patricia Allen, for her patience, counsel, editorial skill and over-all direction.

I would like to mention in particular Dr. Barry Commoner, the Citizens Party Presidential candidate in 1979. Barry was fed the usual smears of my alleged anti-Semitism, but it did not influence him. On a number of occasions we shared the same platform, and I was invited to speak at the last rally of his presidential campaign. During the conflict in the June 12 Rally Committee, I asked Barry to use his influence to mediate the situation, which he did, and should be given substantial credit for the settlement.

Finally, I want to acknowledge all my friends and supporters in the "gorgeous mosaic" that is our world, especially Francesco Canterella, Wilbur Levin, Paul O'Dwyer, Richie Perez, and Mimi Rosenberg, for their long years of friendship and counsel.

# Foreword

Herbert Daughtry is one of the towering prophetic leaders of his generation. Pastor of the world-known House of the Lord Pentecostal Church for nearly forty years, founder and first chairperson of the National Black United Front, and leader of the African Peoples Christian Organization, Rev. Daughtry has touched the lives and inspired the hopes of thousands of people. He certainly has enriched my life—as friend, mentor, comrade, colleague and fellow Christian.

I shall never forget the first time I witnessed his courage and vision. It was on the corner of 125th Street and 5th Avenue in Harlem in 1977. He was leading a march, giving a speech and fusing his fervent Christian witness with radical progressive politics. His profound commitment to overcoming Black suffering was undeniable, and his love for the people was overflowing. I decided to get to know him. By an act of sheer grace and providence, A. G. Miller, a student at Union Theological Seminary (where I then taught) and now a professor at Oberlin College—approached me to give a series of lectures at his place of worship, Rev. Daughtry's church. Little did I know that his invitation would lead to an exciting and enhancing period of nearly ten years of monthly lectures at the House of the Lord. In fact, major parts of my first book, *Prophesy Deliverance! An Afro-American Revolutionary Christianity* (1982), were first heard in Rev. Daughtry's church in Brooklyn. Furthermore, it was the first time I faced the challenge of lecturing (with no notes) to an eager yet weary audience after a long day's work—be it a raining, snowy or sunny day—about Modernity and the problem of evil in America. Under the able leadership of Rev. Daughtry and Charles Barron, Timbuktu School was established.

This grand institution gave free courses by Professors Ivan Van Sertima, John Henrik Clarke, Gayraud Wilmore, James Cone, James Washington, myself and many others. I shall never forget the deep sense of engagement, learning, and inquiry in the basement against the backdrop of the Black Jesus—with Rev. Daughtry and his lovely and brilliant wife Karen on the front row usually with their children.

Like the prophets of old, Rev. Daughtry often has been misunderstood. His sincere outrage against injustice and social misery has challenged the status quo and unsettled the powers that be— at the White House, State House, City Hall, Wall Street, *The New York Times* or *Daily News*. This is especially so in regard to his relations with Jews in New York. We know that any wholesale critique of the vicious legacy of white supremacy includes Americans of all colors, including Jews and Blacks. Any principled opposition to xenophobia requires a wrestling with these evils in our own souls and society. Yet how easy it is for the mainstream media to demonize Black leaders who target American racism in white and Jewish communities. All too often, the stigmas of Black racist demagogue and Black anti-Semite are attached for life.

Needless to say, there certainly are some Black racists and Black anti-Jewish bigots in America. Yet, the false stigmas attached to those like Rev. Daughtry ironically increased their ranks. So I am delighted to see my brother and spiritual godfather set the record straight. His rich stories need to be heard. His integrity and character shine through, and like the cracked vessels we all are, his deep humanity is clearly seen. In this way, he speaks his truth and bears witness in the best of our Black Christian tradition of suffering and love, evil and hope for resurrection.

— Cornel West
*Professor of Afro-American Studies
and Philosophy of Religion at Harvard University*

# Part I

# "I'm Going to Get the Jews . . ."

# Prologue

While I have often been asked whether I had an official statement on anti-Semitism, I have always referred my examiners to my speeches, position papers, etc., encompassing other issues. Uncomfortable with that response, however, I promised myself that I would formulate a written statement, especially in light of the allegations of anti-Semitism leveled against me beginning with the late 60s to the present day.

There have been few statements from the Black community on anti-Semitism. First, many of us were convinced that the established media would not present anything that seemed critical of any aspect of the Jewish community. If we did publish even the most basic accusations in a position paper—however truthful—it was understood that we would have to finance it ourselves.

Second, there were the constraints of time and focus. For Black activists labeled anti-Semitic there are, for the most part, the more pressing issues of survival. Responding to charges of anti-Semitism simply did not seem an appropriate expenditure of time, energy, and resources, and especially so among those who suspected the cry of anti-Semitism to be nothing more than a ruse to draw them away from the real community-related issues.

Finally, there are some Blacks who simply did not give a damn. The issue of anti-Semitism was not one important enough to divert or attract their attention or that of their constituency.

Nonetheless, I, as pastor of The House of the Lord Pentecostal Church, decided that I would at last write my own statement on anti-Semitism, and that I would, if need be, finance its publication myself. There were personal factors that propelled me to do so.

In the main, I wanted a statement for my family and for my friends. I have been blessed with a wonderfully supportive family and with innumerable friends from every national, political, and religious background and sector. I felt I needed to give my children something in writing—something substantive to which they could always refer when the need arose. My name would come up in their classes (in fact, it already had) or in school-related activities, and they would have to explain, clarify, and, perhaps even defend me. It would not be enough for them to say, "My Daddy told me ...." They needed a written statement from me to which they could always direct anyone who might raise the subject of Black anti-Semitism. Then I thought I also owed something to my friends. Based upon what they know of me, these friends have been loyal. To some of them I had given a portion of my side of the story. To others I had said very little, giving them only "bits and pieces," but they remained steadfast nevertheless. I thought it was my obligation to present a defense or, at least, to provide them with the truth as I saw it, to give them something definitive that would justify their unwavering loyalty to me.

Therefore, despite innumerable demands, a multitude of responsibilities, and constant travels throughout the United States and abroad, I could not rest until this statement was completed.

Then, in addition to the above-mentioned imperative, there was my personal crusade, for once the writing had begun I realized that this would be an opportune occasion to document some of the many political and social issues in which I had become involved during the last several years. These are not necessarily removed from the issue of anti-Semitism. There are, however, many people who believe that I spent most of my time fighting

Jews. I find it interesting and sometimes irritating that most people link me with former New York Mayor Ed Koch and with
Crown Heights, an area of Brooklyn with a considerable population of Blacks and Hasidic Jews, in both cases casting me alone
as the contentious, warlike adversary.

For a quarter of a century, there have been many issues for
which I have continuously worked and struggled. There were
struggles with New York City law enforcement regarding the
abuse of police power (i.e., police brutality and assaults and killing
of innocent citizens), struggles with the business community
regarding their social responsibility. There was the creation of
job development programs, scholarship programs, and other
programs to help the needy, including marches and rallies on
Wall Street, City Hall, and the United Nations. There was the
constant effort to build a political power base within the Black
community. There were speeches,[1] sermons, lectures on cam-
puses, in churches and in seminaries, on street corners, and on
the steps of government buildings. There was the organization
of forums, seminars, and conferences, and, most significant to
the subject at hand, there was the formation, in 1978 and 1980,
of the Black United Front and National Black United Front
(NBUF), respectively. In addition to all these, there were and are
my pastoral duties. I sometimes say to people, "I am not doing
or saying anything now that I have not always done or said for
the last twenty-four years." It seems to me that I have always
been concerned about and, for most of my life, struggling for
the rights of the people.

I am the National Presiding Minister of The House of the
Lord Pentecostal Churches, and for more than thirty-eight years,
I have been pastor of a Brooklyn branch of my church.

Peter Haley, reporting for the Brooklyn newspaper *Phoenix*
wrote:

> [1978] was the year of Reverend Herbert Daughtry. The tire-
> less reverend of an Atlantic Avenue church and a Crown
> Heights congregation demonstrated against the Fulton Street

5

merchants, asked Congressman Fred Richmond to resign, pinned his demands for Mayor Ed Koch on the door of City Hall, and demonstrated against the policy of President Jimmy Carter. The local merchants listened. They established a Randy Evans Scholarship Fund in memory of a youngster killed by police. Reverend Daughtry expects the others to come around too.

So to give a more comprehensive picture of myself and my work, I yielded to the urge to lengthen my response to the anti-Semitic charges. As I succumbed to the irresistible drive to keep on writing, I found I had enough material—in volume and content—for a book.

I have lived a rather exciting life, one encompassing the *conquest* of liabilities, disadvantages, destructive habits, and prison; the formulation and dissemination of innovative ideas, institution building, extensive travels, extraordinary associations, dramatic struggles, and confrontations, etc.—many of the things that enthrall the interest of humankind.

While much in my life story touches the common experiences of humanity, I believe my experiences can be an inspiration to many, especially to young people, who are passing through the valleys where I have already sojourned.

I have tried to write this book for all Black people, but particularly Blacks who have also been labeled anti-Semitic. I have tried to express what I believe are sincere feelings, and I hope that I have done the job well. If this labor helps to produce better understanding and stronger solidarity between Blacks and Jews and all people, the time, energy, and resources invested will have been well worth it.

One final important note: the events discussed in Part I of this manuscript transpired between 1977 and 1986, approximately. Part II discusses my role in the 1991 explosion in Crown Heights, and related incidents, including the Korean store boycott and the 1993 re-election campaign of David Dinkins. When a manuscript is laying around for years, or one is dealing with

6

past events, there is an overwhelming urge to adjust the content to reflect contemporary thinking; evaluation of persons and events sometimes change.

But in order to reject revisionism and maintain integrity, one must resist the temptation to rearrange things. I am satisfied that I have achieved this end.

Of course, this means that the reader must wonder if I still believe what I believed when the thoughts were first put to paper ... and maybe I have to wonder myself.

## NOTES

1.  Speeches are available from Daughtry's personal files.

# Chapter 1

# No Monopoly on Suffering

The following text is part of the remarks I made at a theatrical performance in August 1994. At the conclusion of the play, we were asked to suggest means of solidarity. They were intended as encouragement to the audience, but their application is universal.

In 1981, I visited the Sachsenhausen concentration camp in the German Democratic Republic with a delegation that included a Jew, a Chicano, a Puerto Rican, an Indian, and myself, an African. In the discussion that followed that profound visit, we each discussed the level of our people's oppression, finally reaching the conclusion that none of us had any monopoly on suffering.

There are many who may lay claim to the dubious distinction of being the world's number one sufferer. In the competing foray, we sufferers must learn to hear one another.

It has been said: They who have scars can never take another's wounds lightly.

Living together, harmoniously, and creating space to hear one another in the aftermath of slavery, genocide, holocaust, and universal suffering are the subjects I would like to address.

First of all, those who have suffered from the cataclysmic events of history, call it what you will—genocide, holocaust, or slavery, whether in concentration camps, plantations, or reservations—should be given their time of remembrance and a time of recognition for their suffering. Let them build their monuments and establish their memorials. Let the rest of us, when invited, participate and empathize, supporting them in their celebration of survival. To minimize another's suffering, or to attempt to discourage or diminish their history is an act of crass disrespect and dishonesty, pouring salt in wounds of the mourners. As we strive to understand the other's pain, we make possible the opportunity to hear one another.

Second, let the sufferers use the cause of their suffering to educate, not only regarding their own suffering but regarding the suffering of others through genocide or holocaust, taking the opportunity to underscore and examine the depth of human depravity and the height of human heroism. In doing so, we will be creating space to hear one another.

Third, let the sufferers fight for everyone's right to memorialize their pain or fight for everyone's right to be heard regarding their genocide or holocaust. In so doing, we can transcend the horror and ignominy of our own suffering while encompassing the history of other sufferers.

Moreover, there is the potential of producing coalition and understanding, thus setting the stage for continued dialogue, thereby creating space to hear one another.

Fourth, let the sufferers strive to forgive. Those who continue to cling to the past run the risk of poisoning their own spirit, leaving themselves open to illness and a life of resentment

10

and bitterness. Such a condition only debilitates; obstructing the sensitivity and creativity needed to enhance both body and spirit. It can also disallow space to hear one another.

But as we strive to forgive, we do not forget, for *"those who do not learn the lessons of history are doomed to repeat its mistakes."*

On the other hand, let the sufferers resist adopting the behavior of the oppressor. One of the cruel ironies of history is the slave who, having gained freedom, now employs the methods of the slave master to enslave or exploit others. Sufferers who struggle for justice, freedom, and dignity must be vigilant lest they become one with the image of those they struggle against. With so malevolent an attitude, there can be no space to hear one another.

Sufferers must resist the temptation of exacting tribute for their pain from everyone. It is one thing to have everyone acknowledge and respect another's history of genocide or near annihilation, but it is another to demand that some special payment or tribute be forthcoming from everyone, even though the incidents of injustice and inhumanity may have occurred thousands of miles away, in another land, in another time, among another people.

This is not to reject reparations or some form of payback. Rather, my concern here is that the demand for reparations must be focused. Otherwise, the sufferer, with the old "the world owes me something" attitude, appears to be exacting payment from everybody, and thereby, making life miserable for everyone, including the sufferer.

Finally, sufferers must resist the urge, however strong, to argue for pre-eminence in suffering. All sufferers believe they have suffered more than others, just as those who carry a burden believe their's heaviest. Those who strive for monopoly on suffering will never create space to hear one another.

# Chapter 2

# My Personal Experiences with Jews

My personal experiences with Jews have been exceptionally gratifying, beginning with the education of my four children. In the case with my eldest daughter, a graduate of Dartmouth College, a Jewish teacher gave her special attention in her elementary grades and recommended that she be accelerated, paving the way for her entry into a program for gifted children. In 1982, my second daughter was inducted into the National Honor Society while in high school; she also went on to graduate from Dartmouth. This could not have been done without the recommendation of Jewish teachers. The achievements of all my children would not have been possible without significant contributions of their dedicated Jewish teachers.

In business, my dealings with Jews have been excellent. My wife and I purchased our first home from a Jewish couple. The house was reasonably priced, and the expensive furniture, some of which we still enjoy, was left in the house. Seeing the woman who sold us the house vacuuming the rug as we were moving in was a sight I will always remember. She wanted "everything to be clean and nice for us."

The purchase of our second home, where we now live, was facilitated by a Jewish family. We very much wanted the house. It was spacious and close to our relatives, thus giving our children an extended family. As my wife and I were constantly away from home, it was extremely important that our children have the comfort, love, and the protection of grandfathers and grandmothers, uncles and aunts, nephews and nieces, and cousins nearby. The price of the house, though reasonable, was beyond our financial reach at that time. With the New York fiscal crises threatening our meager income, buying the house seemed near impossible. When we conveyed our situation to the sellers, they graciously offered to take a second mortgage, and, they said, if at any time we encountered difficulty meeting the payments, they would work something out for us. As it happened, we never had to request their magnanimity. But had it not been offered, we would never have undertaken such a venture.

Assisting in the purchase of our home was the president of a bank, Wilbur Levin, a friend of twenty years. Our friendship began when I led a boycott against one of his stores. After some heated clashes we reached an agreement. A friendship developed, and now he is not only a trusted counselor in financial matters but in all matters. It would have been easy for this friend to have chimed in with the anti-Semitic charges. But he chose reflection, and a valuable human relationship has continued over the years. We still argue and vigorously defend our respective positions: He says my "tactics stink." I say, "If I were a banker I would probably think so too." We both laugh. What a wonderful place the world would be if all differences were so congenially debated and resolved.

The community in which my family now lives is interracial with a preponderance of Jews. There have never been any incidents of racism. It is a neighborhood of peace and mutual respect.

When I was jobless and with a new bride to support, it was a Jewish man who gave me employment—and more importantly, friendship. Long after I left his employ we remained friends, although we saw each other infrequently. But after the anti-Semitic smears, our relationship ended; one of the few I've had that was adversely affected by the anti-Semitic charges.

My association with the New York Jets football team was, I believe, another casualty of the anti-Semitic campaign. During the middle of the 1975-76 football season, Tom Skinner, the nationally known Black evangelist, invited me to the Jets training camp at Hofstra University in New York. Skinner had been cultivating a relationship with Black athletes, and Coach George Allen[1] had heaped lavish praise on him, giving him credit for helping make the Washington Redskins a winning football team.

When Skinner and I visited the Jets camp, they were in the middle of a losing season. The Head Coach then was Charles Winner, son-in-law of the Jets' first coach, Weeb Eubank. After that initial visit I became friendly with many of the players including Steve Early, Winston Hill, and Coach Sam Rutigliano, who would later become Head Coach of the Cleveland Browns. I started holding Bible Study classes once a week, providing not only a sounding board for those who wanted to talk but also a much-needed friend who was not interested in exploiting their fame. The Jets closed the second half of the season on a winning note.

We began the next season with high hopes. When the Jets opened in Buffalo, my wife and I were invited to accompany the team. The Jets' management made hotel reservations for us, and the next day we joined the caravan on to the stadium. The Jets were trounced and that was the beginning of a horrendous season and the end of Charley Winner as coach. When the next

15

coach, Lou Holtz, was hired, my relationship with the Jets continued. When the season came to an end, Holtz decided that he would return to college coaching, and Walt Michael became the head man. My relationship with the Jets continued as before. Michael impressed me as a strict disciplinarian who knew his football. Another thing I liked about Michael was that he brought a Black coach with him.

During the first two years, I paid frequent visits to the camp. The field, dressing room, offices, and personnel were all accessible to me. I was able to induce several players to visit hospitals and drug centers and to become interested in New York politics. I'd like to think that I provided a positive service to the players. I know I learned a great deal from them. I still have the team-autographed footballs.

At no point in Bible Studies or in our rap sessions, did the subject of race arise. In fact, I consciously avoided racial issues. This was a football team, and unity was paramount. However, when Black players wanted to discuss a situation in which they believed they were being subjected to racial prejudice, I neither encouraged nor discouraged them. My role there was to act as confidant and spiritual adviser. Quite early on, I learned that many football players—and this is true for all athletes, whatever their fame, and perhaps because of it —have serious problems. So I spent most of my time just listening.

As my involvement in the community became intensified, I did not have as much time to devote to the players as before. However, I would always send words of encouragement to Walt Michael. Those first several years were losing years for the Jets, and there were rumors that Michael was on the verge of being ousted. He would always respond to my letters.

Once the anti-Semitic allegations and my confrontations with Koch began, there seemed an inexplicable coolness emanating from the Jets camp. More specifically, Michael no longer replied to my letters. I could only conclude that it had to do with the allegations, and my combative relationship with Ed Koch. I learned much later that the principal owner of the Jets, Leon Hess, happened to be a close friend of the Mayor's. I cannot say definitely that the anti-Semitic charges or Ed Koch were responsible for the change in atmosphere at the Jets camp, or even that my sense of the situation was accurate. But, it was my feeling that there was a definite change, and such allegations—founded or unfounded—led to tensions and misunderstandings, nullifying even the most harmonious relations.

I have a Jewish doctor and a Black doctor, a Jewish lawyer and a Black lawyer, and a Jewish banker to say nothing of the innumerable Jews I count as friends. The three most important areas of my life are, to a large extent, entrusted to Jews: my family's health, finances, and legal protection.

Now that admission might expose me to criticism from the Black community, but the truth, as they say, is the light. One of the reasons for this development is that Black lawyers usually require a fee, which Black activists, at least in my case, do not have. William Kunstler took my defamation case against Channel 5 *pro bono*; without a fee. In fact, we didn't even discuss money. Prior to the meeting with Kunstler, I had approached a Black attorney who requested a substantial retainer before he would make any movement on the case.

I don't want to belittle the contribution of Black attorneys, or to imply that at no time do they serve voluntarily. Indeed, there were attorneys like Randolph Jackson, Clayton Jones, C. Vernon Mason, Alton Maddox, and Joseph Mack who provided their talents for little or nothing. But overall, Blacks simply did not have the financial security to do *pro bono* work. That, again, can be attributed to racism. This society has not given equal opportunities to Black attorneys, or to Blacks, period. Thus, when Blacks are ready to put their skills to work after years of schooling and sacrifice, they need some tangible returns. Who can blame them? Many White lawyers, on the other hand, can afford to do volunteer work from time to time. They know that they will be paid in some way: either with publicity, closeness to the struggle, friendship with Black leadership, or with the price-less feeling of contributing to a worthy cause. Oftentimes, this can be translated into money later, if that is their objective.

I do not want to imply that closeness is derived from service rendered by the attorneys. In my case, and I believe this is true for most Blacks, the attorneys and I enjoy a friendship that tran-scends the usual lawyer-client relationship. Nor do I mean to imply that these attorneys render service out of ulterior or self-ish motives; I am convinced that some, if not all, of the attor-neys I've dealt with were/are motivated by a commitment to human rights.

I have touched briefly upon my personal experiences to demonstrate again that wherever I have criticized *certain* Jews, my criticism can not possibly have been directed toward all Jews.

In addition to personal relationships, organizationally, the Black United Front (BUF) has been the beneficiary of Jewish assistance and friendship. Andrew Moss, a BUF member was attacked by police during the Sydenham Hospital confrontation. He was arrested and charged with verbal abuse and assaulting the police, among other things. Rafael Abramovitz defended him. In another confrontation with the police during a demon-stration against Ed Koch in Brooklyn, three of our members—Adeyemi Bandele, Bob Daughtry, Jr., and Sam Pinn—were arrested. Donny Altman, Terry Selzer, and Stephine Benson respectively defended them. Attorneys John Zurinski and Michael Ratner, President of the National Lawyers Guild, have also rendered invaluable assistance.

## NOTES

1.  George Allen's method of building a team was to take veterans, misfits, and troublemakers, and mold them together as a team. This was contrary to the usual method of team-building, where owners generally construct-ed teams from the draft pool. Allen believed that "the future was now," and he traded away his draft choices for veterans. Allen had leaned very heav-ily upon Tom Skinner to help cement the various attitudes and personali-ties of these veterans.

18

**Chapter 3**

# Ocean Hill–
# Brownsville

In instances where I have been involved in confrontations with *certain Jewish persons or groups*, I have always believed that the difficulties emanated from the perspective of group interests or power. For example, during the Ocean Hill-Brownsville battles of 1969, my position was that the United Federation of Teachers (UFT), for its own selfish interests, blocked community control, while the Afro-American Teachers Association (AATA) and the Black community believed community control would advance their interests, eventually producing quality education for all New Yorkers. One of the ways the UFT helped to exacerbate the tension was by giving wide circulation to several pieces of extremist literature.

On the other hand, the UFT would not give, and Blacks did not have, the resources to circulate positive and constructive literature. Take, for an example, the AATA's position in their November 1968 newsletter, which called for a "responsible Jewish voice" to step forward. At the time there were than 300 Jewish teachers supportive of the Ocean Hill-Brownsville experiment who denied any anti-Semitism in the district. Nor was it widely circulated that many Jews were critical of UFT President Albert Shanker. There were some Jews (and Jewish groups) who did try to bring honesty or clarity to the issues in Ocean Hill-Brownsville. The Rabbi's Committee for Community Control, the Jewish Teachers Committee for Community Control, and the New Coalition Party of the UFT took out a full-page ad in *The New York Times* that was a reprint of an article from *The Public Life* magazine, entitled "Exploding the Myth of Black Anti-Semitism."

Rabbi Martin Siegel, in his book, *Confessions of a Rebel Rabbi*, points out that Blacks do not have the wherewithal to engage in an anti-Semitic campaign, and, therefore, that the whole issue of anti-Semitism was skillfully used by the UFT. He also points out, which surely most people knew, that Black people, even if they wished to, did not have the power to promote anti-Semitism.

Reacting to an attempt to get a resolution passed and stating, in substance, that despite the rise in Black anti-Semitism, Jews were not going to turn against Blacks, the Rabbi wrote:

> I obviously had to object, because the resolution conceded a rise in black anti-Semitism when I feel that this is all an invention of the teachers union and the ADL to serve their own self-interest. The very term black anti-Semitism presupposes a Black community which doesn't exist. With no real unity and no real leadership, they are just a group of individuals who are only slowly gaining a sense of cohesiveness, a sense of belonging to one another. The Jews have been a community for 4,000 years—they have the structure to react to anti-Semitism. What they don't seem to understand is that the blacks don't have the cohesiveness to be communally anti-Semitic.[1]

The issue is power: the right of a people to influence their own lives and their own destiny. Let me quote from a statement I wrote in 1969, which was first delivered to Clergy Vigil, a religious organization comprised of White liberals and Black leaders:

> It is true that anti-Semitism is not the issue. The issue, the burning, inescapable, undeniable issue, is the appalling, inequitable distribution of the nation's resources and an alarming lack of people's participation (particularly Black People) in the decision-making process.[2]

However, I did sharply criticize those Jews "who had elected to cast in their lot with a racist, oppressive, and exploitative system. In such a situation, i.e., when they are criticized, let them not blame it on their nationality or religion. Let them not say it is anti-Semitic," for, as I wrote, "if they choose to fly with buzzards and feast on the cadaver of Black people, let them not cry anti-Semitism when the buzzards are attacked." I have never tried to hide my feelings or my utterances. My statement was given to the Clergy Vigil at their request. They claimed they wanted to share it with their rabbinical friends.

I interpreted their invitation to mean that a statement from me would help to clarify what Blacks like myself were thinking and feeling. Never did I think that they viewed me or any of my remarks as anti-Semitic. But I made the mistake of criticizing the Vigil for attempting to diffuse the hot issues of anti-Semitism, and racial tension and for attempting to strengthen allies and win new supporters for Blacks in the Jewish community. All of these objectives needed to be realized, but not at Black people's expense. The Vigil's approach, I thought, had the effect of tipping lightly by the Black community's legitimate grievances.

I thought I discerned the historic betrayal once again; i.e., that whenever confrontations develop in which Blacks are involved, we are always sold out; or our legitimate indictments are placed in a context of appeasement to other groups. The end result is a reduction of tension with conditions stabilized, that is

21

to say, almost exactly where they had been prior to the confrontation, or where Blacks receive minimum gains and maximum promises; and the other groups involved almost always emerge with substantial gains. In either situation, Blacks are rendered weaker than ever, and the other groups stronger than ever. Looking back, however, I have come to believe that the approach the Vigil initiated was a principled and prudent one, because it was necessary to win allies and broaden our support with the various groups in the city, especially with the Jewish community.

It should be underscored here that I have also criticized the Vigil. We have worked together daily, and I have counted its constituency among our friends. But that did not exclude them from some stinging criticism from me.

We cannot, however, overlook the fact that there was and still is a perception in the Black community that *some* Jews had taken over the educational system; and instead of creating quality education for Black children, they have allowed—perhaps inadvertently—the system to worsen progressively, turning out "functional illiterates by the thousands," the chief culprits in this being Albert Shanker and the UFT.

In addition, unnecessary structures were created, e.g., Board of Examiners, that made it more difficult for Blacks and Puerto Ricans to become certified teachers.

As late as April 1982, a young man with a host of degrees sat in my office and bemoaned the fact that he could not find a job in the educational system. He recited his history as well as that of other Blacks with the Board of Examiners. According to him, an excessive number of highly qualified Blacks have failed the test. He was convinced that passing the test had nothing to do with qualifications, but that it was a matter of race, nationality, and politics.[3] The fact is those who teach and administrate the school system in New York City have done a reprehensible job. According to the 1980 Annual Urban League Report, seven out of ten children entering the public school system will not finish high school, and those who do finish will not be able to read above the eighth grade level.[4]

## NOTES

1. Martin Siegel, *Amen: Confessions of a Rebel Rabbi, The Diary of Rabbi Martin Siegel*, Fawcett, Greenwich, CT, 1970, p. 105.
2. Herbert Daughtry, "Statement Made to Clergy Vigil" (unpublished), Brooklyn, 1969. Available from Daughtry's personal files.
3. Through community pressure (and with the assistance of our many allies), we succeeded in eliminating that system of certification.
4. See New York Urban League Annual Report, 1980.

**Chapter 4**

# Creating a Movement, Empowering a People, Perpetuating a Memory

~~~~~~~~

In the summer of 1977, Sam Pinn, Albert Vann, Jitu Weusi, and I began to meet. At that time, Pinn was chairman of Brooklyn Congress of Racial Equality (CORE). Vann was Assemblyman in the 56th AD, and Weusi was founder and leader of The East, a cultural and educational organization that generated some of the most innovative and progressive programs in the city. All three were educators. Pinn later became a professor at Ramapo College in New Jersey. Vann and Weusi taught in the New York

City public schools, both having played prominent roles in the struggle for community control in Ocean Hill-Brownsville. In fact, both taught at P.S. 271, one of the main schools in the Ocean Hill-Brownsville school complex. Both Vann and Weusi had been smeared by the charge of anti-Semitism, as was anyone who played a leading role in the struggle. Over the years, the four of us had been politically involved with one another in various ways but never in the way that we were then. At that time we were particularly concerned about the deplorable state of people of African ancestry in Brooklyn and throughout the country.

In Brooklyn, despite our numbers, Blacks were relatively powerless, a frustrating situation pervasive throughout the city and the nation. We four decided to set aside one morning a week just to analyze and evaluate our political situation and to plan for better conditions.

> Brooklyn has the largest concentration of people of African descent in the Western Hemisphere. Over 1.5 million of our people call Brooklyn their home today. We have come from many lands and have various stories to tell about our lives. The truth of our condition today is that while our population is vast, we are a powerless people and cannot effectively control the factors that influence our lives.
>
> We want to stop the terror by the police and Hasidim in our community. We want to end the state of oppression and exploitation that ravage our embattled population. We want to create a living memorial to the memory of Arthur Miller and declare that NEVER AGAIN will we allow our people, especially our youth, to be brutalized and murdered without an adequate response.
>
> But we must come together and do more than just talk. We must educate and organize our community. We must agitate and petition for change. We must develop the facility to protect ourselves, our families and community. There is much WORK to be done.
>
> Join the people's movement for JUSTICE![1]

As we compared our knowledge and analyses, we realized that we were learning a great deal about and from each other, that we were becoming more knowledgeable about the true political and social conditions, issues, and personalities of our community. In meeting together, putting our collective heads together, we became far more politically aware. While other individuals and groups were wondering what to do, we had already formulated our strategies. In addition, we knew each other's strengths and weaknesses. We could build upon our strengths and improve upon our weaknesses, and in the process we learned to trust each other. This is so very important in all ventures but especially in political and social ventures, where powerful people and systems will be challenged; where leaders must take risks, in spite of threats to themselves, to their families, or to their friends.

Each of us played a vital role in the group. Sam Pinn was reflective and analytical. Al Vann was thoughtful and theoretical. Vann was to receive the political credibility and power generated from our movement, and he, in turn, agreed to serve the people. Jitu Weusi, a quick, sharp thinker and a long-time activist and organizer, had wide-ranging contacts and credibility within the grassroots and nationalist communities. I was chosen as point man, the spokesperson who would argue our case in public, articulating our direction and policy.

In November 1976, a police officer named Robert Torsney killed a 15-year-old Black youth named Randolph Evans for no apparent reason. A year later, almost to the day, the jury rendered a decision to place Torsney under psychiatric treatment and to allow him weekends at home. The Black community was incensed. Once again, a White policeman had unjustly killed a Black youth, and again there was neither recompense nor apology. There had been others: 11-year-old Ricky Borden from Staten Island; 11-year-old Clifford Glover from Jamaica, Queens; and 14-year-old Claude Reese from Brooklyn. Various kinds of demonstrations followed the Evans killing.

The four of us, calling our movement the Concerned Leaders

and Citizens to Save Our Youth, began to plan an appropriate response that would not only express our anger but would at the same time promote something positive to perpetuate the memory of Randolph Evans. We vowed to build a movement that would eventuate into the political and economic empowerment of our community. We decided on a three-pronged attack:

## 1. Economic Boycott

In December 1977, we launched our citywide boycott of the business community. We called it "Black Christmas 1977." In time the boycott focused on downtown Brooklyn, whose major stores then included Abraham & Strauss, Korvettes, Martin's, and May's.

After ten months of boycotts and demonstrations, we settled for a ten-point agreement:
1. Minority bank deposits
2. Minority media advertising
3. Minority employment in construction and maintenance of the Fulton Mall
4. Randolph Evans Community Crisis Fund (RECCF)
5. Randolph Evans Scholarship Fund (RESF)
   (The business community would fund both the RECCF and the RESF for a five-year period. Abraham & Strauss, under the leadership of vice president Robert McMillan and Francesco Canterella, who is still active, continued the scholarship fund until it merged with Macy's.)
6. Minority employment
7. Brooklyn fair for minority vendors
8. Peddlers—space for peddlers to set up tables to sell their products.
9. Community advisory committee
10. Entertainment complex
   (Presently, there is a multi-million dollar development under construction in downtown Brooklyn; some aspect of this

development is exactly what we argued for in our initial meeting with the merchants in 1978.)

## 2. Legal Action at the Federal Level

We demanded the U.S. Justice Department indict Officer Torsney on violation of Randolph Evans' civil rights. The Justice Department refused, citing "insufficient evidence."

## 3. Comprehensive Youth Program

We demanded that New York City appropriate special funds and activities for our youth. On January 12, 1978, the Coalition and other community leaders met with Mayor Ed Koch. The meeting grew out of a demonstration we led during Koch's inauguration at the Brooklyn Museum on January 1, 1978. (*See Chapter 7: EDWARD I. KOCH: MAYOR OF NEW YORK CITY.*) Joining us at the meeting with the Mayor were Basil Paterson, who had been appointed Deputy Mayor, and David Dinkins, who was then the New York City Clerk. At the meeting we discussed three issues with Koch.

- *Police Brutality.* Koch said that we should meet with his newly appointed Police Commissioner, Robert McGuire.
- *The Indictment of Robert Torsney.* We asked Koch to write a letter to United States Attorney David Trager in support of our demand for the indictment of Officer Robert Torsney on the violation of Randy Evans' civil rights. Koch agreed to write the letter.
- *A Comprehensive Youth Program.* Koch said a Blue Ribbon Commission on youth had been established. But not too much, if anything, came of it.

The meeting was very cordial, and Koch was very agreeable.

The Honorable Basil Paterson, then Deputy Mayor, was widely respected and helped to negotiate the agreement. Other

29

members of our negotiating team, in addition to the four (Pinn, Vann, Weusi, and myself), included: Safiya Bandele, who would later become head of the Black United Front Women's Section and who currently serves as Director of The Center for Women's Development at Medgar Evers College; Peggy Smith (now Washington), who served as assistant coordinator of the demonstrations; Job Mashariki, who organized the Black Veterans for Social Justice; and Michael Amon-Ra, who coordinated the boycotts and later became executive organizer of the Black United Front, and then became Executive Director of Career Opportunities for Brooklyn Youth, one of the many programs influenced by the movement. Also included was my wife, Karen S. Daughtry, Director of the Alonzo A. Daughtry Memorial Day Care Center, and Annie Evans Brannon, the mother of Randy Evans. Mrs. Brannon had been with us from the beginning and still participates in all the activities related to the Randolph Evans Scholarship Fund.

After the agreement with the downtown merchants, we held a retreat at Ramapo College in New Jersey. We invited every one who had been active to attend, wanting the community involved in any decisions we would make with our gains. This was an important part of our efforts, because it was consistent with our objective to empower the people. The community is usually left out of the decision making once a victory is won! We wanted the people to decide on our programs, on our administrator, and on how we would extend our organizing for optimal growth.

We decided that Professor Sam Pinn would chair the Randolph Evans Crises Fund Board of Directors; Jitu Weusi would administer the program with a part-time secretary, the only paid positions. Assemblyman Al Vann would chair the Randolph Evans Scholarship Fund's board. I would chair the Coalition for Economic Fairness, which would sponsor the Randolph Evans Scholarship Fund Awards Ceremony Luncheon or Dinner. Ms. Brannon would chair the Randolph Evans

Scholarship Committee, and she and I would be ex-officio members of all boards and committees. Karen Daughtry would coordinate the event at which the scholarship would be awarded. I was particularly concerned about this program; the memory of Randy Evans should be kept alive, and the awful crime against him (which in a way symbolized the violence and racism as represented in police behavior), never to be forgotten. I could think of no one more capable of achieving this than Karen Daughtry.

The Randolph Evans Scholarship and Luncheons are still in existence. Since we initiated the program in 1979, we have awarded ten scholarships a year of $1,500 each to selected student who have been accepted at an accredited college.

We had created a powerful movement. Perhaps our most important accomplishment is that it eventuated into many viable organizations, movements, programs, and events.

## THE CREATION OF THE BLACK UNITED FRONT

The Concerned Leaders and Citizens to Save Our Youth was expanding rapidly, and we realized we needed more structure and more clearly defined strategy. In July 1978, we formed the Black United Front (BUF) with a steering committee consisting of:

- Rev. Herbert Daughtry—The House of the Lord Church
- Jitu Weusi—Black Community Congress
- Dr. Vernal Cave—Black Community Council of Crown Heights
- Sam Pinn—Brooklyn Congress of Racial Equality (CORE)
- Andy Gill—Arthur Miller Community Defense Committee
- Rev. Clarence Norman—First Baptist Church of Crown Heights
- Leon E. Modeste—New York Urban League
- Mahmud Ramza—Ramza Associates
- Rev. Heron Sam—St. Mark's Episcopal Church

31

Also, we developed five Principles of Unity:
1. Opposition to racism, bigotry, and racial violence
2. Re-distribution of the resources and wealth of the nation to provide abundantly for all citizens
3. Opposition to genocide through miseducation
4. Opposition to police brutality
5. Opposition to national and international denial of human rights.

The Black United Front became the umbrella organization for a variety of organizations, and many people joined. At a news conference on July 5, 1978, on the steps of City Hall, we formally announced the formation of BUF as "a vehicle to agitate, educate, and organize our community."

We organized countless cultural awareness programs, rallies, seminars, and lecture series. The most eminent scholars in the country participated in our lecture series, including Cornel West, Ivan Van Sertima, John Henrik Clarke, James Cone, and Gayraud Wilmore.

In July 1978, we organized the Arthur Miller Community Patrol, with the motto: "To serve, share, and protect the community in times of siege and crises." The Patrol was ably led by long-time activist Yusef Iman, now deceased, who had served as security for Malcolm X. Eventually, Kobie Ransom and Weusi Iman, Yusef's younger brother, assumed responsibility for the patrol.

Our Police Investigation Unit, organized as an arm of BUF, investigated, monitored, and kept the public informed about police behavior. Dave Walker was appointed coordinator, and later he started his own private investigation agency.

While we viewed all our efforts as related to political empowerment, there were some things that proved more directly political. In addition to working for candidates, we engaged in voter registration and education drives. We also organized political conventions to educate and analyze issues and candidates and to elect candidates. Candidates running for any office eagerly sought our endorsement.

In September 1978, we ran our own slate of candidates:

- Stanley Clarke, Assemblyman, 43 AD
- Katie Davis, Female District Leader, 57 AD
- Bernard Gifford, U.S. Congress, 14 CD
- Andrew Gill, Male District Leader, 53 AD
- Roger Green, Male District Leader, 57 AD
- Horace Greene, Assemblyman, 59 AD
- Velmanette Montgomery, Assemblywoman, 57 AD
- Sam Pinn Jr., State Senator, 18 SD
- Annette Robinson, Female District Leader, 56 AD
- Albert Vann, Male District Leader and Assemblyman, 56 AD

Except for incumbents Al Vann and Annette Robinson, I regret to say that all these candidates lost. However, in 1991, Annette Robinson ran in the 36th Councilmanic District and won. In 1983, Velmanette Montgomery ran in the 18th Senatorial District and won. In 1981, Roger Green ran in the 57th Assembly District and won.

From 1977 to 1986, the organizations associated with BUF and the movements emanating from it were at the center of the most crucial issues in the city. (*See Appendix A* for a listing of other organizations, programs, and events than emanated from the energy created by the National Black United Front.) The Front was not only influential in shaping the life and direction of the city but, through the National Black United Front (NBUF), we exerted influence on national and international issues as well.

## NATIONAL BLACK UNITED FRONT

After our success with the BUF model in New York City, we decided to duplicate it across the country. So on June 26, 1980, the Founding Convention of NBUF met at the Sumner Avenue Armory in Brooklyn, attended by over a thousand delegates from thirty-five states and five foreign countries. We adopted a temporary constitution and we also elected temporary officers:

Herbert Daughtry, National Chairperson
Ron Herndon, Portland, Oregon, National Secretary
Florence Walker, Philadelphia, PA, National Treasurer
Jitu Weusi, Brooklyn, NY, National Coordinator

After the heated atmosphere of the convention, my wife and I immediately embarked on a three-week cross-country drive, visiting the delegates in hope of healing wounds and resolving differences.

In 1981, the second NBUF Convention was held at Boys and Girls High School, in Brooklyn, where we ratified the permanent constitution after debate at the four regional conventions held during the year. This was historic. It was perhaps the first time any organization's beginning was so widely debated, thus exemplifying democracy at its highest.

The FBI's infamous COINTELPRO initiative had created a climate of distrust among Black organizations, turning them into warring camps. But NBUF, perhaps because of its unique constitutional ratification process, marked the first time these factions, along with more moderate and conservative groups, came together to build a truly representative, national Black movement. Participating groups included:

All African Peoples Revolutionary Party
Black Panther Party
Institute for Positive Education
League of Revolutionary Struggle
NAACP (chapter levels)
Nation of Islam
Republic of New Afrika
US

The Convention elected officers for a two year term:
Rev. Herbert Daughtry, National Chairperson
Ron Herndon, National Secretary and
    Western Regional Coordinator
Florence Walker, National Treasurer
    and Easter Regional Coordinator
Jitu Weusi, National Coordinator
Alfred "Skip" Robertson, Southern Regional Coordinator
Rev. Charles Koen, Midwest Regional Coordinator

The importance of NBUF was that it added a deeper dimension to the social, political, revolutionary struggle of people of African Ancestry. More importantly, NBUF was the only national mass-based, independent, progressive, nationalist, Pan Africanist, radical, revolutionary organization in United States of America at that time, perhaps at any time.

I remained chairperson until my resignation in 1984. Dr. Conrad Worrill of Chicago is the current chairperson.

\* \* \*

Overall, without controversy, Pinn, Weusi, Vann, and I made, and still continue to make a significant impact on our world. What we accomplished is far greater than anything any one of us could have done individually.

After 1982, our group no longer met, as the responsibilities of our successes became quite demanding. For example, my election as Chair of NBUF necessitated a rigorous travel schedule. Then, too, there are my duties at The House of the Lord Church. Pinn, in addition, to his professorship at Ramapo College, created the Fort Greene Senior Citizens Center, which sponsors a variety of social services programs. Weusi had the responsibilities of The East and its school, Uhuru Sasa Shule. Vann, one of the most popular and powerful elected officials throughout the state of New York, continues to inspire his organization of Black elected officials in Brooklyn.

35

Inarguably, we achieved our objectives.

- **Perpetuating a Memory**
  Randolph Evans' memory is still alive and will ever remain so as more and more college-bound students receive the scholarship in his name.
- **Creating a Movement**
  As demonstrated, the movement we created had an enormous impact on so many people, organizations, programs, events, etc. around the world that it is impossible to assess the full extent.
- **Political/Economic Empowerment**
  While we are a long way from political and economic empowerment commensurate with our numbers, we are undoubtedly far better off today than we were in 1977, at least potentially so. What we do with it is another question.

The activity we generated put us in a scoring position and helped to place people in positions where they can drive the runs in. Future years will reveal the extent to which we took advantage of the opportunities we created.

## NOTES

1. Excerpt from "How We Can Build A Strong Movement In Brooklyn," a recruitment flier produced and distributed by the Black United Front and the Black Community Congress of Brooklyn, 1978.

# Chapter 5

# "I'm Going to Get the Jews and the People in the Long Black Coats"
## The Facts Behind
## the *New York Post* Article

Where did the anti-Semitic charges begin? I'm not sure. Aside from the Ocean Hill-Brownsville struggles, the only other place would be in Crown Heights and, more especially, in an article printed in the *New York Post.*

On June 20, 1978, the *New York Post,* whose scurrilous

reputation is well known throughout the city (Norman Mailer called the paper "the most dangerous and meretricious element in journalism today,")[1] carried a picture of me, my arms out-stretched, eyes wide and a caption quoting me as saying, "We will get the Jews and the people in the long black coats." I want to state categorically, before God and all humankind, that I made no such statement.

What I said was, "When we organize our patrol, when men meet men, we will see then what the people in the long black coats will do." My reference was very clearly directed toward the Hasidim, and even at that, was not an offensive statement but a defensive one; "... we will see then what *they will do*." I emphasized this point to *The New York Times* writer Selwyn Raab on June 23, 1978:

> [Daughtry's] statements about the political power of the Hasidic community in Crown Heights and his call for the street patrols by Black men to counter patrols "of the people in the long black coats"—many Hasidic men wear black frock coats—have led to charges of anti-Semitism and that the minister is increasing racial tensions.
>
> Denying the charges, he said, "We're not looking for a confrontation. But Blacks have been assaulted by the Hasid patrols, and we think our own patrols will reduce, not increase, tension."

When I approached John Mitchell, a Black *New York Post* reporter, who had attended the community rally, where the statement is alleged, he agreed I had been misquoted, and he was willing to sign an affidavit to that effect. I should also point out that I had a tape of my speech that would provide further evidence of the inaccuracy of the *Post* article. I went back and forth with various personnel—editors and publishers—at the *New York Post,* which was at the time in the process of being sold. The *Post* claimed they had picked up the article from the Associated Press. I did not pursue it, but now I wish I had initiated court action. But that was a year of perpetual crises, and at that time I had no idea that matters I was involved in would mushroom quite the way they did, nor did I fully comprehend the tenacious perseverance and irrational nature of *some* in the Jewish community in their pursuit of anyone charged with anti-Semitism. Letting the issue drop proved an unwise decision; the article haunts me to this very day.

I did approach some of my Jewish friends and remember one of them saying, "I don't believe half of what I read in the newspaper and nothing of what I read in the *Post.*" I took every opportunity to deny and to clarify my stance. An instance of this was printed in the July 13, 1978 edition of the *Phoenix* newspaper:

> [I]t was reported in the New York "Post" that Daughtry had included some anti-Semitic remarks in a strong speech he made in Crown Heights on June 19.
>
> Shaking his head slowly, Daughtry denied the account and labeled it "an awful lie," adding, "some of the most vicious people are in the news media, and they don't care what they print. This story projects me for what I'm not and it's clear defamation of character." Daughtry, who sees himself as a "moral leader," particularly in light of his attack on [New York Congressman Fred] Richmond, was troubled by the "Post" depiction.
>
> "Even if you have a conflict with the Jews, which we do, I wouldn't want to hear anyone say, 'Let's get the Jews, the Italians, or the Blacks.' To be labeled anti-Semitic is an anathema for me," he said.

In fact, several evenings later I vigorously denied the *Post* charges on Channel 11. As we were discussing funeral services of Arthur Miller,[2] Jeff Kamen, for whom I have always had the highest respect, asked me about the quote, wanting to give me the opportunity to repudiate the infamous quote.

While I am grateful to those who gave me the opportunity

to deny the quote, my denials were insufficient to prevent its proliferation.

I cannot overemphasize the distress this misrepresentation by the media has caused me, the *Post* article in particular. In Jewish circles and places where Jews have influence, where I had previously moved with cordiality, I suddenly felt distance, tension, and, in some instances, hostility. Needless to say, I was swamped with hate mail, expressed in the most sordid and vivid language imaginable. The most egregious piece featured a picture of me from the *Post* article with a portrait of Hitler superimposed over my face.

It was particularly hard on my family. In our neighborhood, children play together, spend the night with each other, and parents transport each other's children to and from school, to little league games, etc. I must express deep appreciation to my Jewish friends, for with the exception of a couple of instances, I never detected a change in their behavior and attitude towards me or my family. My children never reported any changes either. We still watched each other's children, invited each other to various functions, moved in and out of each other's homes, dined together, argued furiously for our own interests and biases, organized and formed alliances together. We all proceeded as if nothing had happened. I knew my Jewish friends must have been under a lot of pressure. But they never wavered in their trust, nor did they castigate me.

It is interesting to note that no one ever asked me if the article was true, which forces me to ask: Before such a story is disseminated, shouldn't it be checked with the accused first? Who takes responsibility for fact-checking and monitoring these matters? Who is guilty of peddling these false accusations? Have certain Jews developed an accountability system on the issue of anti-Semitism? Can any Jewish group that feels threatened, start a campaign against a "supposed" anti-Semite? Is there some mechanism to discern and publicize real anti-Semitism? Do Jews feel any guilt for the way some of their number have hounded innocent people, who are trying to speak the truth as they see it, or people who are trying to do for their people what Jews are doing for their own? Do they make *any* effort to validate charges of anti-Semitism? Are they glad when an assertive Black leader is labeled anti-Semitic? A label so fraught with volatility, it seems to me, should make it incumbent upon Jews to monitor its use.

Isn't it ironic that I and other Black leaders, who have known unparalleled oppression at the hands of practically everybody, be charged with anti-Semitism? It calls to mind what Malcolm X used to say when he was accused of being racist: *Here we have a knife in our back, and when we scream, twist, and turn to get the knife out of our back, we are called anti-Semitic or racist.* Black people in America do not have a history of discrimination against any people. However, we do have a history of struggling against those who oppress and exploit us, whoever they may be.

There is, then, a contradiction. I know of no Jewish person who claims perfection. Rather, they would say that they are mortals. Since all mortals make mistakes—and are endowed with a certain portion of wisdom and folly, virtue and vices—it would seem that criticism would be a natural expectation. It cannot be both ways. One cannot claim mortality and exemption from criticism too.

In a pluralistic society, it is inevitable that the interests of the various ethnic and religious groups, unions, and churches collide. But, there are *many* Jews who turn any conflicting opinion, whatever the issue, into anti-Semitism.

Some years ago, New York Senator Jacob Javits called on Blacks to denounce "Black Power" as he had denounced the KKK. (Note that Javits' absurd logic equates the Black Power movement with the Klan.) Roy Wilkins immediately responded, urging Blacks to do just as Javits had suggested. Black people did not denounce Javits as being anti-Black; we simply criticized his logic. But when Blacks criticize Zionism or some other political or religious ideology held by *some members of the Jewish community*, it becomes a case of anti-Semitism. The attitude *some* Jews convey is: We can do whatever we like, to whomever we like, but if you struggle for your own legitimate interests, and they conflict with ours, you are anti-Semitic.

What should concern us here (I hope that it doesn't surprise anyone) is the deep resentment building in the Black community, a resentment harbored by some of the people who are considered ardent supporters of the Jews. This is not always made public, in fact, most of the time it is hidden, but it exists. A people cannot be forced into silence and have their deep-seated convictions expunged as well. When they are strong enough, you will hear from them again. They will not forget that they were once forced to swallow their dignity, their convictions, and their pride.

I wonder if, eventually, some people will say, "Alright, if I am labeled anti-Semitic because I fight for my rights, I will *be* anti-Semitic, and I will wear the label proudly." To call everyone who struggles for human rights and self determination anti-Semitic is to make anti-Semitism a label to be coveted. I discussed an analogous proclivity in a speech made at a March 27, 1983, rally in Washington, D.C., to protest U.S. intervention in El Salvador, where an estimated crowd of 50,000 people attended:

> Every movement for freedom is ascribed to communism. What stupidity! They give their enemies credit for inspiring efforts of liberation, freedom, independence, and self-determination. The highest qualities are ascribed to communist initiatives or involvement. It is comparable to blaming your adversary for sunshine, flowers, music, art and love. They have driven people who were not communists, who would have accepted assistance from anyone, into alliances with communists.

Indeed, the list of persons unfairly stigmatized with an anti-Semitic label is crammed with impressive names, including heads of state, ambassadors, foreign ministers, governors, senators, mayors, state officials, artists, clergymen, journalists, businessmen, soldiers, scholars, etc. Is it too far-fetched to project that a club might be formed as a defense against falsely being labeled anti-Semitic? But once such a club is formed who knows what direction it might take.

 With that prospect, unlikely as it may seem, those of us who try to speak the truth, who say publicly what many say privately, should receive accolades rather than attacks. It seems a large segment of the Jewish leadership prefers to delude themselves. When Black/Jewish conflict erupts, they call on the usual Black establishment leaders who have been selected and sustained with the help of those very Jewish leaders (note I am now criticizing some Black leaders). So the illusion continues: Blacks and Jews love each other. Jews have always been the greatest supporters Blacks have ever had. All Blacks recognize this. There is no serious problem that cannot be resolved with moral and financial support to civil rights organizations, more positive media exposure, and more appointments to prestigious seats of power.

 Then along comes a community-based leader, be it Malcolm X or Herbert Daughtry, who says: *No! We have some grave questions to raise.* We think there are deep, long-standing perceptions, attitudes, and arrangements of empowerment that need to be reconsidered. We believe that if we are honest and candid with each other, and if we work together as equals, we can resolve our differences and make life more harmonious, prosperous, and secure for *all* people. But we will not betray our people, we will not compromise our people's legitimate interests no matter how golden the offer, no matter how loudly or how viciously you attack us as anti-Semitic, and no matter what other forms of covert and overt reprisal you employ.

## UPDATE

As the manuscript for this book was being prepared for publication, F. Donnie Forde wrote a three-part article on Crown Heights which appeared in the *Daily Challenge* (October 5-7, 1996), a Black-owned newspaper published by Thomas Watkins, Jr.

In the final installment Forde wrote:

Reverend Herbert Daughtry of Brooklyn's House of The Lord
Church then proposed remedying the situation [conflict with
the Hasidim], according to the stridently provocative *New York
Post*, by having young Black men "get the Jews and the people in the long black coats."

Observe:
* Forde, while recognizing the reckless, irresponsible
nature of the *New York Post*, nevertheless, insists upon using
the most provocative portion of the quote attributed to me: i.e.,
"get the Jews ...."
* Forde, in misrepresenting the already egregious error in
the *Post*, goes a bit further in his distortion than in the original
publication; he claims that the *Post* quoted my statement as a
*solution* to the problem in Crown Heights. Even the *Post* did
not leap to that conclusion in interpreting the infamous quote
they ascribed to me. Rather, the *Post* writers knew better than
Negroes like Forde that my intention was Black empowerment;
believing that our powerlessness made us convenient targets for
assaults by Hasidim, police, etc.
* Then, Forde turns to "Daughtry's emotionality notwithstanding . . ." Why does Forde, a Black writer, in pigmentation,
mistake passion, activism, and justifiable anger for "emotionality?"
There are two other significant points to be underscored:
First, Mr. Forde doesn't include my denial in his article. As I have
pointed out many times since its initial publication, I have refut-
ed the quote with tape-recorded evidence of the Crown Heights
event. Doesn't fair and responsible journalism dictate mention
of my denial when one has been made, in print?
Second, doesn't fair and responsible journalism dictate interviewing the person who is prominently involved or significantly
quoted in the story? Mr. Forde does interview others, however,
including Hasidic rabbis, "Johnny-come-lately's" to the struggle,

and obscure non-participants; yet the one who has written most extensively about Crown Heights—the one with the longest history of involvement, the one most visible, the one most frequently quoted and misquoted regarding the events there —is unsought for the article. But, neither from my writings nor from conversation does Forde quote me directly. Why not?

Here we are eighteen years later, and a misquote printed in an irresponsible, slanderous rag, masquerading as a newspaper haunts me still.

In the past, I have had to expend precious time and energy writing to the White media to set the record straight. Now I have had to do the same with the Black media, in this instance, expressing a peculiar pain and paradox that a Black writer in a Black newspaper could be as biased and malicious as White writers in White papers.

## NOTES

1. Norman Mailer, *New York Daily News*, January 23, 1982.
2. Arthur Miller was a respected Black businessman who was strangled by the police.

**Chapter 6**

# Crown Heights

By 1978, in Crown Heights, the Lubavitcher Hasidim had usurped the turf Blacks had long considered their domain.[1] In addition, Hasidim were viciously attacking Black residents there. They even assaulted White television cameramen and policemen. In an extensive investigation, City Council President Carol Bellamy, charged that members of the Lubavitcher sect were misusing federal funds to purchase and renovate their property;[2] that there were "fiscal and programmatic irregularities." In the process, Blacks were being harassed and displaced. It would seem that the Hasidim were creating Hasidic settlements within the city. On every occasion during those confrontations, I, along with other Crown Heights leaders and residents, tried to make clear whom we perceived the usurpers to be; not the Jewish people as a whole, but the Lubavitcher Hasidim.

There was nothing new about confrontations with the Hasidim. In a letter to the U.S. Department of Justice, President of the Black Community Council, Dr. Vernal Cave, detailed a long history of abuses.[3] My first encounter with Hasidim occurred in the mid-1960s. I was attending a meeting organized by Black community groups concerned about the Hasidic Maccabees as vigilantes who harassed and attacked Black youngsters.

## CHARTER REVIEW COMMISSION

The New York City Charter requires a review of the Community Planning Board district lines every ten years. (A Community Planning Board participates in decisions regarding all that takes place within its community.) In 1975, pursuant to this mandate, the City's Charter Review Commission drew up plans revising the Planning Board district lines. Under their design, Planning Board No. 8, consisting mostly of Bedford Stuyvesant, would end at Atlantic Avenue to the south; Planning Board No. 9, consisting of Crown Heights, would be bound by Atlantic Avenue to the north, and Clarkson Avenue to the south.

Under pressure from Councilmen Bobby Steingut and Ted Silverman, as well as from the Hasidim, Mayor Abraham Beame, after initially endorsing the Charter Commission's plans, reversed his position and changed the plan in 1976. He drew up his own plan, moving Planning Board No. 9's northern boundary from Atlantic Avenue to Eastern Parkway, and extending its southern boundary to Clarkson Avenue, thus enhancing the Hasidim's power base while diminishing the Black community's power base in Crown Heights.

The Black Community Council of Crown Heights, led by Vernal Cave, tried to resist this encroachment on Black interests. On December 22, 1976, I, along with other community leaders, sat up half the night with Mayor Beame at Gracie Mansion, trying to dissuade him from using his influence to change the planning board lines.

A few days later I spoke before the Board of Estimates, predicting that if the Board voted to redraw the boundaries, they would be establishing a veritable Bar Lev[4] line along Eastern

48

Parkway that would breed hostility for years to come. The Board of Estimates meeting, held at Police Plaza, was literally packed with Hasidim who had arrived in advance. They were exceedingly hostile and constantly screamed insults. On several occasions, security officers had to separate Black and Hasidic advocates.

Despite our protests, the Board of Estimates voted to create the new lines. The venerable warrior, Paul O'Dwyer, then President of the City Council, and Percy Sutton, President of the Borough of Manhattan, voted against the measure. Mayor Beame, Brooklyn Borough President Sebastian Leone, Queens Borough President Donald Manes, Bronx Borough President Robert Abrams, and Staten Island Borough President Robert Connor voted in favor of the measure. (One good thing happened that day: Percy Sutton told us that he'd decided to run for Mayor.) Blacks, I knew, viewed the vote as yet another power struggle between Blacks and *some* Jews; and that Jews had won again. Significantly, no charges of anti-Semitism surfaced during this time.

On our weekly Sunday morning program on WWRL radio the following week, I preached a sermon entitled "The Agony of Powerlessness." I analyzed our situation and attempted to show that the powerless will always get "a raw deal." I urged unity and the development of political and economic power, my continuing theme. I criticized the Hasidim for their misuse of power, and I also criticized our Black leaders for not organizing our people to exercise power for our own interests:

> Let us suppose that the Hasidic Jews had tried to ingratiate themselves or, shall I say, tried to Uncle Goldstein their way to power. Do you think anything would have been gained? Probably here and there somebody would have felt sorry for them and given them a few jobs and some poverty bucks, but nothing really substantial.
>
> However, by organizing themselves first, then making demands, they made success depend upon their own strength.

49

So, when those Rabbis actually went somewhere to negotiate for their people, they had several thousand outside.

When Black preachers try to negotiate, we go by ourselves, then argue about who's going to be the spokesman, who will get the chance to make a television statement.

So we don't get anything, or we get a little if the "power person" is in a good mood, or if he can give us something without hurting himself or going against his own ethnic group.

The group of ministers who went to see Mayor Abe Beame was not about to move him from his position. All we were able to get from him was that we were going to cause him another sleepless night. In other words, we had a just cause, we pleaded with reason and righteousness. We had all the right on our side, we had everything going for us, but power. The Mayor knew as well as I knew that most of us don't have enough influence over people to get ten people anywhere except to a free chicken dinner.

I've got to say it bothers me. Until we can produce people like those in the Hasidim, we will always be begging, fighting each other over who gets to be spokesman, fighting each other over who gets next to the Mayor, or who's suppose to represent power.[5]

From that sermon one can easily discern that there was no animosity toward the Hasidim. They had won because they were better organized and because their people were in power. I was more critical of Black leaders than of the Hasidim. I reckon Black leaders could accuse me of being anti-Black.

In *The New York Times* (December 28, 1976), Francis X. Clines wrote:

The issue clearly is a classic study of a grassroots struggle for power —at least whatever modicum of actual power is to flow from the current reformation of the city's community district lines and processes. The initial plan for a community district centered on Eastern Parkway was changed after the tightly knit

Hasidic community of Crown Heights complained to political leaders.

One interesting aspect of the issue is that Blacks and Jews had lived in Crown Heights, side by side, for years before this fight over redistricting broke out, which some critics view as a secondary point, far removed from the real seats of power in the city.

In 1977, Reverend Heron Sam, Pastor of St. Mark's Episcopal Church and a founding member of the Black United Front (BUF), led a demonstration protesting Hasidic assaults on Blacks. It should be noted that Rev. Sam later betrayed the community by entering into a secret alliance with the Hasidim, who subsequently failed to honor their agreement with Rev. Sam.

## DEATH OF ARTHUR MILLER

On June 14, 1978, Arthur Miller, was strangled to death by the police. Miller was an enterprising businessman, a solid citizen, a stable family man, and an all around good guy who was even friendly with the police. This particular night he had gone to help his brother, who was having problems with the police. There are various accounts of what happened; but when it was all over Miller was dead for no apparent reason.

## BEATING OF VICTOR RHODES

In the early morning of Friday, June 16, 1978, thirty to fifty Hasidic men, women, and children savagely beat Victor Rhodes, a 15-year-old Black youth. I received a call from Victor's mother that night, informing me of the incident and asking me to visit her son, who was then in Kings County Hospital. The next morning I went to see him. Mayor Ed Koch, Assemblyman Al Vann, and Ms. Rhodes were there too. The Mayor appeared visibly shaken and genuinely moved by Victor's condition.

I was deeply saddened but also very angry. Here was a lad who would never be the same again, if he lived, which was questionable at that point. He was unconscious. His face was swollen like a balloon. What kind of people gang up on a 15-year-old kid? I vowed it would never happen again.

Why Victor Rhodes was beaten was never clear. June Jordan's account in *Seven Days* magazine (August 1978) is consistent with our facts:

> The night of the Hassidic attack upon Victor Rhodes, he was walking his girlfriend home from a party to which he planned to return: His friend lived opposite the main Hassidic synagogue on Eastern Parkway. He had to return to the party because his god-sister was there, waiting for his escort back to the home and legal guardian they shared, some few blocks away. It is inconceivable that Vic struck "one of the boys" (i.e. Yeshiva students, in version one, according to Rabbi Rosenfeld) or that "somebody" struck "an elderly Jew" (version two, according to same authority) because no one living in Crown Heights makes any mistake about the paramilitary control of Eastern Parkway in the vicinity of No. 770, the address of the world headquarters of the Lubavitcher Hassidim. According to Captain Katz of the 71st Precinct, Hassidic sect numbers a million and a half followers throughout the world and its nucleus, opposite the home of Victor Rhodes' companion, has been protected, since 1966, by a 24-hour-a-day New York Police Department patrol car, staffed by two cops. The same remarkable protection has been the privilege of the head Lubavitcher rabbi's private home, two blocks south. (Responding to outcry against the special treatment enjoyed by the Hassidim, New York Mayor Ed Koch last week ordered the vigil ended, only to be apparently defied by his Police Commissioner, who said this status quo would be maintained until "an alternative plan of protection with routine patrols" could be devised. It is interesting to note that the taxpayer cost of such singular services, since 1966, amounts to more than $4 million; when last have you heard of comparable monies made available for jobs for Blacks kids Victor's

age, for instance?)

It is unlikely that Victor Rhodes would have chosen to cross the Parkway and thereby pass through patently Hassidic turf: The Black gynecologist Dr. Rufus A. Nichols and his wife, Janet, who lived with their family just eight or nine doors down from "770," readily recount varieties of harassment they suffer as neighbors to the Hassidim....

It is hardly probable that a 16-year old boy, by himself, after midnight, would walk into such an armed, bristling, vigilante-patrolled encampment, per se, let alone accost a young, or an old, or a middle-aged Hassid! According to eyewitnesses to the beating, Victor was chased by no less than 30 Hassidic men and women on foot, bicycles, in cars, and in vans, and finally caught. When Black by-standers tried to stop the beating, they were threatened with guns and told, "Don't come near him, don't touch him."

On June 19, 1978, at a meeting in Manhattan at One Police Plaza attended by community members, police brass, the city administration, and attended by Koch himself, I stated that the Mayor showed great compassion over the Victor Rhodes beating. I also reiterated my theme: *We were being beaten and killed because we are powerless. We must develop power. Every group acts on behalf of its own. We must develop power to protect ourselves and promote our own interests.* I added that *when political and economic power have been equitably distributed, I would gladly stand on the steps of City Hall or anywhere else and declare that creed, color, and ethnicity do not matter. Until then, we must organize ourselves and act with self-interest.* At that point there was no suggestion of anti-Semitism from any quarter.

## POWER AND POWERLESSNESS

Obviously, there were those observing my words and activities who felt threatened by me. This, I believe, was because of my urging, on every possible occasion, that Blacks unite and develop economic and political power. The charge of anti-Semitism that came later was an attempt to isolate and discredit me and to divert attention away from the message that I endeavored to deliver to my people, indeed to all New Yorkers. Selwyn Raab admitted as much in his June 23, 1978 article in *The New York Times*.

> Mr. Daughtry said that the death of Mr. Miller has raised issues other than police brutality. "Arthur Miller died because the police see Black men as a menace," he asserted. "But his death also reflects on the powerlessness of Black people to affect their destinies. It's more than a single issue of the police. The larger issues are how the city's institutions control and manipulate Black people—how, when Mayor Koch gets ready to cut the budget, it's the people with the least political power who get their services cut more than anyone else."...
>
> Many police officials in Brooklyn and at Police Headquarters believe that Mr. Daughtry's coalition has in a short time gained widespread credibility and influence within the Black neighborhoods of Brooklyn.[6]

Other articles reflected the same sentiment. June Jordan wrote in *Seven Days*:

> In Rev. Daughtry's House of the Lord's Pentecostal Church, I have seen my people rise, shouting as one to the call for intensive voter registration which Daughtry deems essential to the surcease of Black powerlessness.[7]

The *Soho Weekly News* wrote:

> "Arthur Miller was the guy society usually tells us to look to," said the Rev. Herbert Daughtry, Black Pentecostal minister who has led a series of protests and City Hall negotiations. "He had a history of working together closely with the Police Dept." ...
>
> "No, there was no visible tension," he says, "but there's always latent tension. What to one community may be severe tension, to us is business as usual."

Daughtry's analysis is like a big lasso, somehow tying together into one package the police violence, Chassidic over-reaction, City Hall indifference to blacks, and sexual procliv-ities of Congressman Fred Richmond.

"Fred Richmond may be a symbol of powerlessness", he says without flinching. He plunges ahead, landing eventually on solid ground. Blacks in Brooklyn have been kicked around for years because they don't vote, Daughtry suggests.

Richmond was elected four years ago in the 14th CD, which—in its zigzagging east-west course across Brooklyn — was supposed to have been tailor-made for a minority con-gressman. But the almost two-thirds majority held by blacks and Hispanics never materialized at the polls, and Richmond—who has confessed to soliciting sexual favors from young black boys—won in a landslide.

Now, Daughtry says, much of Brooklyn's Black commu-nity including parts of Crown Heights - finds itself represent-ed by a white man who has violated "the moral code." "No people can allow that to happen and not respond—and expect to have their self-respect," he says.[8]

## The *Phoenix:*

To Daughtry, the death of [Randolph] Evans and the more recent death of black Crown Heights community leader Arthur Miller are a reflection of blacks' powerlessness.

"Until we develop power through the political process, things like police brutality will continue," said Daughtry, who insists that "things have not changed, that's the same old tale" from blacks in Brooklyn.

The Reverend has also made Congressman Fred Richmond a target calling for his resignation and now urging his defeat at the polls. Daughtry says that "Richmond him-self" is not the issue; the issue is what he stands for. Richmond is the ultimate insult. That he would choose to remain in office after debasing a black child and will run for reelection indicates blacks' powerlessness again.

On a recent Saturday morning, plans for a big voter registration rally were being made and Daughtry was part of them.[9]

In a profile on me entitled "Feisty Preacher in Vanguard of Rights Issues in Brooklyn," C. Gerald Fraser of *The New York Times* wrote:

Sunday service at the House of the Lord Pentecostal Church in Brooklyn is in its last half-hour, and the Rev. Herbert D. Daughtry is roaring to the finish of his 45-minute sermon on "Power, Politics, and Religion."

"The only thing I'm guilty of is battling for my people," he says. He wheels to his left and says he is guilty of wanting an education for his people. He spins right and says he is guilty of wanting to see "our men" working.

His full black clerical robe and a long Ghanaian kente-cloth stole he wears swings back and forth as he wheels and spins, his eyes ranging over the semicircle of pews in which the congregation of a few hundred sits and fans and nods approval.

Mr. Daughtry has become a kind of ecclesiastical point man, his name appearing frequently in newspaper articles and his face on television newscasts as he challenges Brooklyn's businessmen and political and police organizations to end what he perceives as racial injustice...

Asked what he saw as major issues for Brooklyn's Black residents, Mr. Daughtry replied: "Jobs—jobs is what I think is the surface issue, but I think the major issue is the imbalance of power. Jobs go to the powerful. We are powerless, for example, against the police. We don't have any impact."

"And even deeper than powerlessness," he added, "is personlessness—lack of identity. There is no feeling of self-worth," he said, among many Black people. "High self-esteem moves one to power, but you can't make a man powerful—something has to happen to the mind."

Significantly, Fraser also wrote that people found me sincere:

Not everyone is enamored of his style, but one Bedford-Stuyvesant pastor explained that he was unwilling to publicly criticize Mr. Daughtry because "we are arriving at a unity among Black people that we have never had in Brooklyn before."

An executive of a Brooklyn department store who has negotiated with Mr. Daughtry characterized him as "a very sincere, dedicated person who basically wants to help Black people achieve many of the things that white people want to achieve. I found him honorable," said the executive, who asked not to be identified. "I found him highly interested in media coverage. He's interested in power, but I personally believe he's not interested in power for his own personal gain." William Nielson, the 84th Precinct's community-relations officer, said he had been dealing with Mr. Daughtry for four years and had found him to be "a gentleman."

"During demonstrations," Officer Nielson said, "I could always come and talk to him and he was realistic about the problem. He had his cause, and our job is to protect life and property, and he realizes our situation. When I call him, he gets back to me. We have a rapport."[10]

Earl Caldwell of the *New York Daily News*, who also wrote a personal profile on me entitled "Rev. Daughtry Is Fit to Be a King," wrote:

It was warm that day. It was near the end of September and late that morning at City Hall the police began to gather. First they were on the steps out front and then more of them came and made long lines that stretched along both sides of the building.

They came in old green buses and in cars, and their numbers continued to swell, and by noon, the police were everywhere. They built a solid wall of blue around the block.

"What's going on?" someone asked. "It looks like the President must be coming to town." It was the kind of show the police made when something important is about to take place. On this morning though the show was not for a president. It was for a preacher—the Rev. Herbert Daughtry.

Not much is said about it, but there is a movement on the rise now in New York City and the Rev. Daughtry has emerged as the lightning rod for what is building.

It is an old story. Almost always when there is a crisis and leadership is absent, blacks turn to the church.

Once it was Adam Clayton Powell Jr. Then it was the Rev. Martin Luther King Jr. And now, out of Brooklyn, comes Herbert Daughtry.

"He's ready." Sam Pinn, who heads Brooklyn CORE, says. "He's ready to lead and he wants to lead." Sam Pinn has no reservations about Daughtry. "He has charisma, courage and intelligence", he said. "And he's tireless. Those are the traits you find in great leaders. Everybody says there is no King now ... but there is." ...

Some see Malcolm in him. Whites generally do not like him. But they never like leaders who are black and forceful.

Daughtry's background is similar to Malcolm's. He's off the streets. "Dope," he says, "I know it. I was in that jungle. I lived it. I know what it is to be in jail."

He was in jail 25 years ago. If you ask him, he will tell you that he was a street hustler, a manipulator. He was also once an armed robber. His turn around came in jail.

"I started praying," he says. "Getting down in that stinking jail cell - I decided that I wanted to commit my life absolutely to the Lord."

Daughtry is not a politician but he is political. He's into voter registration. He talks politics constantly. But . . . his talk is critical of elected officials. Now they've given him center stage. As Sam Pinn said, when speaking of the elected officials, "They're not about to take the risks. They fear the wrath of the established order."

Daughtry has no political base to lose. His church is with him. And his support is growing. He is in every section of the city. He has a local radio broadcast. He has a newspaper. He has even had a film made, documenting his movement.

"Our church is run down," he says. "We don't have any money and we don't have a lot of people. But so much of what happens in the city goes through here now."[11]

On a number of occasions I led demonstrations composed of hundreds and sometimes thousands of poor, jobless, impoverished Blacks—predominantly young—from Brooklyn across the Brooklyn Bridge, past City Hall onto Wall Street. And I have called attention to the sinful discrepancy. Here were impoverished people, marching into an area considered the financial capital of the world, where executives received incomes in excess of one million dollars a year. How could there be peace with such disparity?

At a community meeting held at P.S. 289, on the night of June 19, 1981, I called for a community patrol to protect our people. I suggested that the Hasidim were a bunch of cowards: *They only attack when they greatly outnumber their victim. But, when we'd organized our patrol and men met men, then we would see what the people in the long, black coats would do.* As I have already discussed, the next day the *New York Post* said that I wanted to "get the Jews."

These were painful times for Black people: 15-year-old Randolph Evans had been killed by a police officer; 15-year-old Victor Rhodes had been beaten to the point of death by the Lubavitcher Hasidim; and now a respected businessman, Arthur Miller, had been killed by policemen. We were still on the street picketing the downtown Brooklyn stores over the Randy Evans killing when Miller was killed and Rhodes was beaten. We called that summer "Bloody Summer 1978." We put out a flyer detailing the attacks and the murders.

# History of the "Bloody Summer of 1978"

- Wednesday, June 14, 1978
  Arthur Miller murdered by the police—77th pct.
- Thursday, June 15, 1978
  Victor Rhodes beaten into a coma by Hasidic Jews.
- Thursday, June 22, 1978
  Charles King beaten and hospitalized by traffic police.
- Sunday, July 23, 1978
  Packed bus returning from Riis Beach attacked by a gang of Whites at Utica and Avenue A.
- Monday, July 31, 1978
  Girard Mark attacked and hospitalized by a gang of Whites in Prospect Park.
- Monday, August 14, 1978
  4 Black youth and 1 Hispanic youth beaten by a White gang in a planned attack in Gravesend, Brooklyn.
- Tuesday, August 15, 1978
  Thurman Robinson beaten and hospitalized by police—73rd Precinct.

In early July, we organized The Black United Front (BUF) and the Arthur Miller Black Community Patrol. (*See Chapter 4*: Creating a Movement, Empowering a People, Perpetuating a Memory.) On July 16, 1978, we held a massive demonstration in front of the Lubavitcher Headquarters and marched to the 71st Precinct. A conservative estimate numbered attendance at more than 5000. It was a peaceful rally. By now accusations of anti-Semitism had begun to saturate the media. Black people were extremely angry; after everything that had happened to us, now we had to defend ourselves against charges of anti-Semitism.

It is true that I personally condemned the Hasidim and the police in the strongest language at my command. I said that I wanted to deliver a message that would reach all the way to Israel so that Golda Meir could hear it. (A large number of the Lubavitcher sect live in Israel). I spoke of Jewish political power, i.e., District Attorney Eugene Gold, Brooklyn Borough President Howard Golden, etc. However, at no point was I critical of Jews as a whole or as a religious group.

I was, however, critical of Black leadership in particular and of Black people in general for allowing ourselves to become so helpless. I emphasized the need to develop political and economic power, and standing on the precinct steps, I added: "The next time the Hasidim touch our kids, we will tear this community up." Clearly, my language was directed toward the Hasidim and to the New York Police Department.

Even so, some of things I said during those turbulent days I would probably say differently in more serene times. One other point of interest: *Village Voice* editor Jack Newfield said he regretted not criticizing me for my "anti-Semitic raving." But, where was Newfield when the Hasidim were assaulting Blacks or anyone else who interfered with them, even as they themselves were interfering with the legal and moral rights of others? Had he taken on the Hasidim before I came on the scene, perhaps there would have been no need to take me on, for maybe there would have been no attack on Victor Rhodes.

## SILENCE OF THE JEWISH COMMUNITY

That the larger Jewish community did not condemn the Lubavitcher Hasidim and the United Federation Of Teachers (UFT) was a disappointment to most of us. They refused to say that these groups were using the anti-Semitic cry to shift the focus away from the real issue—empowerment. We were witnessing the recurrence of the Ocean Hill–Brownsville debacle, where *most* Jews did not condemn certain factions of the UFT and its President, Albert Shanker, who used the anti-Semitic ploy to divert attention away from parental empowerment.

Frankly, in a real sense, some Jews were rather hypocritical. I know the contempt some Jews hold for the Hasidim. I know that some Jews moved away when the Hasidim moved to Crown Heights. I know that John Lindsay (New York's mayor from 1966 to 1973) put a police car in front of the Synagogue on Eastern Parkway and in front of Hasidic Rabbi Menachem Schneerson's home, not to protect the Hasidim from Blacks, but to protect the Hasidim from each other. There had been a feud between the Hasidim in Crown Heights and another Hasidic sect in Williamsburg. Yet, when we pointed to the barbarism of the Hasidim, we were labeled anti-Semitic. Once again, Black people, the victims, were turned into the villains.

Subsequently, in the beating of Victor Rhodes, two Hasidim were apprehended and then acquitted.

In the killing of Randolph Evans, Patrolman Robert Torsney's "defense" was a rare disease called "Psychomotor Epileptic Seizure," an affliction no one had ever heard of before. Torsney was told that he needed two years of psychiatric care, and that he could spend weekends at home. The Epileptic Foundation was infuriated and publicly disassociated itself from any such disease. The U.S. Attorney never indicted Torsney on violation of Evans' civil rights. In fact, nothing more was ever heard about the case.

The policemen who killed Arthur Miller were exonerated. On October 25, 1979, the Grand Jury reached the decision that the policemen had killed Miller "in the line of duty."

Then on top of all that, Brooklyn Congressman Fred Richmond admitted that he had sexually abused Black boys. He also was acquitted. (*See Chapter 13*: Fred Richmond.)

What is significant to remember is that when the dust had settled in Crown Heights, Hasidim ambitions and violence, though contained, were not completely eradicated, and Blacks were viewed as anti-Semitic. Similar to Ocean Hill–Brownsville, most Jews, as well as many others, viewed the whole Crown Heights struggle as a sign of increased anti-Semitism, and those Blacks who fought for their rights, protection and interests (i.e., against the Hasidim's savagery and avarice) were, and are, considered anti-Semitic.

# NOTES

1. For detailed information on Crown Heights, see PART II: INSIDE THE STORM.
2. Carol Bellamy, Report on Chevra Machaziekei Hashcuriah, Inc, The City of New York, City Hall, December 1978.
3. Vernal Cave, Letter to United States Department of Justice, June 28, 1978 (unpublished). Available from Daughtry personal files.
4. Bar Lev is the boundary line separating Egypt and Israel.
5. Herbert Daughtry, "The Agony of Powerlessness" (unpublished). December 1976. Available from The House of the Lord Church.
6. *The New York Times*, June 23, 1978.
7. *Seven Days* Magazine, August 1978.
8. *Soho Weekly News,* June 29, 1978.
9. *The Phoenix,* July 13, 1978.
10. C. Gerald Fraser, *The New York Times,* August 6, 1978.
11. Earl Caldwell, *New York Daily News,* November 25, 1982.

**Chapter 7**

# Edward I. Koch — Mayor of New York City

≈≈≈≈≈≈

## THE FEUD IN THE CITY

It has been said that the feud between Ed Koch and myself is grounded in anti-Semitism. Nothing could be further from the truth. I led the first group that met with Koch in January, 1978. The minutes from that meeting will show that I offered to work with the Mayor for a better New York.[1]

The meeting came after a demonstration I led at the Brooklyn Museum on January 1, 1978, the night of the first Koch inauguration. In November 1976, a White police officer named Robert Torsney had walked up to Randolph Evans, a 15-year-old

Black youth and, without provocation, shot him dead. Randy, a decent youngster, had no police record. Torsney pleaded not guilty by reason of temporary insanity (he claimed that he suffered a "psychomotor epileptic seizure" but was nevertheless able to shoot young Randy Evans in the head point blank). In November 1977, the jury sentenced Torsney to psychiatric treatment. The Black community was furious. (For more detailed information on the Evans case, see *Chapter 6:* CROWN HEIGHTS and *Part II:* LETTER TO THE METROPOLITAN COUNCIL OF THE AMERICAN JEWISH CONGRESS.)

We organized a group called the Coalition of Concerned Leaders and Citizens to Save Our Youth, a group comprised mostly of community-based leaders. Of course, Randy was not the first youngster killed by "New York's Finest." Before Randy there had been 11-year-old Ricky Borden, 14-year-old Claude Reese, and 13-year-old Clifford Glover. The Coalition, which would later become the Black United Front (BUF), would use economic boycott as a tactic to compel the business community to join us in demanding punishment for Torsney. (*See Chapter 4:* CREATING A MOVEMENT ...) Beyond that, we wanted federal investigation of the entire New York City Police Department and development of a comprehensive youth program. We started our boycott of downtown Brooklyn stores on December 17, 1977. We really had no other option because, politically, the city was in a lame duck situation; Mayor Abraham Beame was on his way out, so he couldn't or wouldn't do anything, and Koch wasn't inclined to deal with anything before his inauguration.

In a populist effort to reach the citizenry, the new Mayor held a public inauguration ceremony in each of the city's five boroughs. So on a snowy January inauguration night at the Brooklyn Museum, we decided to try to get the Mayor's attention. We succeeded in catching Koch's security off guard and in capturing the stage, and when Mayor Koch came on, I snatched the microphone and would not allow him to speak as I informed him and the audience of our grievances. Both Koch and the audience seemed receptive enough. Koch asked me if I could quiet the crowd; I told him I could, but that we wanted to meet with him. He promised to meet with us within two weeks. During the intervening period, I had several friendly conversations with Herb Rickman, the Mayor's Special Assistant. The Mayor kept his word, and, as I have already mentioned, it was a cordial meeting.

For that meeting, there were three items on our agenda: police brutality, a youth program; we also sought his support in our effort to have the federal government indict Torsney on the violation of Evans' civil rights. As to the first, Koch told us to meet with Police Commissioner Robert McGuire. As to the second, he said a Blue Ribbon Commission was just finishing a report, and that, once he reviewed it, he would develop a youth program. He said he would write a letter to U.S. Attorney David Trager, regarding the Randy Evans killing, which he did. We came away with high hopes. A week later, we held a news conference to report on our meeting with the Mayor; I even announced to the press that the meeting had been cordial.[2]

On February 1, 1978, we started a series of meetings with Police Commissioner McGuire. We placed before him our list of recommendations.[3] At the first Randolph Evans Memorial Scholarship Fund Dinner, Bob McMillan, Vice President of Abraham & Strauss, said that BUF not only confronted people —challenging business people, elected officials, i.e., the power broker —but also laid out viable programs. The meetings were amicable, but eventually we came to feel that they were unproductive. McGuire could do nothing without the Policemen's Benevolent Association (PBA), and the Black community's perception of the PBA—that it was racist to the core—was certainly not unfounded.

On May 19, 1978, we wrote to Commissioner McGuire, inquiring about the implementation of the monthly meeting we had recommended. (At the time, we believed that, whatever else, if Black leaders and the Police Commissioner, with his staff, could meet periodically, much of the hostility and abuse of police power

67

might be averted.) McGuire never responded.[4]

My disappointment and criticism of Ed Koch were rooted in his policies, programs, attitude, and behavior, which I believed were anti-Black and anti-poor, his on-again, off-again relationship with a handful of establishment Blacks notwithstanding. It is worth mentioning that in a television interview aired on November 29 and December 6, 1980, newsman Gabe Pressman asked if I hated Koch. "No," I replied, "I don't hate him. In fact, I find him rather likable at times. What I resent are his programs and policies."

## ON THE WORLD STAGE: KOCH AGAINST THE UNITED NATIONS

In February 1982, Yehuda Blum, the Israeli Ambassador to the United Nations, proposed to the Mayor of New York that the quote on the Isaiah Wall at the U.N. headquarters be changed, because of the General Assembly's condemnation of Israel's annexation of the Golan Heights. The quote reads:

> And he shall judge among the nations, and shall rebuke many people: and they shall beat their swords into plowshares and their spears into pruninghooks: nation shall not lift up sword against nation, neither shall they learn war any more. *Isaiah 2:4*

Mayor Koch indicated that he would not remove the quote, but that he would speak to the hypocrisy at the U.N., which he referred to as "that cess pool."

First of all, the quote from Isaiah articulates the hope that war would end one day. What better statement from the site where the nations of the world meet.

Second, the United Nations is just that; a union of nations. It is the place where the family of nations meet to debate, to plan, to arbitrate, etc. How can the mayor of the host city presume to act so precipitously toward that world body, to deface a structure, inscribed with the Holy Writ, and that signifies the desire for world peace? Ed Koch would, nevertheless, add words to his liking.

Third, Koch and Blum demonstrated incredible disrespect, not only for the distinguished members of the United Nations, but also for the various ethnic groups throughout the city and the nation.

It is one thing for the Mayor to have temper tantrums in New York, the city where he was elected to office and where his antics are encouraged by a doting press. But, it is another to carry this supercilious attitude onto an international forum.

Koch disgraced New Yorkers before the world. There is already a perception in the international community that Tel Aviv initiates U.S. foreign policy. Now the perception might be conveyed that New York City's mayor steers U.S. policy.

Fourth, it is significant that the reason behind the furor was Israel's annexation of parts of the Golan Heights. One would have to look long and hard to find a posture as arrogantly ethnocentric as Koch's and Blum's.

It is outrageous enough that when the nations of the world condemn a member state for annexing land, the accused member state turns around and calls its critics criminals; but then that foreign state persuades a U.S. city official, the mayor of New York, to agree. One is driven to ask: What would happen if it were the other way around; what if Syria or Jordan had taken land from Israel? But, here again we see the old game of making the victim the villain.

Why does Koch react the way he does? Surely it cannot be his concern for justice. The unconscionable acts committed by South Africa's racist regime, unquestionably criminal, received not a whimper from City Hall. Koch reacts the way he does because he is Jewish, and for him it is not a question of right or wrong, of international propriety, or of statesmanship. So tied is he to Israeli interests that he uses his influence to help Israel wherever and whenever he can, at the expense of anyone else. And if anyone dares criticize Koch or Blum, I guarantee that he or she will be labeled anti-Semitic.

## RADIO POWER

On February 18, 1982, Mayor Koch made a statement criticizing President Ronald Reagan for supporting South Africa, and he called on Blacks to support Israel. That same day I did a radio interview on WLIB, in essence thanking the mayor for his support but pointing out that the situations were vastly different.

Our brothers and sisters in South Africa were removing no one, annexing no one's land; they want only what is theirs. Second, Israel is a staunch supporter of the Apartheid regime in South Africa. To be consistent, Koch would also have to criticize Prime Minister Begin. I went on to say (this part of the interview was never played) that most Blacks would support Israel if there were an independent Palestinian state and a termination of Israel's support for South Africa. I was certain that an avalanche of anti-Semitic charges would follow. A few days later Koch dropped his U.N. venture. Perhaps my radio interview had something to do with it.

## NOTES

1. See Minutes of Meeting with Mayor Ed Koch, January 12, 1978 (unpublished). Available from Daughtry's personal files.
2. See Press Conference at City Hall and Press Release, January 7, 1978 (unpublished). Available from Daughtry's personal files.
3. See recommendations to Commissioner Robert McGuire, 1978 (unpublished). Available from Daughtry's personal files.
4. See Correspondence: Daughtry/McGuire (Re: Periodic Meeting), May 19, 19788 (unpublished). Available from Daughtry's personal files.

**Chapter 8**

# Town Hall Meetings with the Mayor

～～～～～～

## TOWN HALL MEETING NUMBER ONE: KOCH COMES TO HARLEM

When tensions between Koch and the Black community were at their zenith, the Mayor decided to hold a Town Hall meeting in Harlem. These Town Hall meetings were theoretically a good idea, and Koch should be commended for inaugurating them. They gave the communities an opportunity to meet the Mayor and his aides, an opportunity to present their complaints and to express their desires. Koch invariably had his top aides with him, giving the impression of bringing government to the people.

But because of the perception in the Black community that Koch was a racist, many people thought it was not a good idea for him to come to Harlem at that particular time. Koch, however, always determined that he would "not be intimidated," insisted upon holding the meeting.

To ensure attendance at the meeting, ministers agreed to urge their parishioners to be present. As most had predicted, the meeting was a farce. It was attended only by the elderly, most of them regular, obedient churchgoers. Blacks protested both inside and outside. There were probably as many policemen present as there were community people. Koch had to be ushered out the side door. I was not in Harlem on that occasion; however, Jitu Weusi, Chief of Operations of the Black United Front (BUF), offered some interesting comments on Koch's visit.

But, unlike the meetings in Forest Hills, Bay Ridge and other White, middle-class areas, the Harlem gathering was not going to be a town meeting but a "constituent assembly." Taking no chances of being embarrassed and blowing his image-building performances, Koch and his cortege of commissioners and department heads engaged in a rare form of "plantation politics." Instead of an open forum of questions and answers asked by informed citizens, the gathering relegated the disenfranchised residents to a low level gripe session. Those who wanted to speak with Koch and his corp personally had to come forward to small tables and privately state their problem and then hear what the city could do about it. It was the Master calling in each of the slaves individually for a private chat about their hardships as they suffer collectively.

Neither Koch, nor any of his staff attempted to deal conclusively with a variety of mass issues which affect the lives of our people as a whole. As the residents came up one at a time, photographers and newspapermen were taking pictures and getting small tidbits of human interest data that would provide the image of a "Mayor who cares." This circus continued for the better part of two hours. Many within the audience were dissatisfied with this format and realized that Harlem and its people were being exploited once again. However, the obvious presence of plainclothes, undercover policemen and the confusing assurance of the Harlem political elite prevented any massive display of discontent and obstruction.

An angry group of participants resorted to a steady chorus of "Koch is a racist" and "Recall Mayor Koch." While these tactics were effective, they were not enough to completely cancel this sham session, and the afternoon ordeal ended promptly at 5 pm with Bull Koch and his contingent completing their mission.

This fiasco heightened an already intense atmosphere, and the next day brought more name calling.

## TOWN HALL MEETING NUMBER TWO: KOCH COMES TO BROOKLYN

Koch, still aiming to prove his courage, came to Brooklyn. On November 12, 1980, Town Hall Meeting No. Two took place at Boys & Girls High School.

Again, there were as many policemen as community people at the meeting; the total attendance was approximately 200 people. Koch amiably but condescendingly opened with introductory remarks on random subjects, and then opened the floor to questions. One questioner asked: "Being Mayor of New York, why do you show more compassion for Jews in Russia and never speak out on behalf of Black youth killed by New York Policemen?" Koch hastily replied that the question was anti-Semitic. The meeting, already extremely heated, abruptly ended.

The next day and for many days thereafter, Koch and the press focused on the Jewish-related question that had been asked, emphasizing that it was anti-Semitic. Some members of the press said that the meeting was broken up by Blacks screaming malicious anti-Semitic rhetoric, and, of course, I was the designated ring leader. But, in fact, during the entire meeting the only reference to Jews was the perfectly legitimate question raised by the elderly man to whom I have already alluded. (It was reported that within a month this man was fired from his job, and later there were even attempts to prevent him from receiving his unemployment checks.)

My only input at the Meeting was to jump from my seat in response to Koch's statement and rush to the microphone to charge the Mayor with insulting the community. When I reached the microphone, I discovered that the plug had been pulled. So, my voice could not have carried very far.

## Town Hall Meeting Number Three: Koch Replay on Brooklyn

After the Boys & Girls High Town Hall Meeting, Koch said he would not come to the Black community again unless he was invited by responsible Black leaders. Several Black ministers took that as their cue. They arranged for a meeting with Koch and invited him to return to Brooklyn. Koch agreed to come but required that the audience be screened. Meetings were held by some community leaders to develop a screening plan that would satisfy Koch.

These "screening" sessions broke down. The overwhelming majority of the community believed that it was improper for Koch to dictate the composition of a community meeting. If he wanted to meet with certain leaders, that was his prerogative. But to call a community meeting, inviting only screened attendees, was, to put it kindly, bogus. The ministers, however, were insistent that the meeting take place. They went back to Koch and persuaded him to come anyway, promising that they would take full responsibility.

We, the Black United Front, began to organize against the meeting. We thought the meeting would be counter-productive for the Black community for several reasons:

- First, the ministers who were trying to arrange the meeting had little credibility in the community. A couple of them were known opportunists. An orderly meeting would not only give

74

Koch credibility, but would further the ambitions of these ministers.

- Second, we thought Koch was only trying to use these meetings for his own propaganda purposes, when what we needed was some concrete demonstration of the Mayor's intentions to deal honestly and substantively with the Black community.
- Third, we thought that the meeting would make for greater fragmentation and ill-will within the Black community at a time when we desperately needed unity.

If the meeting were held the Black community would lose. If the meeting came off well, it would appear that Koch was a good guy, and the majority of the Black community—the "responsible" Blacks especially—viewed him as such. After all, it was only a handful of anti-Semitic radicals who opposed Koch. Obviously, this would encourage Koch to continue his anti-Black, anti-poor policies, and the only Blacks who would benefit would be these opportunistic ministers and their ilk.

If, on the other hand, Koch came to the meeting and met stiff opposition, he would then be viewed by the White community as tough and fearless, "standing up to the niggers" who had wrested control from the cowardly "responsible" leaders. More votes and White support would encourage Koch in his then current policies.

Given the above possibilities, we felt it was still better to demonstrate, and risk misrepresentation of our actions and motives, and perhaps fueling Koch's cannon, than doing nothing, and thus convey the impression that the Black community was satisfied with Koch. We would have to make a statement, a statement that said: *Most Blacks are dissatisfied and angry, and we represent them. Those who attend the meeting are a few naive souls and the meager followers of these opportunistic ministers.*

We also risked cultivating misunderstanding among our own

people. The meeting was scheduled to be held at a church, for the leaders who organized it were ministers. Koch was the Mayor, and many of our people—particularly the elderly—still respect authority, no matter what those in authority do. And there were people asking, "Why not come to the community meeting and tell Koch what you want?" No organization, at least the kind we were attempting to build, wants to alienate the people.

Another risk involved the number of attendees. If we did not have a good crowd, or if there were more people attending the meeting than demonstrating against it, we would lose. And a defeat at that time would have been critical for us. We had repeatedly demonstrated our capacity to mobilize great numbers, and therefore, BUF had become the organization to which people looked to express their wishes with mass action. The continued viability of our organization depended upon our ability to rally people. We would have to have a good gathering outside, while discouraging people from attending the meeting.

The only victory of sorts would be if the Black community would, in effect, say to Koch: *We appreciate your wanting to come back to Brooklyn, but we have decided to meet among ourselves and develop an agenda that would reflect the needs of our people. At such time, we will be back in touch with you.* Such an approach would say to all: *We are willing to meet with the Mayor, but we do not want to participate in a nonproductive meeting. When we have organized ourselves and developed our proposals we would gladly meet.* Other than the opportunistic ministers and their cohorts, who benefit from back room deals and a divided community, no one could argue against that approach.

This is precisely the same approach we used when we met with Koch in July 1978. I believe that when community people meet to talk with elected officials in power, it should be done only after consultation with the broadest representation of the community, and a delegation selected or elected by the community should attend the meeting. Only in the rarest instances should there be private meetings and then only after extensive consultation with the advisors and members of the community. Perhaps this is one of the reasons why BUF had been able to gain pervasive credibility.

For all the reasons alluded to, we initiated a meeting with the ministers through Assemblyman Al Vann. On December 8, 1980, we met at the Restoration Plaza. We had a proposal to put before the ministers. We would agree to the meeting under the following conditions: that I could make a short statement; that Koch would agree to meet within a reasonable period of time following the meeting; and that we would continue to meet with the ministers with a view toward building greater unity in the Black community.

We thought this was a reasonable compromise. I would have an opportunity to state our position, evincing a show of unity. The question of a future meeting with Koch gave us the greatest difficulty, for it had the sound of asking for another meeting with Koch—the very thing we were against. Heretofore, we had argued that we wanted something concrete before attending another meeting. Now, we seemed to be departing from that position. But we really didn't want a confrontation, especially with our own people, so we were prepared to compromise. But at least in calling for a future meeting, we knew we could organize the community, create an agenda, and elect a delegation to negotiate, which as I have indicated, was our approach. And, further meetings with the ministers were an expression of our desire for a better relationship.

The ministers said that they would meet with Koch and get back in touch with us. We gave them a deadline; we had to know in enough time to organize if the answer was no. Word came from Koch: "No deal."

The Black United Front proceeded to mobilize the overwhelming majority of Blacks in our Brooklyn community. On December 13, 1980, a Town Hall meeting was held at John Wesley Methodist Church. Passes had been given to those ministers who wanted to attend. There were a few dignitaries attending; one stayed outside with us. Inside about a hundred elderly people were seated as if in a church service; the crowd outside numbered approximately five hundred. We surrounded the church. In the middle of the street, I stood on an oil drum and addressed the people, as was my custom. What I did and said that day is what I always do and say when addressing outdoor crowds in a confrontational situation. I explained why we were there, why we adopted the stance we took. I emphasized our sanity and our credentials. Then I expounded on our powerlessness, putting it all in an international and historical context, and concluded with an admonition on our past behavior and on what we needed to do for the future.

Frankly, I enjoy talking to people in the street. To capture and hold their attention inspires me. Many of these people represent the excluded, the dispossessed. As a result of these sessions, we increased our visibility and associations with all our people, and our membership also increased.

When the meeting inside ended, the police set up a ruse. They moved nearly all their forces to a side door, giving us the impression that Koch was coming out of that door. We were all set to give him an earth shaking howl, but Koch furtively escaped through another door.

On our way back to our cars, an altercation erupted between police and the community. Community people were beaten, and three of our members were arrested. They were later acquitted by a Brooklyn Grand Jury.

The police have their side of the story, but one thing is clear; we did not intend a confrontation. (I have already discussed how Koch would use this meeting, i.e, that he was accepted by "responsible" Blacks, and that I was an instigator. However, it would be more difficult for him to use an orderly protest, than a disorderly one.) We had women and children with us. The last thing we wanted was a confrontation. We had made our point: the Town Hall Meeting was sparsely attended, and we had a good crowd. Clearly we had persuaded many to stay away, and we counted this as a victory. We did not want a confrontation. We believed the police initiated it; many of them had been after us for a long time. We had constantly criticized their killing of Blacks and Latinos, and their brutality and insensitivity toward people of color. And on this day, they were particularly angry, because they had been forced to remove their helmets and their sticks.

After receiving the report on the arrests and on the wounded, I took a flight to Washington, D.C., to attend the Founding Convention of the D.C. Chapter of the National Black United Front.

Over the next several days, the press continued to pound away at the so-called rabble rousers, the disrupters, the attacks upon the police, and, of course, I was the ring leader. Even the *New York Amsterdam News* criticized us. Doug Ireland of the now-defunct *Soho News*, typified the more malicious variety.

This [meeting] created a natural opportunity for Herbert Daughtry, the Mayor's favorite rabble-rouser, to take to the barricades outside, there to give vent to the rage and anger most black citizens feel at having been written out of the political process by the Mayor of a city in which a majority of the residents are not white. A cold winter can provoke tensions as surely as a hot summer, and particularly in the context of a mayoral appearance before the TV cameras and behind closed doors from which, at this alleged "community meeting" the general public and the poor were effectively excluded.

Not since Joseph Goebbels invented incendiary Van Der Lubbe has there been such a symbiotic relationship between alleged antagonists as that between Koch and Daughtry. It is as if Koch had telephoned his pal David Garth: "Hey Dave, we think we would liven things up a bit if you could find me someone good to play off of—you know, the kind of guy the white middle class loves to hate? He should be black, have a criminal record, make a lot of references to Zionism that we can label anti-Semitic, be a hot platform demagogue. Somebody who makes good TV..."

Even the normally perspicacious Gabe Pressman succumbed to the carefully contrapuntal way in which Koch has used Daughtry by making the passionately reckless minister the major black spokesman in his recent WNBC-TV series on "Blacks and the Mayor." Koch governs the city to satisfy the needs of two groups: the bankers, the real-estate magnates and other folk in whose hands lies moneyed power; and the producers of television news. He is the first mayor of New York City to have captured the cadences of the 45-second news clip. Only the impression, the style, matters—not the substance.

Television's legacy to us is a generation raised on information overload: there are too many facts to remember, so people don't. Thus, Koch knows that what will be remembered from the television accounts of his appearance in Bedford-Stuyvesant last weekend is not the measured indictment from Dr. V. Simpson Turner that, on a scale of 1 to 10, the Black community gave him a "failing grade"—a sentiment enthusiastically applauded by the well-dressed middle-class audience. No, what will be remembered is the contorted face of Herbert Daughtry hollering into a bullhorn, the sudden eruption of violence, the word "riot," and how the implacable Ed "I Won't Be Intimidated" Koch once again stood up to niggers. Another 50,000 White votes for our perpetual Mayor.[1]

"Reckless!" How would he know? He had never talked to me. I have already discussed how and why we made the decision. Disagree with it, but don't make it appear that it was a reckless, individual decision. When Mr. Ireland recklessly suggests that Koch contrived the whole thing and I fell neatly into his scheme, he is really saying that I am a dumb, anti-Semitic, rabble rouser, who cannot think for himself. I have already indicated that we (not I) knew the risk involved and we deliberately decided on what we thought was the lesser of two evils. On February 12, I wrote Doug Ireland expressing my fury at the malicious representation.[2]

Fairness moves me to cite here the impartial reporting of Jim Ascendio at WINS radio. He reported directly from the scene and gave both the community and the police a chance to tell their sides of the story. I wrote to Mr. Ascendio, on this occasion to express my appreciation.[3]

Let me relate another, little-known fact that may help to explain why we demonstrated, which also gives insight into what we are up against with some Black leaders, and further demonstrates why White outsiders should never try to pass judgment on Black leadership. The principal speaker at the Town Hall Meeting was Rev. Dr. V. Simpson Turner. According to all reports, he delivered a thoughtful statement, sharply critical of the Mayor. Everybody applauded him except Koch and his supporters. Many sincere people, some we counted as friends, asked what was so unacceptable about the statement.

In his article, Doug Ireland compared the two of us: Dr. Turner, the "responsible" minister; Herbert Daughtry, the racist, anti-Semitic militant, a foil used by the Mayor. We agreed with what we read of Dr. Turner's statement. Our position, as I have already discussed, was that we needed something concrete. We had had powerful statements before, far more "thoughtful" than Dr. Turner's. If we did not get something concrete, Koch would use this meeting to his advantage, and Blacks would get nothing.

(It takes so little to satisfy some of our people! It reminds me of the meeting a group of Black ministers is reported to have had with President Carter. He said, "I don't have much time. [The ministers should have worked out details before the meeting.] We can discuss issues or take pictures." The ministers elected to take pictures.)

In a statement to the press, following the Town Hall Meeting, Koch said that Dr. Turner, after excoriating him, sat down and said, in essence: *Don't worry. I had to do that for their sake—* "their" referring to his own people.

That, I believe, says a great deal about the two men, both

turn coats. Koch so easily reveals what was supposedly a private confidence to the public, and, as I have mentioned before, in a community where many do not trust "these preachers," where many viewed the meeting as the ministers' strategy to promote their own interests, Dr. Turner simply confirmed their impression.

I do not believe that the private behavior of this man, Dr. V. Simpson Turner, in the presence of Ed Koch is an exception. Rather, I believe that his behavior is the norm for most Black leaders. And that is one of the reasons our people in New York are in their present state of powerlessness. It also explains why a Black leader who is honest, committed, and assertive is overly scrutinized and mistrusted. Others have already sold out and can, therefore, be used to block, isolate, and vilify the most viable and popular Black leaders. These self-serving leaders are the ones the White establishment love to call "responsible leaders."

Most of us would understand their vulnerability and would have no problem with them if they would simply be quiet, get whatever they are trying to get for themselves, stay out of the way, and not allow themselves to be used against the interests of their people.

But when you eat crumbs from the master's table, at some point you will have to obey the master's call.

## NOTES

1. Herbert Daughtry, "Open Letter to Community," December 13, 1980, (unpublished). Available from Daughtry's personal files.
2. See Herbert Daughtry/Doug Ireland Correspondence, 1980 (unpublished). Available from Daughtry's personal files.
3. See Herbert Daughtry/WINS Correspondence, 1980 (unpublished). Available from Daughtry's personal files.

## Chapter 9

# Koch Wins Big But Still Acts Small

—〰〰〰〰—

After his second election as Mayor, which he won in grand style, Ed Koch turned his concern to his relationship with minorities, Blacks and Latinos in particular.

Koch pledged that he would make an effort to cultivate better relationships with the Black community. Nevertheless, he refused to meet with Assemblyman Al Vann or Bronx Borough President Herman Badillo, revealing once again a graceless, petty disposition. Here was a man who had just won a stunning victory. Apparently, the majority of the electorate had voted for him. He had won on both the Democratic and Republican lines. He had won more Black votes than most had expected, sixty percent, according to some statisticians. However, we knew that the victory was not as great as the Mayor and others wanted to believe, for several reasons:

- Historically, Blacks in New York have always voted for Democrats. As the saying goes: "If the devil ran on the Democratic line, he would get the Black vote."
- There was no worthwhile candidate around whom Blacks could rally. Frank Barbaro, an unknown in most of the Black community, did exceptionally well in the Democratic Primary.
- After the primary, which Koch won, Al Vann switched parties and voted for Mary Cobb, the Liberal party candidate. This fragmented the already-fragile coalition that was building around Barbaro. Black Congresswoman Shirley Chisholm supported Koch. So, there was no clear signal or direction given to the Black Community. They had the unattractive option of Mary Cobb (Liberal Party), Ed Koch (Democratic and Republican Parties), and Frank Barbaro (Unity Party) or none of the above; stay home, or go fishing—which most Blacks did. The Latino community was equally divided.
- Then, there were Blacks working in the Koch Administration who had something to protect, and those who were trying to *get* something to protect: i.e. the Reverend Calvin Marshall, pastor of Varick Memorial AME Church, for his own reasons, was the lone Black minister to open the doors of his church to Koch.
- And on top of all that, once the determined voter arrived at the polls, there was difficulty even locating Barbaro's name among the list of candidates. I received innumerable calls from frustrated would-be voters.

The wonder is not that Koch received 60 percent of the Black vote, as he claims, but that he did not do better!

The decision to exclude Vann and Badillo was not the first

time that Koch sought to dictate the composition of a meeting with Black leaders. In 1979, when antagonism between Koch and Blacks intensified after a series of incidents, Koch summoned several Black leaders to Gracie Mansion. After what appeared to be a friendly meeting the participants talked to the press: Koch said that he was going to be meeting with other Black leaders, and that he was sure these relationships would improve.

When asked if he would also be meeting with Rev. Daughtry, Koch's response was an emphatic "no!" I immediately criticized the Mayor for his arrogance in dictating to Black people which delegates were acceptable to him. If he were sincere about wanting to better relations with Blacks, he should be satisfied to meet with whomever Blacks decided to put forward. At any rate, the romance with those few select Black leaders was short-lived. It wasn't long before the temperature heated up again.

Under the electoral conditions existing in 1981, a Democratic incumbent running for Mayor in New York should have reaped ninety to ninety-five percent of the Black vote.

Be that as it may, Koch had everything going for him that year. The pollsters declared that he was the most popular Mayor in the city's history. His garrulous "shoot-from-the hip" style made him an icon in the New York media. Reporters waited expectantly to catch any word or expression, however insipid, that "Hizzoner" would condescend to drop their way. *The New York Times* found him fascinating enough to print a photo of him on their sacrosanct front page: Dressed in a turban, seated on a camel, there was the Mayor of New York exuding the bearing of an idiot. Koch was vacationing in Egypt at the time.

Another New York newspaper ran a page featuring Koch mugging with various facial expressions, and a caption that asked, "Which is your favorite Koch expression?" It was a baffling exercise in narcissism. Yet, a hero was born to the middle and upper classes, and the White media became the oracles who fed their fantasies. Koch was New York's most popular mayor, they said. "With whom?" was the question most Blacks kept asking.

During the period of this vulgar display, I was in Paris, enjoying a week with my eldest daughter, who had won a scholarship to study for a semester in France. Even the *International Herald Tribune* carried this racist nonsense. Writing was my response. (*See Chapter 10*: The Mayor and the Media: Reflections from Paris.)

So, at the height of success, with New York in the palms of his hands, some would suppose that Koch would forget old injuries. He could afford to "bury the hatchet," and urge all New Yorkers, even his political adversaries, to join with him to build a greater New York for all the people. But, not Ed Koch; he can never forget and/or forgive. While basking in a magnificent victory, he still sulks. He will work with Blacks and Puerto Ricans ... but not with Al Vann and Herman Badillo—a sad but telling qualification. Still, Koch has many qualities that could make him a truly great politician. He is hard working, determined, fearless, resilient, intelligent, enthusiastic, witty and loves his work. But his pettiness, paltriness, pugnacity, and impetuosity all shackle him. His re-election campaign was successful now because of a confluence of negative factors. But these factors will disappear, so will Ed Koch. He will be remembered as dinosaurs are remembered, i.e., with bewilderment and curiosity.

## Chapter 10

# The Mayor and the Media: Reflections from Paris

—━◁◁◁▷▷▷━—

Paris, France, has always held a fascination for me, so I was quite excited to be there again in 1981. Adding to my excitement was the pride I felt, for I was there to escort my daughter, who was beginning a course of study in France for a semester. I also looked forward to being away from the battlefields of Brooklyn, to spending a few days relaxing and sight-seeing with her. I was determined that the only serious reading I would do would be related to France under the newly elected Mitterand government.

There we were, standing on the Place De Gaulle, under the shadow of the Arch of Triumph when, against my better judgment, I decided to buy the *International Herald Tribune*. As I glanced through its pages, the last article I saw referred to the election in New York. The columnist discussed the lawsuit that might have delayed the statewide election, and his article touched on Koch's reactions to a provocative Frank Barbaro commercial contending that race was a factor in redistricting, and that Koch had had problems with minorities. Barbaro was a Brooklyn Assemblyman who was running against Koch.

Then, and this is what ticked me off, the writer went on to say that Koch was a very popular Mayor. Now I know that he was simply expressing the media-accepted approbation that Koch's popularity, according to some, exceeded that of any other Mayor throughout the country. I was infuriated by the sheer racism of the evaluation, and now this racist opinion was being touted to the world. It was all I could do to bring my thoughts back to my daughter's expectations and back to the allure of Paris. However, the only way to gain my equilibrium was to promise myself that I would put my thoughts in writing, arguing assiduously against Koch's popularity and therein show the subtle and de facto workings of racism.

*Ed Koch is popular!* Why is that statement racist? First, we must ask another question: Popular with whom? Surely not with Black people and, although perhaps to a lesser extent, not with Latinos. There are, to my knowledge, only a handful of Blacks who actually like Koch. There are Blacks who work for him, and there are those who believe they have to relate to him to get what they want. But they would be the first to tell you, privately, if not publicly, that it is all political. They dislike him, even dislike being in his presence. The overwhelming majority of Blacks have publicly expressed their antipathy for Koch. No Mayor in the history of the city has created as much racial antagonism and division.

Gabe Pressman, a respected local newsman—who is Jewish

—admitted as much on his TV program. So, with the Black and Latino populations making up over 50 percent of the city, and this majority population having expressed their dislike for him, how did Koch become popular? It is important that we assess the demographics of the city at this juncture, because the 1970 U.S. Census gives an interesting ethnic breakdown; with Blacks making up the single largest ethnic group. If then, the question regarding Koch's popularity were put to Blacks alone, there would be an entirely different evaluation.

This, then, is where the issue of racism comes in. The only way anyone can say that Koch is popular is to disregard the sentiments and thinking of Black and Latino people; in effect, *what Blacks and Latinos think really does not matter*. It is what Whites think that counts. This is the way racism has always worked. It ignores blackness, i.e., the other. Racism works itself out in a process I call NED (negation, emasculation, and decimation). Racism says that the other doesn't exist—negation. The other is invisible; the other does not count. The other exists only when racism says it exists. Consider the 1977 primary election, when Percy Sutton was running for Mayor on the Democratic ticket. The media all but ignored him, treating him as though he didn't exist. Yet, according to the White media, *There is no Black leadership!* In Ralph Ellison's metaphorical novel, *The Invisible Man*, published in 1952, the Black man was rendered invisible because of the pressures of racism and poverty.

The second manifestation of racism in the NED process is *emasculation*. That is, destroying our manhood, our dignity. While negation pretends that Blacks do not exist, emasculation acknowledges that Blacks do exist, but seeks to strip away our humanity: denies us the vote, denies us employment, physically abuses us, and uses the media (printed and electronic) subtly to confirm our nothingness.

The third manifestation of racism is *decimation*. When Blacks or non-Whites resist or retaliate, racism destroys us. Consider the plight of Native Americans. Consider the annihilation of the leaders of the Black Liberation movements, i.e., Marcus Garvey, Malcolm X, and Martin Luther King, Jr. But let us set aside Blacks and Latinos for the moment.

Koch is popular among which ethnic group? Irish? Jews? Italians? And with which class? The working class? The middle class? The ruling class? If we could identify the group from which his popularity is derived, we would probably see that the preponderance of one ethnic group and class has produced the results. It is possible though that if every class and ethnic group expressed itself, we might discover that Koch is the most *unpopular* Mayor the city has ever known.

Now bear with me while I interject a little about myself. I feel as the Apostle Paul might have felt; I don't really want to do it, but I must make the point, and this is the best way to make it. So, forgive me, for I have a serious charge to prove.

I am often referred to as controversial. I am often referred to as anti-Semitic. But who accuses me of being controversial? Surely not Black people, and I am not sure about Latinos. Allow me to give you the benefit of our findings. In 1981, New York radio stations WWRL and WLIB each sponsored a citywide poll. Bob Law, the host of WWRL's *Black Dialogue*, asked his listeners on three occasions whom they would prefer as Mayor. On each occasion, I received the majority vote. WLIB asked its listeners which Black organization they considered the most effective. On three occasions the winner was the Black United Front (BUF), an organization I was instrumental in creating, and which I chaired. I should emphasize that both polls were taken without my knowledge or my participation.

These polls bolster what I and my BUF colleagues know to be true. Wherever I go I am recognized (in spite of White media attempts to negate this) and greeted with respect and affection. Oftentimes as I stop at a red light or ride alone, people in other cars wave to me. On occasion they have pointed me out to their children. In many gatherings, I am sought for advice and for autographs, even by sophisticated adults. At the annual African-

American Day Parade in Harlem,[1] I was surely one of the most recognized marchers. All along the route, people waved and greeted me, again proud parents pointing me out to children. At the conclusion of the Parade, a distinguished long-time Harlem resident remarked with amazement, "The people really recognize you... Some people live in the community all their lives and are never recognized." I remember smiling and saying, "Yes, I know it, and my enemies know it too."

So, if it is not Blacks, not Latinos, and not the many Whites whom I am pleased and honored to count among my friends and supporters, i.e., Irish, Poles, Jews, Muslims, etc., who is it that "filches my good name?" Among Black people especially, and the majority of Latinos and some whites, I am admired, respected, and, yes, even loved.

Yet, according to most in the White media, I am controversial, a rabble-rouser. This is an interesting characterization, for not only does it degrade me, it also dismisses me, my friends, and my supporters. Seldom do I get a positive write-up.

On the other hand, Koch is disliked among Blacks and Latinos, but he is never referred to as controversial or as a rabble-rouser. *He* is popular. The world does not know him as a vindictive, divisive, insecure, petty racist, but as a popular and beloved leader, and that is so because racism wants it that way.

More evidence on the workings of racism: Racism abrogates to itself the authority to name and to label people, irrespective of what people name or label themselves. That is an integral part of emasculation. During slavery, Blacks could not name themselves, sign contracts, enter into marriage, elect their own representatives. When Black people say, *He is our leader*, racism says, *No, he is a racist, he is controversial. This White (or Black) person is your leader.* And because racism is supported by wealth and power it can make these things appear real. Racism can buy and bribe enough Blacks to agree with its policies.

One of the most glaring instances of the White media's

racism was manifested in negation during the Organization of African Unity Conference in Libya in 1982. This was a momentous event for Africans and for so-called Third World peoples, and, therefore, for the entire world. While these annual conferences had been in existence for a number of years, that year, all the African Foreign Ministers assembled for the 49th Council of Ministers, and all the African Heads of States assembled for the 19th Summit Conference.

The 1982 conference had an added significance: Because of the conflict between Morocco and the Polisario,[2] many African countries threatened to stay away. The number of African nations then totaled fifty. Thus, a quorum of thirty-four nations was in jeopardy. African people everywhere watched expectantly, yet the White media gave very little attention to this historic gathering. In fact, more space was given to Princess Diana's baby in one day, than to the entire conference.

That year, the OAU invited me to the conference for the second time—one of the highest honors an African-American leader can receive. From the dribble of news here, I could not ascertain whether the conference had been postponed; rumors to that effect had been circulating. I finally decided to go, but the conference was held unofficially, with only thirty-two nations attending.

Nevertheless, we see again and again that no matter how important the person, the issue or the event to Black people, if Whites do not deem it relevant to them, they try to discredit it or negate it.

The White media inundates us with the myth of Ed Koch as a popular folk hero. I charge those who postulate this premise without qualification, with racism. I will, however, be gracious enough to say that perhaps it is unconscious, for surely the White media, and pollsters, and spin doctors—the creators and sustainers of the "Koch is popular" hype—would never commit a conscious racist act.

But unconscious racism is like unconscious sin. It is an activity that can result in devastating consequences. We can rectify that which we are conscious of, but we will persist in a course of action if there is no awareness of its harm. Racism, KKK-style, is "White sheet" racism; conscious, raw, flagrant, vicious. But "Koch is popular" is "white collar" racism; subtle, sophisticated, often unconscious, but equally damaging. Both forms have the same objective, both sustain power and privilege for Whites, and both maintain Blacks in a state of powerlessness, thus perpetuating subjugation.

When we say then that the United States is a racist society, it is not necessarily the white sheet variety that is under consideration, rather the white collar variety that pervades all of America's institutions, traditions, and mores.

—*Paris, September 21-28, 1982*

## NOTES

1.  The African-American Day Parade draws hundreds of thousands of participants each year. In 1981, I was elected as permanent Honorary Parade Marshall.
2.  The Polisario was a progressive force in Western Sahara rebelling against neocolonial and right-wing rulers of Morocco. These Black freedom fighters wanted to establish a democratic nation, the Sahrawi Arab Republic, formerly known as the Spanish Sahara. Most of the African nations supported the Polisario.

93

# Chapter 11

# Koch and Auletta: Partners in Perfidy

During the confrontation with the Hasidim, Mayor Koch sent me an infuriating letter indicating that the Hasidim would meet with "responsible leaders from the Crown Heights community." (See Koch/Daughtry correspondence at the end of this chapter.)

The Hasidim had driven us from our land and property, had harassed us, and beaten us (the most recent victim having been a 15-year-old), and now they had the effrontery to dictate with whom they would meet. I replied to Koch along those lines, asserting, among other things, that the Hasidim were savages, adding that "these savages" had unleased thirty to fifty of their members upon one lone youngster, and that now they wanted to determine the composition of the representatives of the people they had offended. Ridiculous! No self-respecting leader, Black or White, would agree to a meeting under such a stipulation. To facilitate any kind of accord, the Hasidim would have to express some degree of remorse to the community, families, or individuals involved. Then it would be up to the offended parties to determine the nature of further talks.

Though it was clear that the issue concerned mainly Crown Heights Blacks and the Hasidim, Koch showed the letter to Ken Auletta, a writer of sorts, who rendered a shoddy, vicious misrepresentation of my statements second only to those printed in the *New York Post*. Auletta did not merely misquote or rearrange material; he took words out of context. For example, where I used the word "savage" with reference to the Hasidim, Auletta has me calling all Jews "savages." I wrote to the two publications that carried Auletta's articles, *The New Yorker* and *The New York Daily News*, calling attention to the hatchet job to which I was being subjected. But my response was never published. The courtesy usually given to anyone who is quoted—to defend, clarify, or correct a statement—was never extended to me.

Let me draw this out a bit. Some months later I was browsing through the library at Dartmouth College, where my eldest daughter was an undergraduate. I spied a book written by Ken Auletta and slowly pulled the book from the shelf, hoping against hope that it did not contain his Koch article. But to my dismay and sorrow, there it was, just as it was previously printed. I stared for a long time and eventually returned the book to the shelf. I, then, forced myself to sit down. Here it was in the library of this prestigious college! My daughter might have to contend with Auletta's horrendous distortions, and vicious attacks on her father. There and then I determined to write this book.

In the September 10, 1979 issue of *The New Yorker,* Ken Auletta wrote:

Koch is not one to turn the other cheek. One of his louder feuds has been with Herbert Daughtry, of Brooklyn, a black minister. It began in June of 1978, after Arthur Miller, a black businessman and civic leader in Crown Heights, was choked to death by policemen under mysterious circumstances. The police subdued Miller after an altercation and were alleged to have accidentally strangled him with their nightsticks. The black community was enraged and suspicious. A grand jury was impanelled. Daughtry's Brooklyn-based organization, the Black United Front, wrote to the Mayor urging a meeting. The group also forwarded a copy of its "agenda," including demands that "all police officers at the scene of Arthur Miller's death be suspended immediately and remain suspended until a thorough investigation of the murder be expedited and the killer or killers be brought to justice;" that "three Black psychiatrists be appointed to examine all police officers involved;" that "the entire investigation, including psychiatric findings, be made public;" that "a screening board be set up to evaluate the files of policemen who are to begin assignments in all Black communities and that the Black United Front be part of the selection process;" that the Seventy-seventh Precinct have "immediate changes" and the "staffing pattern be altered to represent 50% Black and Hispanic policemen;" that, because of "frequent allegations" of assaults by the Crown Heights Jewish Community Patrol, an organization of Chassidic Jews, "all federal money" to this organization be "discontinued;" and that "the practice of regularly closing off of service roads on the Jewish Sabbath and other special Chassidic days be stopped immediately."

Clearly, white police officers and Jews—perhaps most white citizens—would feel threatened by this agenda. A reader of the Bill of Rights might conclude that the agenda, if it were adopted, would violate the rights of privacy and due process, among others. For many years, City Hall had been the recipient of fevered agendas and demands. Most had been

97

ignored. Mayor Koch, however, took this one seriously. He dictated a three-page response, picking apart the agenda and asserting, "Your demand that officers involved in the Miller case be examined by three Black psychiatrists not only violates the spirit of the civil-rights movement, but is racist in character..."

The conflict heated up. A few weeks later, Daughtry dispatched a three-page retort charging that City Hall was pro-Jewish. He complained of "Jewish fund-raising," of Jewish "savages," of "Chassidic arrogance and contempt," and of "people who are guilty of the crimes that the Chassidim have perpetrated," and he stated that "most Black people wonder how you and other Jewish people would react ...," and so on. Substitute "black" for Jewish "savages," and it is easy to image the screams of "racism" at such stereotyping. Enraged, Koch wrote back calling the letter "abusive" and concluding, "I see no point in a further exchange of letters."

Daughtry's letter confirming Koch's darkest fears—struck a raw nerve. "I'm very conscious of being Jewish," says Koch. He is also conscious of and threatened by what he considers wide-spread black anti-Semitism. As a member of Congress, he seethed at black colleagues who voted against aid for Israel; he feared that their votes were an expression of their hostility to Jews.

I cannot blame Jews if they were angry when they read Auletta's article. But, before this was added to the list of anti-Semitic charges against me, should I not have been consulted? Should the newspaper or magazine editors have asked if I wanted to respond? I have asked newspeople whether, when printing a personal attack, they are diligent and conscientious in searching out facts. "Do you ever talk to the person in question? Do you think about the person's family, friends, and the impact on innumerable lives?"

When Auletta's article and my letter are compared, it is clear that I was referring to the Lubavitcher Hasidim and not to all

98

Jews, as Auletta would have people believe. In the letter to Koch, when I mentioned "Jewish fund-raising," it is what Hasidim said regarding the ambulance in front of their headquarters which, by the way, is a lie, according to June Jordan. (See Koch/Daughtry correspondence: August 21, 1978.) Where do I say City Hall was "pro-Jewish?" Why doesn't Auletta complete the sentence? I wrote: "Blacks wonder how you and other Jews would react if Jewish kids were beaten by other ethnic groups." To me, that is a perfectly legitimate question, one often used to sensitize someone to the feelings of others. There is nothing anti-Semitic about it. I have used the same language with reference to Italians and Irish, and I wasn't called anti-Italian or anti-Irish or anti-Roman Catholic.

Much later I learned that *The New Yorker* is very meticulous about checking quotations. In the Auletta article, the quotation marks in my case, only enclose a word, a phrase, or a clause. Never does he quote an entire sentence from me. If he had, the magazine would have called me for verification, and Auletta would have had to change or delete his references to me.

Using Auletta's method of quoting, a person could be made to say anything. If I took the liberty of quoting only a word or phrase from someone else's speech, conversation, or correspondence, that person could easily be made to say anything that suited my purpose. And that is precisely what Auletta did. He must have had some purpose in mind, for no matter how inaccurate his quotes, the pain or damage he caused the person "quoted" did not seem to concern him. To refute Auletta's inaccuracies I have enclosed the complete correspondence and the Black Agenda (See APPENDIX B: THE BLACK AGENDA). Readers can judge for themselves.

Now, regarding the Black Agenda: First of all, it was not mailed, but hand delivered. Following the massive July 16 Rally, a group of community leaders, after a period of long debate, finally reached consensus on the Agenda.

We agreed to deliver the Agenda to the Mayor and leave it with him. There would be no discussion; we would depart and await the Mayor's reply after his people had time sufficient to study it. This was a compromise of sorts. There were some among us who felt that a meeting with Koch would be useless. I should point out that I had received word that Koch wanted to meet with us, but I deliberately waited until after the July 16 Rally. If there was to be a meeting, I wanted a community mandate.

On July 31, 1978, a group of community leaders, comprised of clergymen, elected officials, and civic leaders, did finally meet with Koch. Consistent with our plan, I presented Mayor Koch with the Agenda, giving him the history of its development. I asked him to study it, adding that we could meet again, at his convenience, to negotiate. We only asked the Mayor to allow his staff time to study the proposal and then to get back to us. I thought we acted responsibly and respectfully. On August 21, 1978, I received a letter from Koch attacking the Agenda. His next response to it appeared in Auletta's article.

## THE AGENDA
### BLACK AND HISPANIC PRECINCT AND PSYCHOLOGICAL EXAMINATIONS

Let's review a couple of the Agenda suggestions that were ridiculed. We suggested a Black and Hispanic police precinct as an experimental project. Since there had been such widespread abuse of police power against Blacks and Hispanics, why was this suggestion deemed so unreasonable or, as Koch would have it, "non-productive?" If a system does not function well or even if you want it to function better, isn't it usual to evaluate it, to conduct experiments, to test new methods, to create new strategies to change it?

We suggested not only that the officers involved in the murder of Arthur Miller be examined by three Black psychiatrists, but that all police officers be subjected to examination periodically. To us that seemed generally prudent, for the very nature of police work is often conducive to alcoholism and/or drug abuse and to neurotic or psychotic behavior.

What we wanted in the Miller case was suspension of the officers involved. Suspension of officers under suspicion of a crime is not unusual. In fact, the week following Miller's killing (June 22, 1978), a White police officer was suspended after beating Charles King, another Black businessman.

The Black United Front was always trying to suggest ways to improve things. For example, we made many proposals to the business community, to Mayor Koch, to the police, etc. Some of these were implemented; others were simply not feasible.

For the sake of argument, let's say that our proposals were utterly preposterous. Still, should there not have been another meeting to thrash out those ideas and to negotiate? Is it not the common practice in collective bargaining to set forth an agenda and then to negotiate each item? Are labor leaders denied arbitration meetings when their proposals seem outlandish to the opposition? No! Both sides meet with mediators to negotiate their proposals. But the courtesy of a further negotiating session was never extended to us. Our proposals, and myself in particular, were ridiculed in the media. And when we tried to point out the truth, these same newspeople would not give us the opportunity respond.

Significantly, a few weeks later, when I criticized Jewish and Black leaders in an article for the *New York Amsterdam News*, the paper gave a Jewish man space to respond and criticize me—as well it should.

## KOCH'S PRIVATE THOUGHTS

What is also notable about Ken Auletta's article is that Koch's "private thoughts" were intended for the Columbia University library and were not to be made public until some future time. Also included in the article are Koch's views on Black attitudes towards Jews. He believes that "most Blacks are anti-Semitic."

This may explain why Blacks believe that Koch is against them and may further explain why Koch is constantly insulting to Blacks. He has called Black politicians "poverticians," "poverty pimps." He has called the *New York Amsterdam News*, the nation's largest Black newspaper, "an anti-Semitic rag."

On WLIB, a Black-owned radio station, Koch said, "Eighty percent of the people who are murdered in the city are Black, and the people who murder them are Black." But the facts are that in 1980, the last year that a statistical breakdown was available to him as mayor, 47.7 percent of the city's murder victims were Black and 55.5 percent of those arrested for murder were Black, according to the *New York Daily News*, March 2, 1982.

When one believes that he is the victim (i.e., that the people are against him), it is easy to understand the name calling and the misuse of statistics against the perceived enemy. Of course, the selfish, spineless, Tomish behavior of many of New York's Black "establishment" leaders provides a variety of valid reasons for his distrust and disrespect. With that understanding, isn't it reasonable to expect that the "victim" will be on guard at all times, ready to attack that perceived enemy? In that mental state, isn't it reasonable to imagine being attacked when no such thing is happening? And, in such a climate, isn't it reasonable to expect that the perceived enemy will meet strong retaliation in response to the mildest criticism or even where there is no criticism intended?

Significantly, there is no Black leader in New York whom Koch has not attacked, from United Nations Ambassador Donald McHenry to the President of the National Association of Black Social Workers, Cenie Williams.

Moreover, Koch's statement that most Blacks are anti-Semitic evoked several questions in the Black community, among them: *Is Koch a solitary, eccentric voice in the Jewish community? Or is he speaking for the majority of Jews? Do most Jews really believe Blacks are anti-Semitic?* The last is an important question, for one reacts radically different towards a supposed enemy than towards a supposed friend.

I can be criticized for the sharpness of my letters. Even Koch's language, "abusive" and "non-productive," may apply. But I want to make two points: First, the letters were written during a time of intense stress. Anyone who is as committed to their people as I am to mine, who has been as close as I have been to their murders, beatings, molestations, and humiliations would probably respond the same way. I was justifiably angry and make no apologies for it. Second, whatever one wishes to think about the letters, no fair-minded person can say they are anti-Semitic.

•  •  •

The City of New York
Office of the Mayor
August 21, 1978

The Reverend Herbert Daughtry
House of the Lord
415 Atlantic Avenue
Brooklyn, New York 11217

Dear Rev. Daughtry:

Before responding to your United Black Front Agenda, I feel that I should tell you that your attempt to disrupt the visit of the President to City Hall was productive of nothing except ill-feeling.

President Carter played a crucial role in keeping New York solvent. If New York had gone bankrupt, the people who would have suffered most would have been the poor, the minorities. Hundreds of thousands who depend on aid from the city would have had no place to turn, many thousands more, including great numbers of minority municipal employees, would have lost their jobs, or, if they were lucky, merely have had their wages cut.

Considering how important a role the President

played in keeping the city afloat, he had the right to be heard without the competition of your bullhorn. The only purpose your action served was to add a minute to the television coverage. You did your cause no service.

Now, I would like to address a number of points the United Front brought up in its agenda. Clearly, the police situation looms large.

Understandably, you are greatly concerned with the death of Arthur Miller—I am, also. The Brooklyn District Attorney is presently investigating the case, and I am certain that he is doing so assiduously. I can understand why the United Front feels as intensely as it does, but it has not been determined, up to now, that Mr. Miller's death was a murder. Until a determination has been made as to the cause of his death, disciplinary action against the officers would be inappropriate, and until the results are in, there is no basis for giving the officers psychiatric examinations. Your demand that officers in the Miller case be examined by three Black psychiatrists not only violates the spirit of the civil-rights movement but is racist in character.

As to the Victor Rhodes case, two arrests have been made and the investigation is continuing. The demands in your Agenda that the Rhodes family be "awarded all benefits under the "Victims Law" need not have been put in the form of a demand, a simple telephone call to the Victim Service Agency or City Hall would have sufficed. As this was apparently not done, I called the Agency concerning the situation.

As to the Hasidic situation, Police Commissioner McGuire has made an investigation and has decided to alter certain patrol assignments in the 71st Precinct. No doubt you know that the Commissioner has removed one stationary patrol car and will remove another by November 1. The practice, to which the United Front objects, of closing off the service lane for one block along Eastern Parkway, on occasions in which large numbers of people congregate and spill onto the roadway, is considered a necessary tactic in preventing injuries. Commissioner McGuire further tells me that traffic is not adversely affected on the main roadway of Eastern Parkway. The tactic is not peculiar to 770 Eastern Parkway but takes place in numerous locations throughout the city when conditions warrant.

You say the Crown Heights Community Patrol is responsible for assaults on citizens. If that is so, you should take your complaints to the police. Uninvestigated allegations will not change a situation. The City does not fund the Patrol. Your agenda states that the "Crown Heights Community Board in no way reflects the composition of the area it purports to service." Commissioner Haskell Ward of the Community Development Agency tells me that a study, in conjunction with Washington, is currently underway concerning the shifts in demographic patterns among the poor. The purpose of the study is to revise the designated poverty areas—established in the mid 1960's—to bring them up to date. In addition, the criteria upon which these designations were made are being reviewed for the purpose of revising them to insure that all the poor are served in the Community Action Program. Commissioner Ward suggests that you submit a detailed description of the Albany Houses area designations. Your proposal will be carefully reviewed.

At the moment, the City is in the process of restructuring the Community Action Program. CDA will call on community groups, including the United Black Front, to give their critical evaluations.

You have expressed a concern as to how public assistance resources are distributed. The Human Resources Administration informs me that in the area of Aid to

Dependent Children (80% of the entire caseload) the portion that goes to non-whites is 88%. As for the latest figures on home-relief/singles, it is 79% for non-whites. Although we do not have specific figures for Crown Heights, HRA tells me that they would not vary significantly from the city-wide percentages.

As for re-uniting Crown Heights, as you put it, the Charter calls for community boards boundaries to be reviewed within one year after the 1980 census. If you still wish to do so, you should pursue the matter at that time.

You also refer to "land takeover and abuse" in your agenda. The Tax Commission, the Department of Buildings and the Department of Housing Preservation regularly checks into the kinds of situations you refer to. If you have information to bring to their attention, you certainly should do so.

Let me conclude. As you know, I have met with members of the Hasidic community, as I have with you, on some of the same questions you have raised. On more than one occasion, the leaders of that community have indicated that they would be willing to meet with responsible leaders of the Crown Heights Black community to discuss matters of common concern. It seems it would be better for all and do more for the well-being of the community if Crown Heights could agree on steps to resolve the issues that divide it.

All segments of the community are concerned with public safety and the relationship between police protection and community patrols, the effectiveness of Planning Boards, enforcement of housing codes and zoning regulations, and the proper distribution of programs and services. I am sure there is common ground on these issues as well as others mentioned in your Agenda. What is needed, apart from anything the Mayor can do, is a serious attempt to find that common ground at the local level. I would hope that your coalition and the Hasidic community would make that effort. It probably will not resolve all the issues, but it will be a start.

In the future, if you have problems that require resolution, you should pursue them with the relevant commissioners.

Sincerely,
Edward I. Koch
Mayor

• • •

Black United Front
Brooklyn, New York
September 20, 1978

Mr. Edward Koch
The City of New York
Office of the Mayor

Your Honor:

Since your opening remarks addressed me personally, I will respond. A response to your reaction to the Black United Front's agenda will be forthcoming.

Firstly, you criticized me for the Black United Front's demonstrations when President Carter was here in August. We demonstrate, not because we want to, but because we have to.

We had written to Drew Days, Griffin Bell and the President twice in an effort to obtain a response to a request for a Federal investigation of the violation of Black people's human rights by the New York City Police and the Hasidic community. We did not even receive a note acknowledging receipt of our correspondence and when normal channels do not produce even a form letter from those who are supposed to service us, we have no choice but to take our grievances to the streets, in accordance with our constitutional rights. I might add, that we were even nice enough to warn the President of our impending demonstration should they choose to ignore our correspondence. If a response had been forthcoming, the demonstration would never have occurred. However, since the demonstration, we have received several replies from the Justice Department as well as the White House.

Now, to you, sir, in the light of the cowardly way you insulted the President of the United States a few months ago when you shoved a note into his stomach expressing your concern about a matter regarding Israel, thousands of miles away, one would think that you would be the last person to chide a frustrated, wounded people, who, openly, after forewarning, attempt to get their case heard—which case I might add is in their own community here in the U.S.A. and not across the ocean.

You stated that the only purpose our action served was to add a minute to the television coverage. Perhaps our actions did get a minute on New York television. I wish it had been an hour. As I remembered it, your little pusillanimous act got you hours of coverage all over the world.

Secondly, you said that our action was productive of nothing but ill-will. Your statement implies that there was good-will before our actions. Nothing could be further from the truth. Black people have, since the beginning of their holocaust hundreds of years ago, been the victims of ill-will.

Thirdly, you stated that our action "did our cause no service." We disagree. As stated before, we have received several replies which suggests that we were heard even though we had to use a bullhorn and out-maneuver your policemen on horseback who rode zealously into women and children. Moreover, the positive impact upon an oppressed people's self-esteem as they struggle for justice is incalculable. But beyond all that, whether our actions did our cause any good—which cause is that justice might prevail—must be left to the Almighty to judge.

It is my conviction that all of us must give an account of our personal as well as our public lives and I try to order all that I do and say both privately and publicly with reference to the Almighty. I am prepared this moment to stand with you before God to have our lives and actions adjudicated in His Court.

Finally, you stated that the Hasidic Jews would meet with "responsible leaders from the Crown Heights community." Since you have brought a message, would you kindly take one back. Remind them that they have insulted and attacked Black people, Victor Rhodes being the culmination of a long list of abuses. They have attacked policemen in pursuit of their duties; vigilantes seized the 71st Precinct; prevented a doctor from using a publicly paid for ambulance for a patient and then lied about it claiming the ambulance was provided by Jewish fundraising. This ambulance still remains in front of 770 Eastern Parkway.

Call to their remembrance that they have threatened newsmen and stormed television stations. They have misused public funds for sectarian purposes; and in collusion with the City, hacked up a traditional Community Planning Board 8 for themselves.

Call to their remembrance that they uncaged 30 to 50 of their members upon one lone 16-year-old kid and initially concocted a lie that the kid knocked off an old man's hat; then later modified the lie saying he attacked an old man. These people, along with the entire Jewish community, have neither expressed any remorse nor demanded the apprehension of the other savages who did this horrible deed.

Now you say these people want to meet with "responsible leaders in Crown Heights." The only thing they need to do is repent and demonstrate that they are civilized enough to interact with decent people; that they are worthy of the victim's trust. It is the victim, the decent people, who must decide the nature, the time and the place of the interaction, if there is to be one, with those who have shown themselves to be savages.

People who are guilty of the crimes that the Hasidim have perpetrated have forfeited their rights to dictate the nature of a relationship and as long as they attempt to do so, I guarantee you that self-respecting Blacks will vigorously reject their offer and view the whole thing as another example of Hasidic arrogance and contempt.

One final word, most Black people wonder how you and other Jewish people would react if Jewish kids were being killed by policemen and attacked by other ethnic groups with the City officials unwilling or unable to do anything about it.

Sincerely,
Rev. Herbert Daughtry

• • •

The City of New York
Office of the Mayor
October 3, 1978

Reverend Herbert Daughtry
The House of the Lord
Pentecostal Church

Dear Reverend Daughtry:

I have your letter dated September 26, 1978 with regard to the Atlantic Antic Parade held on Sunday, September 24, 1978. Your letter, I regret, is inaccurate in virtually every regard.

To begin with, I did not "lead a parade." I neither organized nor was I an official of the parade or its committee. I was simply a public official invited to attend, and I did so after expressing my appreciation for the invitation. You ask whether I would "lead a parade in front of St. Patrick's Cathedral during a mass." The fact is that as Mayor, I am frequently called upon to participate in public proceedings, including parades, and I do so with pleasure. This past Sunday, October 1, I did, indeed, participate in the Pulaski Day Parade which passed in front of St. Patrick's Cathedral during a mass which was then in progress. On that occasion and on every occasion I was and am sensitive to the needs of those attending the religious service.

I refer to the Pulaski Day Parade for three reasons. First, because it addresses a question raised in your letter (as to whether I would participate in a parade in front of St. Patrick's Cathedral during a mass). Second, because it occurred during a period of mourning for the passing of Pope John Paul I. Third, I refer to the Pulaski Day Parade because that parade, like the Atlantic Antic Parade, was both orderly and sensitive to the needs of the parishioners.

I do not believe that the remaining matter in your letter deserves or requires a response. I would point out, however, that your reference to Section 240.21 of the Penal Law is particularly ill conceived. That provision appears in the disorderly conduct section of the Penal Law. Clearly, the provision has no applicability since none of the elements referred to in the law occurred at any time during the Atlantic Antic Parade. There was neither any unreasonable noise or disturbance nor was there any intent on anyone's part to cause annoyance or alarm to any person.

Contrary to the implication in your letter, it is my intent to conduct the affairs of this City with due regard for the interests of every segment of the community and every citizen. I have the utmost respect and, indeed, sensitivity to the needs of the parishioners of the House of the Lord, Pentecostal Church, and they may be assured that as long as I am Mayor, they will be afforded the same protection and respect afforded every segment of our community.

Finally, I also want to acknowledge receipt of your letter dated September 20, but postmarked September 26. Because that letter, and all other correspondence I have received from you is generally abusive and non-productive in tone and content, I see no point in a further exchange of letters. If you have specific concerns, please raise them directly with the Commissioner having jurisdiction over those matters.

Sincerely,
Edward I. Koch
Mayor

• • •

The House of the Lord Church
Brooklyn, New York
October 18, 1978

Dear Mayor Koch:

Your response to my letter regarding the Atlantic Antic parade was very inadequate to say the least.

Firstly, it is not the parade or marching which I question, but rather the noise which makes it impossible for a religious service to proceed. Did the noise make it impossible for the mass at St. Patrick's Cathedral to continue?

Secondly, since I also made reference to the Jewish Sabbath and services, it is interesting that conspicuously absent in your reply was any reference to that portion of my letter.

Thirdly, with respect to the double standard with which the City deals with its Black citizens—while in preparation for our Crown Heights demonstration, the law which I mentioned was cited to us by the Police Department and hundreds of policemen were deployed to make sure it was obeyed and yet the same Police Department never informed us that we, as other groups, had a right to protest any noise that would disrupt our religious service. To add insult to injury, you, the highest official in New York City, consent to be a Grand Marshall in a parade which breaks the same law and when you are approached concerning this fact, you proceed to launch a personal attack upon me.

Now, respecting my letter dated September 20, 1978, let me remind you that the Black United Front gave you its assessment of the situation in Crown Heights and what it understood as corrective action. You, in your reply, took liberty to address me personally on another matter, giving your perception of my actions. However, when in my reaction to your letter, I gave you my candid perception of your actions, you stated that it was abusive and non-productive and did not warrant a response. It does seem that you initiate personal attacks and when responses come you try to run and hide and haughtily admonish me to relate to your appointees.

Let me repeat, with all the emphasis I can command, THE ONLY PLACE I LOOK FORWARD TO SEEING YOU IS BEFORE THE JUDGMENT SEAT OF GOD. I, personally, do not care to relate to you or your appointees, but you happen to be Mayor of this city and a large segment of the same city happens to see me as leader and spokesman, and whether I speak to you or your commissioners will be dictated by them. That, sir, if you will permit me to be pedagogic, is the hard truth that those of us who assume leadership must abide by, if we would be leaders.

There is one other point I would like to call to remembrance. Back in January, after we had been marching for over a month in the cold and snow trying to get a hearing on the Randolph Evans case and having to engage in some unorthodox action at the Brooklyn Museum, to your credit, you agreed to a meeting. On January 12, 1978, I led a diverse delegation to meet with you and said on behalf of that delegation that we were independent leaders representing people, who for the most part, had been excluded from the city's thinking and since we noted your claims of independence we wanted to work with you to build a better New York. We had some ideas regarding the police, youth, etc. At the conclusion of that meeting you told us to meet with your newly appointed Police Commissioner, Robert McGuire, which we did on several occasions. But nothing happened and a little later Art Miller was killed, other Blacks were beaten by the police; vigilante attacks on Blacks increased; and you, sir, seemed set upon a course that has been described by others as a "war against the poor and against Black people."

Black people have always demonstrated extraordinary patience; have always been willing to go another mile. However, when conditions grow worse instead of better and those in power are unwilling or unable to reverse trends, patience wears thin, and it becomes necessary to employ tactics to dramatize the injustice.

It seems strange to us that when this happens, it is never the perpetrators and/or sustainers of the injustice who are called to account, but the victims, who, in their frustration and despair were forced to adopt words and actions that might cause the normal flow of things to cease for a moment.

What those who condemn people like myself, you included sir, seem incapable of comprehending is that there are those who argue for a more violent approach to change and their position is strengthened each time people in power such as yourself deny progress and attempt to discredit those who are struggling for justice within the Constitutional perimeters.

The demonstrations which I have led all over this city have surely been angry at times; indeed they must be. However, they have to a large measure been disciplined. How much longer this continues depends to a large measure upon you. The ball is in your hands. If we lose, the society is in for catastrophic times; and when and if this city explodes, I want the record to show that you repeatedly resisted appeals from reasonable people who discerned the approaching disaster and sought to obtain some justice or at least an alleviation of the deplorable state of affairs. I will conclude with a quote attributed to Robert Kennedy.

"Those who make evolutionary change impossible, make violent revolution inevitable."

Sincerely,
Rev. Herbert Daughtry

# Chapter 12

# Victory at Last! Al Vann and Roger Green

～～～～～～

In the 1982 election, we achieved two significant political victories with the election of Al Vann and Roger Green. Assemblyman Al Vann, a long-time activist and a long-time personal friend, won the race for the 56th Assembly seat in the heart of Bedford-Stuyvesant in Brooklyn. Roger Green, a relative newcomer to the political scene, won in the 57th Assembly District, in the Fort Greene/Boerum Hill section of Brooklyn.

Vann had been the assemblyman for that district for six years. He had served the community well. His independent, honest, effective political work had endeared him to most Blacks, even to those beyond the confines of his district. Grassroots Blacks in particular admired him. Al Vann was a troublesome crusader to Machiavellian Black politicians, and he was a thorn in the side of White machine politicians. Koch viewed him as an implacable foe. Even after winning the election, Koch's antipathy for Vann was in evidence.

For reasons that are not completely clear, the Democratic Party jettisoned Vann, deciding that it no longer wanted him to represent the 56th Assembly District. There were rumors that Black politicians, those more faithful to the party than to the people, wanted Vann removed. White politicians who always viewed Vann with suspicion were more than eager to cooperate.

Rightly or wrongly, lawfully or unlawfully, the Black community viewed the whole episode as a shoddy attempt to get rid of Al, that is, to override their electoral decision. Whatever the problem, for that reason alone, the Party should have rectified it. Vann decided to run on the Liberal Party line. We knew the battle would not be easy; Blacks, for the most part, blindly voted Democratic. But we still thought Vann could win. Basically, it would be the White political machine and Black Uncle Toms against the Black community personified in Al Vann. It was a hard battle that would require a tremendous effort from everyone. When the votes were counted, Vann had won.

It was one of the greatest victories the Black community had achieved in a long time. While we often refer to this battle as a people's victory, it would be unfair to overlook Vann's commitment, integrity, availability, political wisdom and over-all effectiveness. The fact is that Vann had always been a friend and brother to all of us; and we wanted to win it for him and for ourselves.

Anti-Semitism did not surface during the campaign. But Vann, an activist who had been battling for Black peoples' rights on many fronts for a long time, must have stepped on many toes. There are many Jews who have never forgotten his involvement in Ocean Hill-Brownsville. In a *Village Voice* article,[1] Jim Sleeper resurrected Ocean Hill-Brownsville, connecting Vann with the developments there. At the time of the conflicts, Vann was the President of the Afro-American Teachers Association and a teacher at Junior High School 271.

The notorious file of the Anti-Defamation League must have been shared around. But whatever his past may have been, Al Vann has never been anything else but a sincere and courageous battler for Black peoples' rights; a Black man who would never deny any other people their rights, or participate in any unprincipled organization or activity.

The second 1982 election victory was in the 57th Assembly District, which is where my church was located at the time. (In 1990, the district's lines would be redrawn and the church would be in the 52nd Assembly District.) It takes in most of the downtown section of Brooklyn, a most vital district, and its population is predominately Black and Puerto Rican. For many years, the district had been represented by Harvey Strezlin, an obscure Assemblyman who had never done or said anything of significance; he was just there, the Machine Man. Roger Green, Vann's young protégé, had, despite his years, garnered deep respect within the Black community because of his hard work and devotion to the people. Green was the insurgent. A couple of years earlier he had run for District Leader and had been defeated by Abe Gerges after a hard-fought campaign. Immediately afterward, Green began to put together an organization and to mobilize a network of supporters. When the time came for the Assembly race, Roger Green was ready.

Green campaigned diligently, and the community went all out for his victory. We knocked on doors, handed out literature, took to the sound trucks, organized and attended rallies, talked to people on street corners, in shopping malls, and work places, *and* we raised money. When the votes were counted, they said, "It's too close to call." The anger in the Black community led to a confrontation at the Board of Elections; and we initiated a law suit. We were certain they were trying to steal the election from us.

They said there had to be another election to determine a winner. So we had to start all over again. The odds were with the incumbent: his organization and money were already in place. It would be harder for us to generate enthusiasm again. But people rallied to the cause, and we did it again! And again, the vote was too close to call and a third election had to be held.

If the second round was hard, the third would be harder still. Time was on the side of our opponent, we thought, because the resources of the Democratic machine were on Strezlin's side.

We put our shoulders to the grindstone for this third election and we made history. It was the first time a third election was called, pointing up the determination of entrenched political and economic power. The district was predominately Black, which should justify a Black candidate, and besides, Strezlin had done nothing for the district. Some of us thought that he was weary of the whole business anyway and wanted out, but that he was kept in place by certain groups whose interests he served.

Green, an intelligent, honest, young man, with a glowing future, was the very kind of candidate Whites love to support and push forward. But Green, however, is not White. Still, the determination of the Black community and progressive Whites (including Jews) was equal to the occasion. This time we organized people not only to watch the polls but to battle, if necessary, to prevent chicanery. We were particularly concerned about the Hasidic community in Williamsburg. There were reports that they were trying to register people who were not even citizens and threatening voters whom they thought might be Green supporters. But when it was all over, Green had won. It was a great victory! Black people had shown once again when they believe in a candidate, they can put forth maximum effort to get him or her elected.

With the victories of Al Vann and Roger Green, hope surged in Black communities, in Brooklyn and beyond. Perhaps, at last, we were building the kind of honest political power reflective of our numbers, that is, 700,000 in Brooklyn, according to the 1970 Census. And it is agreed by all that the number has increased.

Vann and Green were not ordinary politicians, made in the image of the political machine. They had both been accessible, candid, and conscientious young men whose roots were deeply and firmly entrenched in the Black community. To say that is not to say that they are against other people. No! They are sensitive to the needs of all people. They believe in fairness for everyone. They represent a new breed of politician. And not only do Black people need what they represent, all Americans need what they represent.

## MASS ACTION

While mass action largely contributed to the Vann and Green victories, there were many individuals and small groups that responded to our appeal. There were, for example, the residents from the housing developments who came out, I am told, to vote for Roger Green because they heard my message on the sound truck urging them to do so.

The Black United Front (BUF) was particularly active, supplying, among other things, man- and woman-power and various kinds of resources. With a mixture of sadness and pride, I can say that NBUF is the *only* viable Black organization whose existence in completely rooted in Black people, that is, ultimately dependent upon Black people. I say with sadness and pride because, if this is so, it underscores the fragmentation and divisiveness existing in the Black community, and, perhaps, the very reason for Black powerlessness.

Without organization, we can achieve very little. Understanding that an unorganized people is a powerless people, I was driven to organize. (Since the Black community is so unorganized, it is highly unlikely that a concrete campaign of anti-Semitism could be launched.)

On the other hand, I am proud of the fact that I had a hand in creating BUF, and I am also proud of what that organization has been able to accomplish in a very short time, against great odds. The Black United Front has validated my assessment of our people and our history. I believe we want unity, and we are ready to struggle against any and all oppressive forces to achieve it.

## INVOLVEMENT

I want to underscore the effectiveness of the political action group associated with The House of the Lord, my church. They campaigned and went above and beyond the call of duty to ensure victory for Vann and Green. But it should be made clear that political involvement is not the only area in which the members of my church have been with me. I believe I can boast of getting more members of my church to participate in social activism than any other minister in the country.

We have become veterans in political elections. We have gone to Buffalo to help Arthur Eve in his bid for Mayor in 1977. On two separate week-ends we filled chartered buses, paid for from our own funds, and walked the streets, knocked on doors, and worked in campaign headquarters. Some people believed that the number of people we registered gave Eve the margin of victory in the primary. Only entrenched racism denied him victory in the general election. His defeat marked the first time in recent memory that a Democratic candidate had been beaten in a general election in Buffalo.

In addition to Al Vann, Roger Green, and Arthur Eve, we also supported and worked for Assemblywoman Ann Davis in the Bronx, Assemblyman Charles Johnson, also in the Bronx, State Senator Joseph Galiber in his bid for the Bronx Borough Presidency, David Dinkins for the Manhattan Borough Presidency, Percy Sutton for Mayor, and the list goes on.

I elaborated somewhat on my political involvement, or support for political candidates, to emphasize a point. Political leaders who have been observing me over the years know what I am about: unity, political and economic power for my people. And my activism, in some crucial way, poses a threat to my adversaries, and so they have tried to slander me.

## NOTES

1.   *Village Voice*, week of December 9, 1981.

# Chapter 13

# Fred Richmond

The 1978 re-election campaign of Congressman Fred Richmond presented still another political occasion for charging Blacks with anti-Semitism. Yet a *New York Amsterdam News* article entitled "Myth of Black Anti-Semitism," reported that a Brooklyn weekly had called Richmond's opponent, Bernard Gifford, a "Black nigger" who wanted to implement a second holocaust:

> Even more reprehensible tactics were used in 1978 when Bernard Gifford, former Deputy Chancellor of the New York City Board of Education, running against Congressman Frederick Richmond, was labeled in an ad placed in the Brooklyn Weekly DER YID as "part of a plot to implement a second holocaust against Jews." The ad also said: "We need Richmond as a representative of our interest in Congress and for this we cannot survive a pitch Black nigger from the heart of Kenya (sic) who supports all our enemies...."[1]

In the early 1970s, federal courts ruled that New York City should carve out another congressional district specifically designed to encourage minority representation on the federal level. Thus, the Fourteenth Congressional District was created in Brooklyn, New York, and Fred Richmond, a wealthy Jewish councilman, ran for election and won the seat.

As the 1978 election year rolled around, Richmond's re-election was considered an easy victory, but by April 1978, the news broke that Richmond had been apprehended while sexually propositioning Black male youths. He subsequently admitted to this charge in an open letter to his constituents. Ed Koch was one of the first to come to his defense.

In response to Richmond's admission, on Sunday, May 7, 1978, I led a group of about thirty-five community leaders and residents to meet with Richmond in his Montague Street office. As planned, we respectfully urged him to resign. With incredible arrogance, Richmond said that he would not resign, adding impatiently that he was going to run and win.

A week later a number of the most prominent Black clergymen in Brooklyn publicly announced their support for Fred Richmond. It was deeply painful and disillusioning for me. Many of the ministers supporting Richmond were clergy whom I had admired for years. Nevertheless, in an article, published in the *New York Amsterdam News*,[2] I continued to demand Richmond's resignation and criticized Black politicians and others who were supportive of Richmond, or who remained silent or neutral.

Candidates for Richmond's seat began to come forward, and after a series of community meetings that culminated in a meeting at The House of the Lord Church, Bernard Gifford was selected as the Black community's candidate from the pool of four, which had also included Rev. Samuel Austin, Simeon Golar, and State Senator Vander Beatty. Gifford was ultimately unsuccessful in his bid to unseat Richmond.

Later, Fred Richmond was under investigation for questionable business dealings. There was also a fugitive who was using Richmond's car while attempting to solicit sex from a man who turned out to be a police officer. In April 1982, Richmond's former aides testified before a federal grand jury that they had purchased cocaine and marijuana for Richmond.

In February 1981, another Black group held a news conference to demand Richmond's resignation. At no point, neither in the first nor in the second demand for his resignation, was the subject of Fred Richmond's Jewish heritage raised, although anti-Semitic allegations were still being hurled at the Black leadership. Most of us believed that the man was simply unfit to hold public office. In addition, since the seat was originally created for a minority we believed that it should be held by either a Black or Latino representative. Succeeding developments have validated our position. Interestingly enough, the *Village Voice* carried an article with the caption: "Hasidim Find Richmond Non-Kosher."

On August 25, 1982, Fred Richmond pleaded guilty to federal tax evasion and to drug charges, and he resigned. It should be noted that both these charges were arrived at through plea bargaining, so the public remains unaware of the extent of Richmond's crimes.

\* \* \*

In September 1982, following Richmond's resignation, Brooklyn Deputy Borough President Edolphus "Ed" Towns won the Democratic primary for Richmond's congressional seat. Towns subsequently won the general election and became the district's first African American Congressperson.

## NOTES

1. "Myth of Black Anti-Semitism," *New York Amsterdam News*, March 13, 1982.
2  "The Moral Dilemma of Fred Richmond," *New York Amsterdam News*, May 6, 1978.

# Chapter 14

# Citywide Rally

On September 28, 1978, we held a citywide rally at City Hall to place our "ten demands"[1] before Mayor Koch. This rally, organized by a cross section of community leaders, had been months in the planning and ultimately attracted approximately 10,000.

The demands were the culmination of weeks of intense debate and deliberation by these citywide community leaders. I posted the document on the door of City Hall. We sought no meeting with the Mayor. The organizing committee comprised of the Association of Black Social Workers and the Black United Front, decided that it was best not to meet with the Mayor at that time, but we placed a full page ad in the *New York Amsterdam News* to publicize the event.

Again, the media portrayed this as a continuation of a personal feud, and therefore simply the ravings and rallying cry of a Black anti-Semite. My guess is that Koch was well aware of the media's view, and that he or his advisors conspired with them to devise a militant scenario of Koch vs. the Black anti-Semitic. It all made political points for him; he was seen as standing firm against an anti-Semitic hoodlum. As the months wore on, however, Koch continued to pick fights with everybody, that is, everybody whom the majority of White middle class apparently resented—for example, unions, judges, Blacks, Latinos, elected officials, such as City Council President Carol Bellamy, whom he dubbed in a *Playboy* interview, a "side show"and a suburban American "sterile." Koch's demagogic stance severely polarized the city.

## Media Compliance

### Channel 5

All the TV channels carried the story of the rally, but Channel 5 had a most peculiar slant. Although I cannot recall exact words, Channel 5 reporter, Christopher Jones' announcement was to this effect:

> We have it from Police sources that the man who calls himself
> the Rev. Herbert Daughtry has been arrested six times in the last
> fifteen years for number slips, forgery, rape, and selling dope.

I could hardly believe my ears. As I sat with my wife and four children, we all stared at the TV, and then at each other. The problem was not the reference to the penitentiary; my youthful years of lawlessness and incarceration were known. But I had never been arrested for rape or for selling dope, nor had I been arrested six times. Even more importantly, at the time of his allegations, I was celebrating my twentieth year of pastoring the same church. I had been arrested during that period for civil rights activity, which is considered a misdemeanor.

Note the way Jones led into his malicious character defamation: "the man who calls himself the Reverend Herbert Daughtry ...." Why, "the man who calls himself ....?" I am an ordained minister. I was ordained over twenty years by a religious institution that was incorporated in September 1930, in Augusta, Georgia. The New York branch was incorporated in Brooklyn, New York, in 1942.

On that "Reverend" note, it has always amused me to observe the difficulty that many White people in power—particularly news people—have in calling me "Reverend." But, this reporter had departed from the rest, giving me the title, but with the implication that I had conferred it upon myself. Thus, he shrewdly insinuates that, along with the other deviant behavior, I had usurped something and therefore that I am a charlatan, an imposter.

I consulted my attorney, William Kunstler, and announced at a news conference that we were suing Channel 5.[2] We won the case, with the proviso that the details would not be discussed publicly. Character defamation suits are particularly difficult to win because one has to prove not only that the media lied, but that they did it with malicious intent.

That was not the first time that Channel 5 had evinced its animosity towards me. After Black businessman Arthur Miller was killed, Brooklyn District Attorney Eugene Gold called a news conference at his office. I, along with others in the community, decided that we would attend. As we listened intently to Gold's report, Channel 5 reporter Martin Bowman pointed to me and asked Gold to remove me. He refused, reminding the reporter that these are tense times and whatever could be done to engender confidence in the law, should be done.

On another occasion, in 1978, Channel 5 sought to vilify me. A newscaster was reporting on the Black ministers' call for Richmond's resignation. He said that one of the ministers was an "ex-convict."[3]

## Channel 7

Let me expose one more endeavor by the media to discredit me. On August 22, 1979, policemen shot Luis Baez over twenty times. The facts were as follows. Luis Baez' mother called the police because her son was acting strangely. He had a history of psychological problems, and the police knew this.

On this particular day the police cornered Baez in the yard. The officers said that he had a pair of scissors or a knife, and as he climbed over the small fence, where he had fallen from the fire escape, apparently headed toward the policemen, they opened fire and pumped over twenty bullets in his frail, 124-pound frame.

On the same day of the killing, with members of the Black United Front, I visited Mrs. Baez. She appeared numb with confusion and sadness. Through an interpreter she explained what had happened. We agreed that we should go to the police precinct to ascertain what had happened and what the police proposed to do about it.

When we arrived with Mrs. Baez at the precinct, police officers met us at the door. We requested permission to enter and talk to the captain, or to whomever was in charge. They would allow only a couple of us inside, they said. Knowing the experiences of many Blacks and Latinos who were beaten in police precincts, we insisted on a larger delegation. They were adamant about the number, the dialogue became heated, and the police began pushing against us. We began pushing back, and after a brief time of shoving and shouting, we departed.

That night on Channel 7 reporter Roger Sharp, giving step-by-step commentary on the incident, referred to me as a professional "rabble rouser." There were no harsh words for the police who had brutally killed a man. No references to the history of the New York City Police Department's killing of Blacks and Latinos under the most suspicious circumstances. No attempt to imply that, given these circumstances, my reaction might have been justified or perhaps constructive, i.e., providing an occasion for people to vent their rage, with no one physically injured. But, no! I was a "rabble rouser."

On Monday evening, August 27, hundreds gathered in

Tompkins Square Park, across the street from the precinct. There were reports that there had been earlier incidents of confrontation and bottle throwing. The body of Luis Baez had been brought to the park. After a number of fiery speeches, the "black coach of sorrow" carried the body away. By that time, the crowd was in a "fired up" mood, as was reported.

The plan was to march to the precinct when the rally was over. But we had received word that provocateurs were in the crowd, and that the policemen were fortified and ready for confrontation. If we marched away from the precinct, it would give us time to identify the provocateurs and to evaluate the over-all situation. So, we took the long walk away from the precinct, circled, and moved in the direction of the precinct. Still blocks away, the police ran through the crowd with their cars, chasing and beating the marchers with their clubs.

The media, with the exception of Wayne Barrett of the *Village Voice*, blamed the demonstration's outcome on me in particular. Barrett pointed out that I had taken the long way around to avoid confrontations,, and quoted me as stating before the march began: "I will not lead you into a slaughter." In anticipation of police violence, and to provide further validation for our nonviolent intent, we had organized a contingent of attorneys who had volunteered to be present for the demonstration. Their unanimous report placed the blame on the police.

In the end, with financial assistance from The Randolph Evans Crisis Fund, Luis Baez was laid to rest. The policemen were exonerated.

Some weeks later, I talked to a vice president of ABC (Channel 7) news. I complained about his station's character assassination of me. He tried to downplay my accusations and said I was misquoting the reporter. I pulled out the cassette that had recorded the precinct standoff, offering to compare it with the news report. "Do you want to hear it?" "No," he responded, "that's not necessary." I proceeded to talk about how carelessly and maliciously the media handles a person's reputation and then I pushed the question of fairness in journalism: *Do news people have any feeling about character assassination? Do they ever consider a person's family and friends or the harm their unsubstantiated reports can do?*

"We will do better," he promised.

So much for the two great American Institutions—law enforcement and the media.

## NOTES

1. See Citywide Rally Demands and Flyer, 1978 (unpublished), Available from Daughtry personal files.
2. See Correspondence: Daughtry/Channel 5 (Character Defamation). Available from Daughtry personal files.
3. See Correspondence: Daughtry/Channel 5 (Convict). Available from Daughtry personal files.

# Chapter 15

# Atlantic Antic 1978

Another Koch-related incident occurred on September 24, 1978. A group of Atlantic Avenue business and community leaders had organized an annual street fair called the Atlantic Antic. Atlantic Avenue was closed off from the Hudson River to Flatbush Avenue. Since our church is on Atlantic Avenue, we made an agreement with the organizers that there would be no amplified instrumental sounds during our worship service, which took place from noon to 2:00 pm.

On the Sunday of the 1978 Atlantic Antic, as I stood in the pulpit preparing to deliver my sermon, loud noises emanating from the outside drowned out my voice. Needless to say, I was angry. When I was informed that Mayor Koch was leading the parade, the congregation and I made the decision to ask for an explanation from the Mayor on the violation of the agreement and on the violation of the law itself. In July 1978, when we were planning to hold a rally in front of the Lubavitcher

Headquarters on Eastern Parkway, the police told us that there was a city ordinance prohibiting the use of amplification equipment within 105 feet of a religious service in progress.

Now, here was the Mayor leading a parade, a choir of brass instruments—drums, horns and all—directly in front of our church, in the middle of our Sunday worship service! To us it was another clear example of a double standard. Still dressed in my pastoral robes, I, with members of my congregation, went out to meet the Mayor. After several blocks, we caught up with him as he hastened to his car. He requested an opportunity to speak. "I am your Mayor," he said, "and you can't intimidate me." When he had finished his comments, I said, "Fine, now let me say a word," but instead he jumped into his car and sped off.

As we headed back to the church, there were a couple of incidents with the police. It was only the cool professionalism of one particular officer that prevented a full-scale confrontation, for a "1013" had already been issued. The 1013 code means "policeman in trouble," and when throngs of police officers arrive on such occasions, they assault first and ask questions later.

I went to the platform and asked the organizers for a moment to speak to the crowd about what had happened. They reluctantly granted me a few minutes. I explained that we had no intention of disrupting the street fair, but that we had been in the midst of our worship service when the noise drowned us out. I pointed to the violation of the agreement, called their attention to the city ordinance and the double standard. We, then, returned to the church and continued our service.

Needless to say, the next day the media had a field day. I was accused of attacking the Mayor, disrupting a community fair, and hurling anti-Semitic invectives. Only Geoffrey Stokes of the *Village Voice* bothered to ask me what had happened. He wrote:

> By the time Ed Koch reached it [the car], the crowd had thinned. Daughtry called for silence, giving the mayor a chance to speak. Standing on the doorsill of the car, visible to the hundred or so onlookers, he did so.

He spoke not to the disturbed worshippers but to the jeering Whites who had followed them. "I want to assure you," he said, "that anyone who tries to break up a parade is out in my book."

"Talk to us, talk to us."

"All right," he said turning to face the Blacks. "I just want to tell you that when you indulge in anti-Semitic remarks, you do your cause no good." He sat, a police officer slammed the door, and the car sped off.

It is important to note that in 1980, according to the *New York Post*, the city ordinance was nullified:

So when Rev. Herbert Daughtry, the Black political leader from Brooklyn, jostled Mayor Koch at an Atlantic Avenue festival that passed in front of his church two years ago, he claimed Koch violated the law by disrupting his church services. Last weekend, a bill backed by City Hall, repealing the law, was passed by the Legislature.[1]

The Atlantic Antic confrontation between Koch and myself produced some sharp exchanges in correspondence.[2]

## NOTES

1. *New York Post*, June 17, 1980.
2. See Correspondence: Daughtry/Koch: Atlantic Antic. Available from Daughtry's personal files.

# Chapter 16

# June 12 Rally

One of the most significant events ever to have taken place in New York was the June 12 Rally. A million people gathered to sing, pray, speak, and march against nuclear weaponry. The rally began at the United Nations and culminated in Central Park. At that point, it was the greatest demonstration in the city's history.

The National Black United Front (NBUF) became involved in January 1982, several months after Whites had begun to organize. We immediately recognized that there should be a substantial increase in Third World involvement, and that the issues of race and nonintervention needed to be addressed in such a forum. An intense struggle began around Third World participation and the aforementioned issues. The debate became so heated at times that the demonstration itself was threatened.

On April 20, 1982, the *Village Voice* printed an in-depth, advance article on the rally, with Dave Lindorff interviewing most of the major figures involved. The article was, for the most part, sensitive and accurate, but inevitably, the question of anti-Semitism arose. According to Lindorff, one of the rally organizers he interviewed had raised the issue. However, even he admitted that it had never surfaced during the debate or in any of the pre-rally meetings. He wrote:

> What was the problem with BUF that made these mainstream peace and environmental groups feel they had to quit rather than work with Daughtry, who represents one of the most active mass black organizations as anti-Semitic? That may or may not be true; certainly anti-Semitic statements have been made in years past by members of BUF. But that issue was never raised at the various coalition meetings, so BUF could not address it. Still, it was raised privately by some leaders and must have played a role in the coalition's breakdown.

On April 30, 1982, I responded to the article.[1] In my letter, I sought to make one point: What did anti-Semitism have to do with the rally? It would seem that somebody on the June 12 Rally Committee (assuming Lindorff's account to be true) chose the issue of anti-Semitism to discredit or to isolate NBUF and me, and achieve an objective that had little to do with Jews per se. Thus, there was, again, an unscrupulous attempt to manipulate a highly sensitive issue to disparage the opposition and to promote the interests of the accusers.

There was a two-pronged conspiracy involved. On one side, there was a conspiracy manifested in helping to circulate the allegations. Then, there was a conspiracy of silence. To my knowledge, no one on the Committee took a public position against the charge.

One final point must be emphasized. The June 12 Rally Committee consisted of liberal, progressive forces. These were not the "red necks," "the crackers," the conservative, reactionary racists. No! These were, supposedly, the open-minded, unprejudiced liberals who had won their spurs in the Civil Rights movement, and in the Viet-Nam War.

My conviction was confirmed—repeatedly argued in this book—*no one willingly gives away power.* Liberal progressives, for the most part, act like conservatives, racists, and imperialists when it comes to Third World people exercising self-determination.

\* \* \*

In spite of all of the opposition, BUF played a major role in the rally and its organizing, particularly Michael Amon-Ra who was my chief representative at the organizing meetings. Also, I was one of the few persons to deliver speeches at both June 12 events, the one at Central Park, and the one held at the United Nations.[2]

## NOTES

1.  See Correspondence: Daughtry/*Village Voice*, 1982. Available from Daughtry personal files.
2.  Copies of Daughtry June 12 speeches are available from Daughtry's personal files.

# Chapter 17

# International Considerations

~~~~~~~~~~~~~

## ANDREW YOUNG

In August 1979, Black-Jewish relations reached an all-time low with Andrew Young's "resignation" as U.S. ambassador to the United Nations, precipitated by his meeting with the representatives of the Palestine Liberation Organization (PLO). Most Blacks believed that pressure from the Jewish lobby had led to Young's dismissal, creating a palpable tension between the two communities. Blacks and Jews were meeting everywhere, separately and together to discuss the matter. Black establishment leaders met in New York and issued a statement, "A Declaration of Independence," they called it. Shortly thereafter, some of these same leaders repudiated or sought to modify their statement.

Many in the Black community believed that once again Jewish pressure had accomplished what they had done many times before when Blacks tried to assert themselves.

I, along with others, organized demonstrations at the Israeli embassy and at the United Nations. The focus of our concern, as articulated in our news release, was Young's unjust treatment and Israel's support of the apartheid government in South Africa.[1] Subsequently, I wrote two articles for the *New York Amsterdam News*, one on August 25, 1979, and the other on November 3, 1979, criticizing Black leaders, various Jewish leaders, and the Israeli government. The gist of both pieces was that people act in their own interests, and that we should be wary of affections without respect for self-determination. I emphasized that Black people had to organize themselves and seek allies based on mutual respect and shared interests. For this honest appraisal, various Jewish leaders responded with labels of anti-Semitism, a stigma they obstinately refuse to examine or rescind.

It is interesting to note that the succeeding UN Ambassador, Jeanne Kirkpatrick, was caught meeting with South African officials, one of whom was head of military intelligence. Kirkpatrick, however, held onto her post. Blacks pointed to the inconsistency and called on friends to force Kirkpatrick's resignation, but to no avail. What Kirkpatrick did wasn't of major concern to most Jews, because it was not in their interests to do so, contrary to the situation with Andrew Young.

## Israeli-South African Alliance

Let me be clear. *Never* have I argued for the annihilation of Israel. Although I am cognizant of the deception, cruelty, annexation of land, and human slaughter that brought Israel into existence, I am also cognizant of the fact that no nation was born in purity, honesty, or bloodlessness. My position on the Israeli-Palestinian conflict is spelled out in the resolution adopted by my church at the 51st Convocation of The House of the Lord Churches.[2] I have denounced the inhumane treatment of

142

Palestinians, and I have argued for a Palestinian State. At the same time, I have argued for Israel's right to exist in secure, internationally recognized borders, and I have criticized so-called Palestinian "terrorist" tactics. I have criticized many of the Israeli government's policies—and so have *many* Jews. When Prime Minister Menachem Begin visited New York, the Hasidim held a demonstration to mark opposition to the Israeli government's policies. The editorial in the May 1982 issue of *Jewish Current* also discusses political differences among Jews.

Moreover, many Black people know that from 1967-1980, Israel received $19 billion in grants and loans, averaging $400 per capita. A substantial portion of this sum came from Black people's tax dollars. Just consider: Black folks are losers on three fronts:

1. Monies that could be used to alleviate some of our misery in the U.S. were going to Israel.
2. Monies from our tax dollars were going to Israel, which in turn gave support to South Africa's Apartheid government, which in turn oppressed, exploited, and murdered Black people.
3. When we criticized this arrangement, there were Jews who called us anti-Semitic. The allegation and the counter allegation created tension and sometimes alienation, among old friends and potential allies, both Jewish and non-Jewish.

I have criticized the Israeli government's alliance with South Africa's Apartheid regime. I have also criticized the Israeli government (as I have criticized the U.S. government) for supporting other oppressive regimes: Samoza in Nicaragua, Pinochet in Chile, and Duarte in El Salvador; all have the support of human and material resources. Israeli and U.S. support not only helped to sustain the racist government in South Africa, it also hindered African liberation efforts. But, in the eyes of many Jews, any criticism of Israel makes Blacks anti-Semitic. But why shouldn't Blacks oppose any government that oppresses, exploits, and slaughters our people?

Then there is the historic relationship, dating back to the dawning of the 20th century, between Zionist and Apartheid leaders. This relationship is documented in the book *Israel and South Africa: The Progression of a Relationship*. Significantly, the authors claim that the Jewish community in South Africa has the highest per capita income in the world.

In December 1981, Sam Nujoma, then President of the South West Africa Peoples Organization (SWAPO), made a scathing indictment on the Israeli-South African relationship in a speech at the Afro-Arab Conference in Luwanda, Angola.

The scope and gravity of Zionist participation in arming the apartheid regime with the most dangerous weapons, nuclear weapons, came to light when Israel and South Africa jointly exploded a nuclear device in the South Atlantic after it has been known that Israel was helping South Africa to produce a nuclear bomb.

The construction of a nuclear submarine is currently under way at the South African naval port of Simonstown.

Tel Aviv also supplies South Africa with conventional arms, she sells SA 105mm mortars, air-to-air rockets and anti-tank missiles. One important characteristic of the military collaboration between these agents of imperialism is their joint venture in the manufacture of arms, like in the case of the US-designed Scorpion helicopters that are partly built in South Africa and then finished in Israel. The South African Panhard armed cars were refitted by Israel. The racist commandos responsible for slaughter of innocent women and children and for sabotaging economic infrastructure of progressive African states are trained by Israeli officers. The racist army is heavily dependent on the Israeli experience and training in fighting national liberation movements as well as launching aggressions against progressive neighboring states. No wonder thus that the racist South African regime is currently following the Israeli tactics in the Middle-East by trying to create another southern Lebanon in Southern Angola with the UNITA bandits playing the role of the "Christian Militia." Israeli officers not only plan operations against the combatants of PLAN the military wing of SWAPO, but Israeli mercenaries participate in fighting our guerrillas. They also participated in the planning and execution of the South African war of aggression against Angola in 1975. The racist troops are equipped with Israeli techniques for evacuating casualties which help cover up their heavy losses.

Besides, the racists also possess radar and other surveillance equipment supplied by Israel to counter attacks by ANC and SWAPO freedom fighters. In return for what it receives in arms, the apartheid regime sells Israel strategic raw material like coal, steel, and uranium. The racists pump large sums of money into Israeli military projects.

They finance the building of the newly designed Israel Lavi fighter bomber that will ultimately be built in South Africa as well as the construction of a military complex in the Negev desert. South Africa also participates in the construction of an oil tank in Israel farm for the storage of oil. Racist South Africa ran to the aid of their Zionist friends during the Israel aggressive war of 1973 against progressive Arab countries by supplying them with mirage bombers, weapons ammunition, spare parts and South African mercenaries. The racist provided Israel with steel for the production of the chariot tank.

The collaboration of apartheid and Zionism in the economic field has the specific character of mostly composing items directly linked with their military build-up. Pretoria and Tel Aviv have been removing every barrier in the way of the growth of their trading ties. Israel also invests in the South African so-called homelands thus boosting the apartheid policies of South Africa.

(The collaboration between Zionist Israel and racist South Africa is, however, directly linked to the support of the western imperialist countries, especially the USA, render South Africa and Israel respectively. Israel's ability to sell South Africa sophisticated weapons is a direct result of the long US military and technical support of Israel. The huge sums of money South Africa invests in Israel military projects comes from western banks.)

The latest US/Israeli strategic agreement and the openly declared friendship of the US with racists in South Africa has given more encouragement to the two diabolic regimes to continue with their criminal policies against the just cause of Arab and African peoples for freedom and self-determination.

Besides, western imperialist countries find it convenient to channel their support to South Africa through Israel as does, for example, West German and the US based Space Research Corporation.

If I condemn Zionist Jews and the Jewish community in South Africa, does that make me anti-Semitic? Am I bad because I want good for my people everywhere? If I am called bad because I want good for my people and all people—but not at the expense of denying any other people their legitimate rights—what does that make those who call me bad?

Supposing African countries had supported Hitler and supplied the Nazis with men and material. How would Jews have felt about African countries? The Jews would have poured out a flood of invectives and would have immediately terminated any relationship, and rightfully so. And it would not be a case of Jews being anti-Black or racists. If Jews would compare that hypothetical situation to ours, it should not be difficult for them to understand why Blacks criticized Israel's liaison with South Africa's Apartheid regime.

But even having to defend one's right to criticize the Israeli government shows the power of the Jewish influence in the media. It is the Israeli government that is guilty of supporting and sustaining one of the most brutal governments history has ever known. It is the Israeli government that should be on the defensive, not the other way round.

## "DAUGHTRY ROASTS ISRAEL"

It would be unfair of me to leave the impression that I only had problems with White media. On occasion, I have also had difficulty with the Black media.

On December 6, 1980, the *New York Amsterdam News* carried an article concerning my speech at the United Nations. The headline article read, "Daughtry Roasts Israel." It angered me because it misrepresented my message. The article went on to say that the main emphasis of my speech was Israel, when, in fact, the reason for my appearance at the UN was to address the issue of Apartheid. There was only one line in the entire speech that referred to Israel.[3]

After receiving my indignant letter,[4] the publisher, John Procope, invited me to meet with him. Once there I vigorously expressed my irritation that the article had not only shifted the primary focus of the speech but had also misquoted me. Given the slant of the piece, my adversaries would undoubtedly place it in their file as additional evidence of my anti-Semitism.

The paper did agree to publish an apology with an erratum.

## NOTES

1. See Press Release: "Ambassador Andrew Young and Israel," 1978. Available from Daughtry's personal files.
2. See Resolution Passed at the 51st Convocation of The House of the Lord Churches, 1981. Available from The House of the Lord Church files.
3. See United Nations speech, 1980. Available from Daughtry's personal files.
4. See Correspondence: Daughtry/*Amsterdam News*, 1980. Available from Daughtry's personal files.

# Chapter 18

# Can You Criticize Jews Without Being Anti-Semitic?

It has been said: *Be careful of what you say so that your enemies have nothing to use against you.*

I have been told much the same thing: *Not only must you not appear to be anti-Semitic, you must not use language that others may interpret as anti-Semitic.*

While both admonitions may be advisable, they are nevertheless burdensome in that they can render a person ineffective.

I have met with many Jewish groups. The meetings have

been helpful and productive, especially when we have tried to be honest and candid with one another. At one point, I was advised not to use the word "Jews" when referring to the Hasidim, for then all Jews would think I was referring to them. I said, "Fine." I never meant *all* Jews when I referred to Hasidic Jews, so I determined not to use the two terms interchangeably again.

Then I was informed that I should never use the term "Jewish control," for example, in connection with the media, etc., for it was one of the cornerstones of Nazi propaganda, i.e., "Jews control everything," and then the Nazis tried to exterminate them. I said "Okay, but I wish I could say Blacks control something." In any case, I have never used "Jewish control" since. But when I asked, in these meetings, how could one constructively criticize Jews or Jewish leaders and not be called anti-Semitic, invariably silence followed, and that, it seems to me is a towering obstacle to Black-Jewish solidarity and one that is grossly unfair. Jews can criticize any person or groups as a matter of right, but when criticism turns in their direction *many* Jews cry anti-Semitism.

In his book *The Zionist Connection*, Alfred M. Lilienthal devotes two chapters to anti-Semitism, arguing that it is relied upon by many Jews to promote their interests. Furthermore, he states, the Anti-Defamation League (ADL) has employed all kinds of undercover tactics to destroy any alleged anti-Semite. "They name the dog, then hang him," he writes.

> The ADL's earlier emphasis on stamping out genuine prejudice and bigotry gave way long ago to acts of defamation, spying, and publishing spurious literary productions, motivated by support of Israel and effected by eliminating critics of Zionist tactics. [p. 405]

He then quotes a number of Jewish leaders to prove their desire for a climate of anti-Semitism. One, Theodore Herzl, the father of Zionism expressed the hope that any anti-Semitism would "act as a propelling force which, like the wave of the future, would bring the Jews into the promised land." At the same time he also wrote: Anti-Semitism has grown and continues to grow-and so do I." [He further predicted]: "The governments of all countries scourged by anti-Semitism will be keenly interested in assisting us to obtain the sovereignty we want." [p. 410–411]

Dr. Judah Magnes, the first President of Hebrew University, said, "We had always thought that Zionism would diminish anti-Semitism in the world. We are witness to the opposite." Dr. Nahum Goldmann, former President of the World Jewish Congress warns:

Current decline of overt anti-Semitism might constitute a new danger to Jewish survival. . . . The disappearance of "anti-Semitism" in its classic meaning, while beneficial to the political and material situation of Jewish communities, has had a very negative effect on our internal life. [p. 412]

Leo Pfeffer of the American Jewish Congress said, "Such discrimination may well be a blessing. It is possible that some anti-Semitism is necessary in order to insure Jewish survival."[1]

The above quotes remind me of a story I once heard about a priest who found the devil dying on the side of the road. The devil pleaded with him for help. But the priest hastened on gleefully. Then he heard the devil citing his contribution to the priest's existence; had he not produced pestilence, hatred, disappointment, alienation, betrayal, etc., all of which made the priest's job necessary? The priest slowed his steps, stopped, and thought for a moment, turned back and began to tend the devil's wounds, finally placing the devil on his shoulders and taking him home for additional care. I confess, I wonder sometimes, if this isn't a true description of anti-Semitism and Jewish leadership. Anti-Semitism, the devil, is nurtured by *some* Jewish Leaders who feel threatened or undernourished without it.

Admittedly, I have criticized Jews as well as other ethnic and religious groups, including Irish, Italians, Catholics, Christians, Muslims, etc., but I've never been called anti-Irish, anti-Italian, anti-Catholic, anti-Christian, or anti-Muslim. In fact, I have criticized African Americans and African leaders, including Black religious leaders, but no one has ever called me anti-Black or anti-African. And to take it to its ludicrous conclusion, I have criticized myself, I don't think I am anti-me.

The point is there seems to be no nice, proper way to criticize any members of, or institutions of the Jewish community without being labeled anti-Semitic. I think it would be more accurate to say anyone who has been critical of what might be called a Jewish position, policy, or program will be labeled anti-Semitic by certain Jewish people. And neither the sensitivity nor the accuracy or even the supportive history of the critic matters one iota.

The person who bears the anti-Semitic label is relentlessly pursued across the globe, whether that person is actually a "Jew hater" is of no consequence. If certain members in the Jewish community perceive, for whatever reason, that a person has "anti-Semitic tendencies," that person's life will be made untenable. Television, radio, publishing houses, newspaper, speaking engagement, jobs, political aspirations, conferences are blocked to that person. South Dakota Senator James Abourzek makes a powerful indictment on this subject:

> Israel has so wrapped itself in its state religion, Judaism, that any criticism of its politics is immediately branded as criticism of its religion. Thus the critic is accused of anti-Semitism, a charge that has served to silence even the mildest questioning of Israel's policies. In fact, it has become much easier for American politicians to criticize their own government.
>
> The Israeli lobby has neither qualms nor scruples when the objective is to silence an effective critic. It has used direct threats of political reprisal on recalcitrants. It has contacted Jewish contributors, warning them that the politician in ques-

tion does not deserve the support of American Jews. It generates hate mail to target politicians, and even bomb threats have been used to prevent speeches critical of Israel from being given.[2]

Rabbi Martin Siegel also comments on labeling every critic an anti-Semitic:

First is their fixation of anti-Semitism. Every individual Jew has a tendency to think of himself as a Jew. If he suffers personal discrimination he calls it anti-Semitism.

Even when it does exist, anti-Semitism is in the natural order of things. Jews are different—they recognize this and they thrive on it—and as long as they are going to be different, they should be prepared for the fact that they are going to encounter prejudice. As it is, their neuroticism about anti-Semitism prevents Jews from understanding that there may indeed be people who have valid grievances against them.

Second is the reality that the Jewish establishment is so self-involved and so terribly busy with its own internal politics that it finds itself unable to make the basic changes required to deal with the new situation. At this point, the most constructive thing some of the establishment organizations could do would be to eliminate themselves.[3]

I have been told that certain Jews have tried to prevent my speaking engagements, my participation in conferences, and in alliances. Some years ago, I was informed that there were some Jews who tried to block me from speaking at a Martin Luther King, Jr. program. Once I met with the people involved, 99 percent Black, they decided in my favor. The rabbi who had been invited dropped out and discouraged involvement by members of his Temple. After the program took place, a Jewish elected official came to me, gave me his card, and said, "You are not what I was told you were."

Sadly, I am driven to the conclusion that most Jews believe Blacks are anti-Semitic, and I believe that this is due (in part) to segments of the Jewish leadership and to *opinion makers*.

A prime example of Jewish belief in Black anti-Semitism can be found in the book *Ocean Hill–Brownsville: A Case History of Schools in Crisis*.[4] The authors discuss two kinds of anti-Semitism—"classic" and "situational"—then proceed to discuss why Blacks are anti-Semitic.

> Anti-Semitism is not a new phenomenon in the black community. Although its precise extent is not known. As many Negro and Jewish leaders have long recognized, its roots are as deep as they are complex. [p. 74]

It must be noted that the authors do not say who these "Negro ... leaders" are who recognize the complex and deep anti-Semitic roots in the Black community. Surely such a charge should require naming names. The authors continue:

> ... [T]he causes of anti-Semitism among blacks today are various, combining both "classic" anti-Semitism with the more recent phenomenon of "situational" anti-Semitism. [p.74]

So, after indicting us with the causes of our transgression, the authors proceed to give us a lesson on classic and situational anti-Semitism. Classic anti-Semitism, they tell the reader, allows Blacks to identify with the dominant culture.

The truth is, Blacks despise the racist system, culture, and mores in which they are the prime victims. But, according to the authors of *Ocean Hill–Brownsville*, when it comes to Jews, Blacks can be as bigoted as their oppressors. What an absurd proposition!

Situational anti-Semitism derives from proximity, the authors claim. In urban centers, Jews work closely with Blacks (i.e., with Jews as creditors, small merchants, etc.) so we naturally hate them: the authors would have the world believe we hate not only those we come in contact with everyday—no, all Jews.

That there is conflict between Blacks and Jews is indisputable. But that the conflict derives from racial or religious bias is dubious. In similar political and social situations there would be conflict, no matter the race, or nationality, or religion. Would this be so if the creditors, merchants, etc. bore the same appearance generally identified with any group or nationality that had created and now benefited from a system of oppression? Blacks have conflict with Latinos, but I have never heard that Blacks were accused of being anti-Latino.

In the book *Ocean Hill–Brownsville,* the acknowledgment facing the title page reads:

> The study on which this book is based was made possible by the American Jewish Congress but the conclusions are those of the authors and do not necessarily represent the view of the Congress.

The assumption here and throughout the book is that Blacks are anti-Semitic. Yet, almost unanimously, Black people vigorously continue to deny Black anti-Semitism.

## DOES BLACK ANTI-SEMITISM EXIST

At times of confrontation, to support their contention of Black anti-Semitism, many Jews use arguments similar to those proposed in the *Ocean Hill-Brownsville* book.

These arguments may be due to Jews' historic experience with anti-Semitism. But I would remind them of the Black holocaust, when they think of the phenomenon of the Jewish holocaust. I don't want to argue for hierarchy of holocausts. But it is estimated that 50 to 80 million African people died during the last 400 years of their capture, enslavement, and middle passage to the Americas, and that does not take into account institutional slavery and lynchings. In times of anger, scattered statements such as Levine's and others from the Jewish leadership, form a rather feeble trellis on which to construct so weighty an argument as anti-Semitism. Would we were consistent in applying the same attitudes to other areas of our lives. Are we bigoted when we speak harshly, insult, or verbally castigate others from time to time, especially when we are angry?

Would it be accurate to say that Jews are anti-Black because a few Jews make pejorative statements in the midst of an altercation? It saddens me when Blacks play a word game called "the dozens" in which each participant refers to the others' mother in the most derogatory fashion. Are the participants so enraged against mothers? Definitely not. I think it is counter productive to take a few words, uttered during the heat of battle, and to use them as examples of anti-Semitism, or anti-anybody or anti-anything.

When a child screams *I hate you* to its parents, it is understood that the child does not mean *hate* in the sense that we generally understand the word. Nobody would argue that the child is anti-parent. There are those who might say that the child's outburst can be a healthy release.

Often, under tension-packed conditions, when adults hurl invectives at one another, it can be viewed in the same way as we view a child's outburst—a temporary expression of dissatisfaction.

The danger of the use of indiscriminate smear tactics is in creating a monster impossible to destroy, and all of the enemies of fraternity and solidarity can use this monster for their own interests.

When there is antipathy, we must ask: Is it against the individual or the individual's behavior? And if that behavior were to change, would there be a change in attitude toward that individual?

One final point, and it is probably the most delicate and difficult to deal with. Are there certain traits, characteristic of a nationality, that elicit resentment? And, if there are, is that an example of being biased against those people, or is it being against a particular trait. This is not to say that the trait actually exists, but that it is perceived to be a racial trait, although to impute a trait to a people, can be a sign of prejudice. But to say that the trait can be positive removes that possibility at least for the moment. If another people hated that particular trait, would that mean they are racist?

The point is that it is exceedingly difficult to ascribe racism—

or anti-Semitism—to an entire people. We can say a particular behavior, word, system is anti-Semitic or racist. But to say that one ethnic group is biased against another, especially in the case under discussion is unjustified, prejudicial, and egregious.

While it is true that all of us create systems that promote the interests of one group of people over another, one can unconsciously—or by omission—diminish the latter group by simply enjoying the benefit of the status quo at that group's expense.

But that very premise argues against Black anti-Semitism, for Blacks haven't accepted a system that promotes the interests of Black people to the detriment of Jewish people. On the contrary, Blacks are more victimized than anyone else. Jews benefit far more than Blacks from the present order of things.

From every standpoint, it is impossible to sustain an argument that any Black is anti-Semitic, to say nothing of an entire people. Black people's history would argue the opposite. We are pro-everybody.

## WHEN IS JEWISH PARTICULARITY ACCEPTED WITHOUT ANTI-SEMITISM?

Rabbi Martin Siegel raises another problematic point:

> Jews are different. They recognize this and they thrive on it— and as long as they are going to be different, they should be prepared for the fact that they are going to encounter prejudice. As it is, their neuroticism about anti-Semitism prevents Jews from understanding that there may indeed be people who do have valid grievances against them.

Jews have a particular history, culture, sense of value, etc. not identical with those of White Europeans. But there are times when Jews want to be lumped in or identified with Europeans. When and how does a non-Jew make the distinction? A mistake in judgement there can open one to anti-Semitic charges. For example, when Blacks accuse Whites of racism, most Jews want to be excluded from the designation of White. When, on the other hand, Blacks have a particular criticism that they want to level against *some* Jews, then these Jews do not want to be set apart from White people. To do so is anti-Semitic. Consider how Ed Koch deals with what he call Black anti-Semitism and White anti-Blackness.:

> I find the black community very anti-Semitic. I don't care what the American Jewish Congress or B'Nai B'rith will issue by way of polls showing that the black community is not. I think that's pure bull .... They'd like to believe that. My experience with blacks is that they're basically anti-Semitic. Now, I want to be fair about it. I think whites are basically anti-black.... But the difference is: It is recognized as morally reprehensible, something you have to control.[5]

Notice that Koch finds the Black community "very anti-Semitic" and his experience with Blacks "is that they're basically anti-Semitic." Then he says, "whites are basically anti-black ...."

Well, where are the Jews in all of this? What is the Jewish feeling towards Blacks? Are Jews lumped in with Whites this time, or are they excluded? Subtly then, Koch has left the Jewish position vague.

One can encounter an even more difficult problem criticizing certain groups or ideologies within the Jewish international community.

In my November 3, 1979 article in the *New York Amsterdam News*, I tried to isolate a particular Jewish ideology—Zionism. As I understand it, Zionism is a political ideology that has as a central position the existence of a homeland for the Jews. Originally, where this land should be was debatable. (At one time East Africa was under discussion.) It is not the quest for a homeland that is questionable; rather, it is the barbaric actions they employed to achieve that objective. And once the objective was achieved, the hostility continued towards Palestinians, the people whose land they usurped, and all who question their behavior. While all Jews are not Zionist, many

Jews say, still, to criticize Zionism is to criticize all Jews. And many Jews say the same about the Hasidim; when you criticize the Hasidim, you criticize all Jews.

## Is It Kosher to Say "Jew?"

I recall one meeting with established Black leaders, where we were discussing an alliance with a particular Jewish group. We spent over an hour debating whether to use the word "Jew" or "Jewish" in a statement we were writing. One Black woman in our group was adamant. She said she had many Jewish friends, and she insisted that Jews did not want to be called "Jews." No one argued with her. We just did not want our efforts to be misunderstood. Some time later, we read a statement prepared by eminent Jewish leaders and they used the word "Jew." We sat looking at each other, annoyed and frustrated. So much time had been spent worrying about the appropriate designation, and there seemed an absence of unanimity even in the Jewish community. Protocol aside, more productive time might have been given to content.

## Notes

1. Alfred M. Lilienthal, *The Zionist Connection*, Dodd, Mead & Company, New York, 1978.
2. James Abourzek, "The Relentless Israel, Propaganda Machine," *Penthouse Magazine*, February 1978, pp. 90-91, 122-123.
3. Martin Siegel, *Amen: Confessions of a Rebel Rabbi: The Diary of Rabbi Martin Siegel*, Fawcett, Greenwich, CT, 1970.
4. Naomi Levine with Richard Cohen, *Ocean Hill-Brownsville: A Case History of Schools in Crisis*, Popular Library, New York, 1969.
5. Ken Auletta, "Profiles: The Mayor - Part I," *The New Yorker,* September 10, 1979.

# Chapter 19

# Conclusion: Urgent Need for Solidarity

〰〰〰〰

All of us should ponder the words of Martin Niemoeller, the noted German Protestant minister, and bind them to us with hoops of steel:

> When they came for the Communists, I was not Communist, so I did not speak up; when they came for the Jews, I was not a Jew, so I did not speak up; when they came for the Trade Unionists, I was not a Trade Unionist, so I did not speak up; when they came for the Catholics, I was not a Catholic, so I did not speak up; When they came for me there was no one left to speak up anymore.

There is an urgent need for Black-Jewish understanding. Toward that agenda, I want to underscore emphatically that I am against no nation, religion, or people, but that I am for *my* people! To be truly for one's people, I believe, is to be for all people.

The great Jewish spiritual leader, Hillel, said, "If I am not for myself, who will be for me; if I am only for myself what am I...?" I concur, adding that I am against oppression, exploitation, racism, anti-Semitism, and all the negative, dehumanizing forces. I am against them irrespective of the national, religious, or ideological human flesh they inhabit.

I acknowledge that there are things I wish I had said better, or differently, or not at all—not only with regard to Jews. This can probably be said of any thinking, responsible person, especially one who often speaks in public or who writes continually. In this book, I have tried to be candid. I am certain that misinterpretation will abound nonetheless. I cannot control other peoples' perceptions, and there is no protection against an enemy. Misinterpretation is open to even the most well-intentioned. But, I believe in, struggle for, and am prepared to coalesce with anyone else who believes in a fully democratic world, where resources are equitably owned, developed, and shared, and where all peace-loving human beings are respected. I believe in the Fatherhood of God and in the oneness of the human family.

Now, that does not mean that I will relinquish my right, indeed my obligation, to criticize Africans, Italians, Irish, Catholics, Jews, Protestants, or anyone else. It is precisely because I believe in and struggle for this oneness that I feel compelled to do this.

While I will always believe in the honesty of my motives and intentions, I know I will not always make the right decisions. I will make mistakes, and my language will be as imperfect as it has been in the past. I should hope that at such times my Jewish and non-Jewish friends would criticize me, and that they will always feel free to exercise this right judiciously. And I hope that I will be given the same freedom, without unfair criticism.

But, I should hope that Jews and non-Jews will understand that my mistakes or perhaps my clumsy impreciseness derive from my limitations, having nothing to do with anti-Semitism or xenophobia.

My challenge to Jews and all people is this: If there are still some matters that require further debate, let us meet for discussion, as people of good will; let us cease these unworthy accusations of anti-Semitism, reverse racism, race labeling among friends and potential allies; let us get on with the business of building a better world.

# Part II

# Inside the Storm: My Role in Crown Heights

## August 19-26, 1991

# Introduction

It was my intention to write a brief note to the Metropolitan Council of the American Jewish Congress to express my disappointment and ire regarding their resolutions on Black anti-Semitism. But, as so often happens with me, I could not stay my pen.

I had become the target of a malicious attack and a smear campaign by certain Jewish and White leaders, by powerful organizations and unscrupulous journalists in an effort to discredit and defame me. Some of them were carried along by the hysteria deliberately created by others. Some joined the pack because they would not or could not fight against the groundswell of animosity and hypocrisy. And some, in promoting their own interests, willingly joined the posse.

The smear campaign had taken a decided turn in 1978. Someone had the insidious idea of taking a *New York Post* photo of me, and placing a picture of Hitler's face over mine, adding a caption quote attributed to me: "We will get the Jews and the people in the long black coats." This photo was widely distributed on flyers and in the volumes of hate mail that I received.

Since the initial article in 1978, I have consistently denied the allegations, offering proof and clarification. Still, whenever it suits the fancy or political interests of certain individuals or organizations, the same allegations resurface—again and again.

I am driven to conclude that there are some in the Jewish hierarchy who are not concerned with truth, fairness, and decency. If they perceive that a person is running counter to their interests or is not kowtowing to their wishes, they exhume old allegations—even when they are proven false—or they distort or misrepresent that person's words or actions.

In my letter to the Metropolitan Council of the American Jewish Congress, I discuss these points of contention.

Following that "treatise" is a letter to Ed Koch, part of a correspondence begun in the *New York Post*, in January 1990, where he makes some of the same old charges. Koch is a perfect example of the dossier-keepers who, from time to time, when it suits their purpose, pull some groundless allegations from the files, heedless of denials or circumstances.

This section concludes with my letters to the media, where I address—again and again—the smear campaign and the charges of anti-Semitism and of inciting riot.

Considerable time and reflection went into my letter to the Council. It is a written account of my role in Crown Heights as well as my observations and analysis of events there and related issues.

In the interests of probity, I hope my attempts will help produce better relations between African Americans and Jews.

If there are inaccuracies, blame my human limitations not my motivations. I make no claims to infallibility, but, with honest introspection, I do claim perfect intentions.

## NOTE

I have never received any public or private response of my letter to the Metropolitan Council of the American Jewish Congress.

# A Response to the Metropolitan Council of the American Jewish Congress[1]

~~~~~~~~~~~

October 2, 1991
The Metropolitan Council of
The American Jewish Congress
Brooklyn, New York

Dear Sirs:
The September 25-October 1, 1991 edition of *The City Sun* carried excerpts of resolutions adopted by your organization. The excerpt states:

As the public leadership vacuum, for the most part, was filled

by, Sharptons, Carsons, Masons, Moores and Daughtrys and
*The City Sun* and *Amsterdam News,* it is left to the Jewish community alone to assert that Black racism is no less racist than
white racism. Only the Jewish community railed against the
anti-Semitism of the hatemongers.

It is not clear to whom you were referring as the "hatemongers;"
it would have been helpful if you had named names. However,
from the context of the excerpt, I am forced to conclude that I
am one of the "hatemongers."

With regard to filling the vacuum of leadership, significantly enough, in some quarters I was accused of exerting no leadership. Because I did not publicly join the "cool it" crowd, and
did not spend a lot of time with establishment leadership, I was
accused of letting others take leadership. Now you accuse me
of being with the crowd that filled the leadership void. More
importantly, what is disturbing is that you place me in a leadership category that you define as negative and destructive.

Then there is the resolution in which you condemn:

the actions of Al Sharpton, Sonny Carson, Vernon Mason,
Colin Moore, Herbert Daughtry and the *Amsterdam News* and
*The City Sun* and others, who have, for opportunistic reasons,
inflamed racial tension and hatred.

If the quotes are accurate, words cannot express my disappointment that an organization as reputable as the Metropolitan
Council of the American Jewish Congress could disparage the
character and reputation of a respected national leader, especially one who has given over thirty years of his life in the struggle for human rights and self determination, without reference
to any facts or without conversation with the person in question.

I challenge you or anyone to cite one instance where I said
or did anything that can be honestly said to have "inflamed racial
tension and hatred."

Because of my respect for your organization, I would like to
share with you what I did do and say in Crown Heights; I will

also send you a copy of the transcript and audio tape of the Gavin Cato funeral service, where I made my only real, full public statement during the period of conflict in Crown Heights (from Monday, August 19, 1991, when the incident occurred to Monday, August 26, 1991, the day of the funeral).

Other than my statement at the funeral, the only other public statement I made was approximately two minutes on Thursday, August 22 (the last night of the uprising). There was a potential confrontation between the crowd and the police brewing on the sidewalk. I was asked to urge the crowd to come back into the street. I complied with the request. This two-minute speech was an attempt to prevent violence, not inflame it.

Also during that time I made a few media appearances and statements. I can assure you that there was nothing in any of these statements which can be remotely interpreted as inflaming the crowd or as anti-Semitic. While I organized no marches, rallies, or demonstrations in Crown Heights, I did participate in three marches that might be loosely described as organized.

The first of these marches occurred on Tuesday, August 20th, after I attended a meeting at the 71st Precinct arranged by Mr. Sonny Carson. In the precinct, crowded with police, Assistant District Attorneys, and community leaders, two demands were made: the arrest of the driver of the car that killed Gavin Cato, and the suspension of the officer who was alleged to have assaulted Mr. Cato, Gavin's father. It was a very short meeting as these demands were rejected immediately. It was then decided, outside the precinct, in a driving rain, that we should walk back to Mr. Cato's home. There were approximately 50-100 marchers. We were at the cross-section of Kingston Avenue and President Street, at about 5:00 pm, when bottles and bricks were thrown. It was this incident that Peter Noel of the *Village Voice* made reference to in his article, as quoted on later in this document.

The second march took place on Wednesday, August 21st. I am not sure who called the march, but at about 4:00 pm we gathered at President Street and Utica Avenue, in front of Mr. Cato's home, which had become a kind of headquarters. We started marching down President Street and after several blocks the youth broke into a run. I returned to the starting point, where we were rejoined by the youths about two or three hours later.

As the youth reassembled on the corner of President and Utica to hear speakers, police officers with riot gear came up President Street en masse, beating their sticks on the street. It was a very provocative act. The youth turned and saw the police and began to taunt and curse them. I went to the Commanding Officer to ask him to move the officers back. As we were talking, bricks and bottles were thrown. The officers began to grab whoever was near them. I went in among the flying debris and darting police clubs to rescue one innocent young man. This was reported live by Dominic Carter, reporter for WLIB radio station.

I learned later that there had also been a demonstration in front of the Lubavitcher headquarters with rock throwing and all. The youth were returning from the demonstration followed by police officers.

The third march was after the funeral and, to my knowledge, it was spontaneous. We marched from St. Anthony's Baptist Church (President Street and Empire Boulevard), where the funeral was held, to the cemetery—without incident, I should add.

The fact of the matter is that there was only one march and demonstration organized by the leaders in question. It took place on August 24th, and was organized by Reverend Al Sharpton and Attorney Alton Maddox. Of the leaders in question, the only other who was present was Attorney Colin Moore. The march and rally were peaceful.

Other times I walked the streets, talking to people, sometimes joining marches which appeared to be unorganized. During these times, I recognized no known leaders and it seemed that there was no one in charge. At times, there were some saying "let's go this way" and somebody else saying "let's go that way," but for the most part it was helter-skelter.

It should be made clear that, in a riot, there is no organized group wreaking havoc. Rather there are scattered groups all over the community or city. And because the grievances are many and the anger and frustration are deep, once an act sets things in motion, wide participation follows. During the sixties, it was invariably an act of police brutality. Even in Crown Heights, there was as much anger, if not more, directed toward the police as towards the Hasidim. Not only were certain businesses destroyed, but also police cars.

There are some lessons I learned from the rebellions of the sixties. One of the lessons was not to rush to tell people to "cool it." People who are engaged in the rebellion dismiss such people as either "naive do-gooders," or "errand boys and girls" for the power structure who want peace without justice. There have been times when I have seen the conditions and felt the rage of the people who were alienated, frustrated, and angry. Then when I warned that unless something was done, violence would erupt, I was accused of stirring up trouble.

When the eruption occurred, I and other leaders, particularly clergypeople, were asked to go and "cool it out"—really meaning, "let's get back to the status quo—to business as usual as quickly as possible." This is exactly what happened in Crown Heights. I, along with others, had warned that the seeds being sown would produce a violent harvest. Yet nothing was done to address the frustration and anger of the people.

So come August 19th, an incident that was no more than an accident and which should have been treated as such, because of the years of built up rage derived from a double standard and preferential treatment accorded the Hasidim—which includes everything from immigration laws and services to special treatment by law enforcement, caused the community to explode.

It is worth noting that even though the eruption occurred Monday evening, August 19th, the persons accused of inflaming the situation did not arrive at the scene until the next day,

Tuesday, August 20th. In other words, people in the community had already determined what course of action they would take. They did not need anybody inflaming them or leading them. They were bent on a course of action and no one was going to stop them.

My involvement began with a call about 1:00 am on Tuesday, August 20th from Mr. David Walker, long time community activist and monitor of police behavior. He informed me of the accident, and of the eruption that had followed. He told me he was going to stay in the streets all night. He asked me if I would come out to Crown Heights later on. I replied, reluctantly, that I would try; I would have to check my schedule. I received several more calls from Dave, keeping me abreast of developments.

Mr. Walker, who was first on the scene, spent more time on the streets than I. When I wasn't there he kept me informed. Mr. Walker really should have received one of the peace awards or at least an honorable mention. Nobody worked harder and longer than he did to keep the peace.

On Tuesday, August 20, 1991, after I visited the Cato family, I was walking back to my car with a heavy heart. I was stopped by a group of young men standing on the curb. I did not recognize any of them. They asked what we planned to do. I said, "I don't really know; maybe there will be marches, demonstrations that kind of thing." I said it rather feebly, because I really didn't want another involvement. At the time I was already overextended. In fact, I had come to Crown Heights directly from St. John's University, where I had led a demonstration in support of a young woman who had been sexually abused, a case which had consumed so much of my time in the previous several months. I was also eager to get back to my church work which had accumulated enormously. I especially didn't want to get involved in Crown Heights because we had done all these peaceful things before and nothing had changed; in fact, things had gotten worse.

So when the youth responded, "We are tired of marching

and all that stuff; we got our own plans," I knew I had been talking to the wind. I said, even more wearily for I knew what they meant, "Well, I share your anger and frustration. I've been at it many, many years. But I hope, however, that you vent your rage through constructive channels." They smiled at me and at each other. I shook my head and sadly walked away. I knew there would be another night of violence. It does not bring any satisfaction to me to have to admit that neither I nor the leadership [you] love to hate, could do anything about it. That is a painful admission of failure. We did not start it, and we could not stop it.

What we could do was try to verbalize the rage of the people and provide lawful means for them to express their frustration and anger—and hope that that would suffice, and that major changes would follow.

It is interesting that, while the American Jewish Congress resolution claimed that I along with others, "for opportunistic reasons," inflamed racial tension and hatred, the August 31, 1991, edition of the *Amsterdam News* called attention to another role we were playing. Mr. Bill Tatum in the editorial wrote:

> When leadership did emerge, it was essentially Black Leadership, and that leadership did what it could to contain the violence by engaging the youth in protest marches and prayer. There were incidents of rock-throwing, burning and overturning of police cars and other vehicles as well as some vandalism and looting. Yet there was not the widespread violence that could have resulted from accidents of history such as these.
>
> Much of the credit for this must go to Mayor Dinkins. But more, much more credit must go to those who could communicate with the Black youngsters who had "had it up to here, and didn't give a f—k what happened." Those who spoke and did communicate are some few Black Crown Heights community leaders. Then there were those who effectively led. They were the gentlemen who are now being blamed for the violence and the unrest: Al Sharpton, Alton Maddox, Colin

175

Moore, Vernon Mason, Rev. Herbert Daughtry and Sonny
Carson. It is a false and unfair charge. It is quite likely that
had it not been for these men, the city might well by now be
up in flames.

Let me emphasize that the people, mostly youth, who were
engaged in the eruption were unknown to me. Everybody agreed
that these youth, mostly of Caribbean background, were alienated, angry, and fearless. A statistic worth noting is that, at one
point, of the 90 odd people arrested, 60 or so gave no place of
employment. These young people did not belong to anybody's
anything. I have criticized Black leadership, myself included, for
allowing such a large segment of our community to be unattached.

Let me share with you a five-point program which I follow during times of rebellion. First, before I make any statements about
the situation I try to get to know the people who are involved.

Second, I try to understand what their grievances are. Not
what I think and/or what others think, but what is the thinking of
the people involved. This means you have to get in the streets.
You have to go where the action is. This is nasty business. On one
occasion in particular, Wednesday, August 21, the night of the
worst violence, police officers warned me not to go into the huge,
angry crowd that had assembled on Utica Avenue between Eastern
Parkway and President Street. I ignored the warning and moved
among the crowd. Fortunately, I encountered no hostility.

Oftentimes you are distrusted by all sides. Those on the streets
think you are an emissary of the "man" or City Hall or the power
structure or whoever they perceive to be the people who are abusing them. But on the other side, because you are not publicly saying "cool it" and because you are with the street crowd and/or
in the presence of leaders who are considered unsavory, you are
on their side. With the exception of Mr. Walker, no leader spent
as much time as I did in Crown Heights. Day and night, I walked
with and talked to the people, especially the youth.

Third, I try to suggest constructive channels for anger or discontent. How successful I am will depend on how credible I am with the

people involved on the street, or who are involved in the eruption.

Fourth, I try to prevent violent confrontation; I try to keep people from getting hurt. I do not try to stop every rock that is hurled at a store or every act of looting. But where there is human life riding in the balance, I try to do what I can to prevent violence.

Although Ira Goldman,[2] in the August 25, 1991 edition of *The New York Times*, quoted unidentified sources as saying I stirred-up trouble and ran away, the truth of the matter is revealed in the *Village Voice* and *Newsday* articles. Peter Noel, who was on the scene August 20, 1991 standing and marching close to me most of the time, wrote in his article in the September 3, 1991 edition of the *Village Voice*.

> On the way back to the site of Gavin Cato's death, the crowd of teenagers pelted the Hasidim one more time. This time the Jews retaliated with a fusillade of projectiles. Activists scattered but Reverend Herbert Daughtry stood his ground praying that the revolution of rocks would end with no serious injuries to Jew or Gentile. His prayers went unanswered and Daughtry helped a fallen combatant to his feet.

Mr. Noel's article is correct, except that the person who was bloodied was not a "combatant," implying a warrior in a fight, rather he was an innocent marcher hit by police officers. Not only did I help him to his feet, I literally carried him several blocks down Albany Avenue, then around the corner, all the while keeping back police officers. As I was returning to President Street and Albany Avenue, I encountered an altercation between police and youth. I got between them and persuaded the youth to go down the block, thus preventing more bloodshed.

Also, I am not as certain as Noel about who threw the first rock. As the rocks and bottles were flying, the police waded into the marchers, beating and cursing them even as the marchers fled. I saw several Hasidim with what appeared to be broom handles chasing and beating the marchers. The Hasidim's bottles and rocks were thrown from behind police lines and there was little or no police action to prevent them. While Blacks were arrested, not a single Hasid met the same fate, as headlined in the August 24, 1991, edition the *Amsterdam News*.

I should add that, during the eruptions many of these people were arrested for no reason. They were just caught up in a dragnet. It almost happened to me. On Thursday, August 22nd at about 10:30 pm, two of my assistants and I were standing on Utica Avenue near President Street observing what appeared to be a confrontation between the police and the marchers several blocks ahead.

The marchers were driven back by the police. As they were returning, with the police in hot pursuit, the police started rushing into the crowds of those who were marching and those who were standing on the sidewalk. The police were pushing, shoving, cursing, and swinging their sticks. Suddenly we were surrounded. A young man standing not far from us was struck by a police officer. The youth was furious and made an attempt to go after the officer. We held him back. We were told not to move. We stood still with our backs against the wall. The officers, maybe about ten, moved in for the "collar," i.e. arrest or whatever. Then I was recognized by one of the officers. There were shouts to the other officers to "get back," "cool it." They started whispering among themselves. I overheard one officer say "that is Reverend Daughtry." Then they all dispersed.

(The police officers seemed particularly focused on Black journalists. Mr. Chris Griffith, a free-lance photographer and brother of Michael Griffith, who was killed in Howard Beach by a white mob, Ms. Vinette Price of the *Amsterdam News*, and Mr. Curtis Taylor of *Newsday* were all victims of police violence.)

Moreover, in the Friday, August 23, 1991, edition of *New York Newsday* in the article, "Fourth Night Brings More Violence," there was this paragraph:

[B]ut Rev. Herbert Daughtry stayed with the group, urging them to stay calm. The marchers went to the Hasidic headquarters, calling for the car's driver: "Yosef, Yosef, Yosef."

Daughtry walked with them, urging calm, and the crowd left without incident after about 20 minutes.

One particular incident worth mentioning occurred on Thursday, August 22nd about 6:00 pm, prior to the event quoted in the *Newsday* article. The youth assembled at the usual gathering place, President Street and Utica Avenue. No known leaders were present. Without success, I tried to keep the youth where they were. I saw the mass of police officers in front of and behind them. I thought there would be a confrontation if they moved. A heated argument ensued. The majority wanted to march, even if it meant confrontation. There was one fellow in particular who vehemently disagreed with me. He urged the crowd to move ahead. As we arrived, midway in the block, an elderly Hasid came running through the crowd trying to reach one of the buildings. Some of the crowd began to move toward him. Others of us persuaded the crowd to leave him alone. He arrived at his destination safely.

The dominant character arguing for the Hasid's safety was the same one who opposed me and insisted on marching. I remarked to Mr. Walker and Mr. Paul Washington, one of my assistants, how difficult it is to have a true reading of people in a demonstration. No one would have believed that the same person who appeared to be a super-militant would be the staunchest defender of a Hasid. If we, who are in the middle of it all, can misread a person, how can anyone from a distant desk or office know the real story.

Finally, I try to bring people together. Once I know who is involved and what the grievances are I can better determine who needs to meet. During a riot, there are endless meetings, and everybody starts blaming everybody for doing or not doing something. Generally it adds up to people talking to themselves or "preaching to the choir." More often than not, the people on the streets, the ones who are creating the disorder, are not involved in the meetings. In fact, those who are doing the meeting often don't even know the people about whom they are meeting.

179

It so happens that I take a different approach. Peter Noel and Rick Hornung in an October 8, 1991 *Village Voice* article, entitled "The Dinkins-Sharpton Connection," although questionable in some parts, provided a glimpse of my efforts to bring people together. I tried to be a bridge, and keep the communications line open between the Dinkins Administration and Sharpton, and Carson, etc. Whatever people think of the Sharptons and Carsons—and even Daughtrys, if you prefer—the fact is, they have influence with the people who need to be reached—or at least the people in question don't boo or throw things at them. And if our objective is to save the City, then we need to talk to whomever can help us to achieve that objective.

In global politics we understand this principle. It doesn't matter how a nation or a guerrilla group is viewed, communications lines are kept open. There is someone who can bring people together when the time is right or the situation demands it.

Now that is what I did in the seven days and nights I spent in Crown Heights. I have not been in Crown Heights since, except for the West Indian Day Parade, to give a check to Mr. Cato from the African American Clergy and Elected Officials, and to attend a meeting at the St. Francis Assisi Roman Catholic Church, where a few community leaders were present.

Significantly, a couple of years ago when a 16-year-old African American youth was shot in the back by police in Teaneck, NJ, there was violent reaction by the youth. I implemented the five-point program that I have discussed in this statement, and I was applauded for my action. I was even asked to write an Op-Ed page for the *Bergen Record*, a leading New Jersey newspaper.

## SOME JEWS MARCH IN FRONT OF MY HOME

On September 15, 1991, some Jews marched in front of my home as well as the home of Dr. Leonard Jeffries, in Teaneck, New Jersey. Some local Jewish leaders denounced the march. To my knowledge, of the 100 or so marchers, only a couple were from the community.

At 11:00 am on the same day (September 15), I called a press conference at The House of the Lord Church to discuss the march in front of my home, which was to take place later in the day. The press conference was attended by most of the so-called major press, I conveyed my approach to rebellion ... essentially what I have already discussed above. Only the *Daily News* thought it important enough to give it a fair amount of ink. In its September 16, 1991 edition, Thomas Raftery and Andrea Kannapell wrote:

> " I went to Crown Heights to do five things," said Daughtry, "to find out who is involved... what the issues are... I try to urge constructive channels for the rage... to prevent confrontations... to bring people together who can resolve the issues. At no point did I urge or encourage confrontation. There is a double standard in Crown Heights," Daughtry insisted.

Most of the media gave plenty of space to the "outsiders" who marched in front of my home. And only the *Star Ledger* (September 17, 1991), a New Jersey newspaper, gave me sufficient space to record my response to the unfounded allegations of anti-Semitism and inciting a riot against Jews.

Let me expand on the march in front of my home. It is most instructive how the media treated it. Mr. [Robert] McFadden of *The New York Times* (September 7, 1991), called me "controversial," and narrowed my ministry to race issues with a slant that suggested trouble making. All of the media took great delight in showing pictures of my home. But only McFadden broke all precedents and gave the full address of my home. What made this affront so glaring is that, a week or two before, when Reverend Sharpton marched in front of Brooklyn District Attorney Hynes' home, no address was given. Channel 2 (CBS TV) even went so far as to zero in on the address over my door, making sure the number was visible to all.

It was as if they were saying, here is where the trouble-making, anti-Semite lives—go get him. The hate mail and threats of which I am the constant recipient, which had been directed to my church, were now directed to my home, so that my wife and children had to handle and read the filthy, threatening correspondence.

*Newsday* headlines an article by Chaplin Wright and Christopher Haraden, "Two Jewish Groups Protest Black 'Anti-Semites'." Also the *Star Ledger* headlined an article by Todd Burroughs, "Jews March in Teaneck to Protest 'Neo-Nazis' Daughtry and Jeffries." How do you explain this kind of reckless, irresponsible, biased journalism? How do you explain taking the baseless allegations of a small group of vulgar, outside agitators, who came into a peaceful, integrated town against the wishes of the community, even the Jewish residents, and making their baseless allegations headlines for articles? Notwithstanding putting the accusations in single quotation marks, which few people are going to notice and/or understand when the headline "Anti-Semitic" or even worse "Neo-Nazi," what Jew or any person of decency and fairness is going to pay attention to the small marks around these words which indicates that that is what the marchers, the enemies of the person in question, said.

It was an interesting time. On August 1, 1991, Blacks attempted to disrupt a meeting at my church where a multi-national, multi-religious group gathered to offer support to the St. John's University sexual abuse survivor. They accused me of trying to sell out the movement by bringing whites, Jews, and Blacks together. Then on September 15, 1991, Jews marched in front of my home and accused me of stirring up Black rage against Jews.

On September 16, 1991, after the march in front of my home, I spent the day talking to editors and reporters regarding the sloppy, inaccurate, irresponsible, reckless, and biased journalism to which I had been subjected. All of them agreed, in full or in part, with my criticism and promised there would be greater vigilance in the future.

Now with regard to my inflaming the crowd, it is very important to note that, when I ask people to cite one example where I said or did anything that can be honestly interpreted as inflaming the crowd or as anti-Semitic, the only thing they point to is my statement at the funeral where I appealed for immediate action to prevent similar violence from occurring in Williamsburg. To my knowledge, the only reporters who have, in fact, pointed this out are Lila Weymouth—*Nightwatch* (September 4, 1991), David Evanier—*The New Republic* (October 14, 1991), Eric Breindal—*New York Post* (October 3, 1991), and Robert W. Laird—*Daily News* (August 29, 1991). Mr. Laird is not sure if what I said was meant as a threat, although he admits it was "helpful counsel." In addition, there was Ira Goldman, *The New York Times* (August 31, 1991). Councilman Noach Dear,[3] Assemblyman Doug Hikind, and the outside agitators who marched in front of my home on September 15, 1991, an interesting collection of bedfellows.[4] The attempt to twist my funeral remarks really says that they cannot cite an example of an offensive word or action, therefore, they have to make up something to fit into their sinister designs.

Here are my exact words from the transcript of the funeral, and, while it may be lengthy, I feel it necessary to include the context in which the statement was made.

> Well, I know I have been long on the history and I know some will criticize me but I don't want to see more of these occasions. I've been around a long time. Lord knows I don't want to see it happen again. We have got to rise to the occasion. And if it happens again, and it will happen again if we can't read the signs of the times and move swiftly and do something meaningful. If we can seize the moment, face the truth, confess our sins, our failures and weaknesses and commit ourselves to right the wrongs, to heal the rifts, to bridge the distance that separates us; if we can lay hold on the events of this day and bend them to serve the interest of justice and fairness; if we can take the tension of these days and not diffuse

it but use it, then little Gavin would not have died in vain.

The Chinese character, you know, for crisis, I'm told, is opportunity and danger. We have the opportunity to do the right thing. To end the abuse of police power. To end the double standard, the preferential treatment. Let justice be even handed. Let there be an equitable distribution of goods and services. Put the young people to work. Let's turn this midnight into morning. It is dangerous, yes. It is dangerous if we don't do something about it. If we let the events just drift and drift we will be back here very soon and it may be fire next time. That was just a taste of what awaits on the horizon and the next time it might not be just Crown Heights. Look to Williamsburg. I want to predict that the same ingredients that brought the explosion here to Crown Heights now exists in Williamsburg. Let's move. Let's do something now. Don't wait until it explodes.

Also let me include another statement that I made at the beginning of the speech.

I want to reflect on the injustice and failures of bygone years— It's a thankless task, but I think I have earned the right. I do so not to inflame but to educate and to appeal for change. Someone has said, "those who ignore the lessons of history are doomed to repeat it's mistakes." Let us not ignore the lessons of history. Across the years we have had enough killings and destruction, abuses, conflicts and injustice in this community.

Clearly, it is a statement urging action to cut off the possibility of violence, not to urge violence, justify violence, or exult in violence. In all the marches, demonstrations and boycotts I have led across the years, not once did I ever call for violence. We have always been the victims of violence. I hate violence against anyone, and I try to prevent violence. One of the ways to prevent it is to correct conditions which can produce the unwanted event. Significantly, others have discussed the conflict in

Williamsburg and have warned of potential violence in Williamsburg, including Brooklyn District Attorney Charles Hynes (*New York Newsday*, September 25, 1991), and Jonathan Rieder (*New Republic*, October 14, 1991).

How is it that when those who are not as familiar with the problem as I warn of or acknowledge the possibility of violence in Williamsburg, they are not criticized but, in fact, commended for their concern and foresight. But when I do it I am accused of "calling for violence," "inciting a riot," "threatening Jews," or "wanting to take the movement to Williamsburg."

Surely there must be some racism in this or at least, for whatever reason, a concerted effort to "Get Daughtry," by any means necessary. A white reporter who was at the Cato funeral admitted to me that the treatment to which the press subjected me was as vicious as he had ever seen.

Significantly, Bob Herbert, an African American writer for New York's *Daily News*, who was at the funeral has a completely different version of what I said. In the *Daily News*, August 27, 1991 he writes,

> The most sensible comments at the funeral were made by the Rev. Herbert Daughtry. Way back in the 70s, Daughtry was marching against the double standard that applied on the one hand to the Hasidim in Crown Heights and on the other to the African American and Caribbean people in the neighborhood. Also in Williamsburg.
>
> "We warned that the seeds of discord, if ignored, would reap a bitter harvest," Daughtry said yesterday. The tensions between blacks and Jews in Crown Heights and Williamsburg were not secret. They were written about in every newspaper and covered on television, but still the double standard prevailed.
>
> Daughtry mentioned the notorious occasion in which a police precinct was put under siege by the Hasidim, and he wondered aloud what would happen if a New York City police station was ever overrun by a mob of blacks.

"I warned that there was going to come an eruption." Daughtry said, "that people were not going to take this."

But no one listened.

"If we let events drift and drift and drift, we'll be back here again," he said. He urged whomever was willing to listen to do something now. Don't wait until it explodes.

Let me convey to you the ingredients in Williamsburg to which I was referring.

## DIVIDING THE WALLS IN SCHOOLS

Once there was the struggle around the public schools. The Satmar [a sect within the Hasidim] wanted to set up dividing walls in the public schools to separate the Hasidic children from the other children. The very fact that the Satmar would put up such a struggle to force public schools to conform to their religious laws speaks volumes about their insistence on having their way of life, and bending everything to meet that end.

After a bitter struggle, this effort was rejected.

## HOUSING AND URBAN RENEWAL

Although the Satmar are the minority in Williamsburg, they want the lion's share of the public housing units. They even wanted to implement a quota system, weighted in their favor of course.

The October 22, 1976, edition of the *New York Post* featured an article entitled "Tension in Williamsburg—Housing for Whom?" in which Edmund Newton wrote:

There's a curious tranquility present in Roberto Clemente Plaza. New tenants wander through the hallways of the 25 story buildings, breathing the smell of fresh paint, half smiling at unsmudged walls and uncluttered vistas.

But debate swirls around the community sponsored federally subsidized complex of 534 apartments with a fury greater than yesterday's frigid, 50 mph wind gusts.

On Monday, thousands of black garbed Hasidic Jews from

Williamsburg ringed City Hall demanding protection for their "beleaguered" community. The planned admission of some 400 Hispanic and black tenants to the site would "tip" their neighborhood away from its present racial equilibrium, they said, demanding more of the apartments for whites.

Hispanic community members responded bitterly yesterday, charging the Hasidim with "empire building" in Williamsburg. The Hispanic community had struggled to build Clemente Plaza and "now they want to take over the development for Hasidic families," one Puerto Rican spokesman said.

... the issues are complicated enough to challenge the skills of a talmudic scholar. At least part of the problem, spokesman for both sides say, is the constant rasping contact between the distinct cultures in a claustrophobic community which houses more than 150,000 people.

... The legal debate goes something like this: The Hasidic community sees the narrow swath of real estate south of Division Avenue—on which Clemente Plaza was built—as a kind of home ground.

"For want of a better term, call it Jewish turf," Rabbi Weinberger said. Infusions of large numbers of blacks and Hispanics will cause "white flight," he added. It's been proven on the basis of experience that 30 percent [minority] is the tipping point.

So 70 to 75 per cent of Clemente Plaza's apartments should be reserved for the Hasidim, they say. It's not a matter of "race" but one of fighting misguided "social engineering."

There have also been disputes on who gets what units in public housing developments. Blacks and Latinos have made accusations that the Hasidim are given the lower floors because their religious requirements forbid use of elevators on their Sabbath and Holy days.

If the relationships were harmonious, and if there had been a friendly request made of Blacks and Latinos, probably they would have accommodated the Hasidim. But because of the hostility, and "the my way or no way" approach of the Hasidim, this was seen as one more attempt by the Hasidim to get their way.

In addition, the Hasidim want to control huge areas of urban renewal land to build religious institutions, among other things, which serve nobody but themselves. In the August 2, 1990 edition of *Newsday*, in an article headlined, "Hispanics Battle Hasidic 'Enclave'," Bob Liff wrote:

> Hispanic activists asked a federal judge yesterday to block construction of a yeshiva, faculty housing and new synagogue on urban renewal land in Brooklyn where the Satmar Hasidic movement's grand rabbi's house already sits.
>
> The Hispanics charge that if the city turns over urban renewal land to Hasidic interests, it would amount to an illegal attempt to establish a religious enclave in Williamsburg bordered by the Williamsburg Bridge, the Brooklyn-Queens Expressway and the East River, a triangular area where most of the Hasidim live.

Also Mr. Liff writes that:

> Meanwhile, a Hasidic developer and Hispanic activists have reached a tentative settlement on re-advertising 250 market-rate apartments planned for a nearby urban renewal site. Hispanic activists claimed advertisements for the Brooklyn Villas apartments had appeared only in Yiddish-language newspapers.
>
> Both the dispute over the Brooklyn Villas property and the land on which the home of the Satmar Grand Rabbi Moses Teitebaum sits are part of a federal lawsuit filed by Hispanic activists charging that the city, through its disposition of urban renewal land has tried to create "a city sponsored Vatican City" in the northwest Brooklyn neighborhood.

The practice of developing housing with public funds, and manipulating the process to insure that the Hasidim, though the minority, get most of the units, is but another example of disregard for anything and anybody that does not fit into their plan. The same thing was done in Crown Heights by Lubavitcher Hasidim, which I will touch on presently.

## ATTACKS ON POLICE OFFICERS

There have been attacks on police officers, Ganson Chambers and Hector Arisa, to name a couple. Mr. Arisa arrested a Hasid— a grave mistake—and complained about the double standard. After much harassment within the police department and psychological tests *[after all, you must be crazy to arrest a Hasid]*, he was transferred to night duty at One Police Plaza.

In the October 24, 1990, edition of the *Daily News*, Bob Kappstatter and Don Gentile record the attempt by about 200 Satmar to storm the 90th Precinct, after one of their members was arrested on sexual molestation charges. Thirty officers were hurt. A fire station next door was forced to shut down. Fortunately, no fire occurred during the time of the disturbance. One Hasid was slightly injured, and one Hasid was arrested.

Meanwhile, the slightest violation or apparent violation of the law by Blacks and Latinos results in beatings, jail, and sometimes death.

## HARASSMENT AND ATTACKS ON BLACKS AND LATINOS

There have been other cases of sexual molestation in addition to the one already mentioned. Some years ago a Hasidic factory owner was accused of sexually abusing his female employees. These immigrants, mostly Latinos, were very reluctant to come forward. That was probably the reason the Hasidic factory owner allegedly took advantage of them. He knew that they would be reluctant to discuss the matter. They knew and he knew that the police would not do anything, and it would only make matters worse for them. But no people ever forgets the abuse of their women and children.

There have been persistent complaints of harassment and assaults on innocent residents by the Satmar patrol. Going back to 1976 in the December 22nd edition of the *New York Post*, Latino leaders complained of harassment and assault by the Hasidim.

> Innocent blacks and Hispanics sometimes get caught in the crossfire, Hispanic leaders contend, says Alexis Miranda, president of the new tenants association in Clemente Plaza. If they see any black or Hispanic in their neighborhood, they might beat him up, try to arrest him.

The Hasidim admitted that sometimes innocent people get roughed up.

> " Yes," says Rabbi Yidel Lefkowitz, another UJO leader, "the cry 'Khap ihm!' ('Catch him!') occasionally rings out in Hasidic Williamsburg and dozens of men respond. But it only happens because the Hasidim are 'preyed upon' by petty criminals, and it never happens without cause," he said.
>
> "Many times the people on the street catch a perpetrator of a crime," he explained, "and sometimes it comes to the point where they rough him up."

On April 9, 1990, 50 Hasidim pulled three men from a car and set the car on fire. Three police officers were injured. There were no arrests. It all started over a minor dispute. In 1989, a young man named William Pickney was beaten in Williamsburg by, some say, 100 Satmar Hasidim, similar to the bearing of Victor Rhodes, a 16 year old Black youth, who was beaten by members of the Lubavitcher Hasidim.

Frustrated after a series of meetings with the District Attorney and staff, we decided to meet with the U.S. Attorney for the Eastern District, Mr. Andrew Maloney. In two meetings we implored him to investigate not only the attack on Pickney but also the Satmar community. We tried to persuade him that they were a very powerful group, who were in collusion with city government and other powerful elements and, that they were using their power in violent, discriminatory, and oppressive ways. I reminded him that in the South, when this was done by hate groups like the KKK, the federal government would intercede. Of course, nothing ever happened.

Meanwhile, Mr. Pickney will never return to normalcy. His father died of cancer some months later. I am sure his condition was exacerbated by the savage attack which left his son unconscious and absent of justice. No Hasid was ever arrested.

* * *

In the August 2, 1990, edition of the *Daily News*, Juan Gonzalez in an article entitled, "Unequal Justice in Williamsburg?" discusses a number of issues including housing, sexual molestation, harassment, double standards and wheeling and dealing by city officials.

Moreover, the same allegations of double standard and preferential treatment that are made in Crown Heights are made in Williamsburg. The same anger and frustration that people feel in Crown Heights is felt in Williamsburg—the only difference is Williamsburg's larger Latino population.

Given the history of abuses, double standards, harassment and assaults that I have mentioned, and others space does not allow me to mention, even if one did not know it, it would be logical to assume there is deep frustration and anger. If it is true that there are feelings of anger and frustration on the part of Blacks and Latinos and violence and arrogance on the part of the Hasidim, even a moron could see there is great potential for violent confrontation. So when I point to Williamsburg as a community where a "Crown Heights" could happen and when I appeal for immediate action, why am I excoriated rather than commended.

It is also interesting to note that when I talked about the possibility of violence erupting in Williamsburg, it was not the only community I had in mind. Across this city there is deep despair, anger and resentment about a lot of things including joblessness, bureaucratic abuses and callousness, police brutality, racially motivated violence, and attacks on Black leaders, etc. In spite of his gallant efforts, Mayor Dinkins has not been able to ameliorate the pain, despair, and anger. These feelings are too deep. The previous twelve years of the Koch Administration, characterized by pettiness, meanness, belligerence, and corruption, fanned the flame of racial antagonism, instigating conflict—it was an anti-black, anti-poor administration. Nobody, short of God, could right these wrongs in four years.

In a word, all of New York City could experience the fate of Crown Heights. A citywide eruption was on the minds of everybody I knew. Yet my detractors chose to focus only on Williamsburg. It is true I named Williamsburg, but the problem extends beyond Williamsburg. James Baldwin once said, "there is nothing so dangerous in a society as a man who has nothing to lose." In New York City, as well as in many other cities across the USA, there are innumerable people with nothing to lose.

I do not recall the American Jewish Congress saying or doing anything during these times. Nor do I remember hearing anything from the Jewish community at large. Surely, the prestige of your offices could have been most helpful in bringing peace and justice to that community.

It is my conviction that these misrepresentations and false accusations to which I and others have been subjected, and the prejudicial reportage of the situation in the community have exacerbated the tension between people of African ancestry and Jews and diverted the attention from the real issues. I have stated repeatedly that the conflict in Crown Heights is a local conflict that has been around for a long time. Let's keep it there.

It is incredible how this local conflict has been elevated to the magnitude of Jews against Blacks and Blacks against Jews, with everybody jumping into the conflict, bringing their own ideological, religious, and/or racial baggage. For instance, to refer to the riots in Crown Heights as Khristelnacht and pogroms, as some have done even with an ad in *The New York Times*—with, of course, an appeal for money—not only exacerbates the situation but runs the risk of diminishing the importance of those dreadful experiences in Jewish history. One who is ignorant of Khristelnacht and pogrom could reason that if a narrowly confined, spontaneous eruption for several days in reaction to a traffic accident by people who feel, right or wrong, that they have been victims of years of a double standard is Khristelnacht and pogrom, then those events could not have been all that horrible.

Similarly, the use of anti-Semitism, or racism for that matter, by any Jew or Black who feels injured or wants to promote his or her own agenda, can reduce the awfulness of those attitudes in the minds of some people. If, in the heat of the moment or during a demonstration or confrontation, a person calls a Jew or Black an ugly name, if that is anti-Semitism or racism, then anti-Semitism or racism is a superficial, emotional reaction by a person who may be a lunatic, a foul-mouthed youth, or an immature, vocabulary impoverished imbecile. I thought anti-Semitism and racism were a mind-set, a world-view, an ideology which manifested itself in traditions, customs, history, societal systems and institutions, resulting in discrimination, abuse, violence, exploitation, etc.

There were a lot of ugly things said from all sides; police also engaged in name calling. It does not help the situation to focus on the sideshow. I have been in many demonstrations, most of them peaceful; where violence erupted, it was done by others not associated with the demonstration. In all demonstrations there is always a negative fringe element, unconnected to the organizers and the purpose of the demonstration. They have their own agenda. Sometimes there are people with signs, chanting slogans that are not representative of the groups involved. Someone screaming "Long live the KKK" or "Hail Hitler," may be some lunatic who does not represent anything but insanity. Yet to focus on these people, as the media and some questionable leaders have done, is to exacerbate the situation, detract from the issue, and play into the hands of those who enhance their egos and bank books in these situations.

The editors of *New York Newsday* agree with my assessment. In the Sunday, September 15, 1991, editorial, they wrote:

> First, we must understand what the disturbance was about. Yes, it was a neighborhood fight. The middle-class Caribbean-Americans and African-Americans who live nearest the Hasidim believe the city serves their own interest last. They believe the city favors the Hasidim when it comes to police protection, subsidized housing and other services. They believe the Hasidim look down on them. And they believe the growing Hasidic households want to push them out of their neighborhood. In fact, a recent New York Newsday analysis found scant evidence of blind official favoritism toward the Hasidim—whether in subsidized housing, repaving or social programs. Still, the image persists. Fact must overtake fiction.

Now, while I agree it was a local conflict, I do not agree with their conclusions relative to the absence of favoritism. The accusation is not "blind official favoritism," but wide-eyed, deliberate, and calculated collusion by officials to promote the interest of the Hasidim.

Personally, I go back about 20 years with the Hasidim. My first encounter was a meeting convened by Black leaders because of complaints that Black people, especially youth, were being randomly beaten by the Hasidic patrol.

## A Shift in Community Planning Board Lines

In 1976, there was an effort to shift the lines of some community planning board lines. The effect of this shift was to give the Hasidic community greater power. I, along with other community leaders, stayed up all night with Mayor Abe Beame trying to persuade him not to reverse his decision, changing the community lines. We warned him and others that this act, which we believed was illegal, would sow seeds of discord for years to come. He did not heed our importunities.

## HASIDIC VIOLENCE

The Hasidim have a history of violence against Black residents of Crown Heights. In addition, they have attacked police officers as well as newspeople, both in Crown Heights as well as at news stations. They have assaulted women and children. Seldom, however, have they attacked men, and they always attack in droves. This was the reason I made the statement in June 1978 after Victor Rhodes had been beaten, "When we have organized our patrol and men meet men, we will see what the people in the long black coats will do." I was maliciously misquoted by the *New York Post* as saying, "We will get the Jews and the people in the long black coats." We did organize the patrol and we did frequently walk through Crown Heights. There was no violence. They did not attack us. We did not attack them. As my statement clearly indicated, we were organizing not to promote violence but to protect from violence.

One of the most infamous attacks was on Victor Rhodes, a 16 year old lad, who was beaten unconscious by 30 to 50 Hasidim, according to the press—only a miracle saved him, but he was never the same. There was never any evidence that he had done anything wrong. Two Hasidim were arrested. There were no convictions.

During the trial, the Hasidim pulled one of their trick plays. On those rare occasions, when one of their members must stand trial, they all show up, obviously in black, thus making individual identification virtually impossible. So they walk away laughing and joking, demonstrating again their utter contempt for the people that they have assaulted and for the law that they have violated. The question which must be asked is, if they are so religious, why do they flaunt the law? Is there none among them who insists that those who violate a nation's law must be brought to justice even if the violator is one of their own?

During those years I was the point person. I organized marches, demonstrations, and a community patrol. Standing on the steps of the 71st Precinct, July 1978, I warned that if changes were not forthcoming, there would be violence. I confess that I implored the strongest language in an attempt to give verbal expression to the rage I knew people felt, hoping that it would not be necessary for them to take a violent expression. In the meanwhile, serious discussion could take place with a view toward making significant changes. The approach was partially successful. There was no violence but neither was there any meaningful change in the conditions. Those in power elected to do little or nothing. By the way, that is why I don't put much store in these so-called peace overtures; I have seen it all before. I predict that in a few months the community will return to business as usual and await another confrontation. Then someone will be found who can be slapped with anti-Semitism and inciting a riot charge. Of course, during that time, 1978, I was called all the usual names, "outsider," "racial racketeer," "agitator," and an "anti-Semite."

## Special Treatment from Law Enforcement

Significantly, the day before Victor Rhodes was beaten, Arthur Miller, a respected businessman who went to see about his brother, who was in an altercation with the police, ended up dead, killed by the police. But in July 1977, the Hasidim, trying to capture three innocent Black youths they believed had committed a crime, took over the 71st Precinct. There were no arrests, not one Hasid was injured. In Borough Park, the Orthodox community destroyed the police precinct—literally destroyed it. Forty police officers were hurt. Ed Koch, who was Mayor at the time, went out and pleaded with them. He even pleaded with them in Yiddish. There was no tough talk, no "get more police on the case" as he urged Mayor Dave Dinkins to do during the recent eruption in Crown Heights. Not one Hasid was hurt or convicted of a crime—unbelievable!

There is special consideration given to the Hasidim by the law enforcement system. Special instruction is given to the police on how and when to arrest a Hasid, and these orders come from the top. For example, if a Hasid is arrested on his Sabbath he cannot be put into a car. He must be walked to the precinct. Incredible! Can you imagine an African American pleading for special consideration on his or her Sabbath? And if a Hasid is booked on the violation of law, the process is accelerated especially to accommodate Hasidic religious requirements. Can you imagine the ridicule or scorn and even violence inflicted upon an African American who would have the audacity to say, "Hurry up with this business, my Holy day or Sabbath is near?"

On a Channel 9 (WOR) television program, November 6, 1991, the host, Richard Bey related a conversation he had had with police officers in New York City. He asked them if there were a double standard in their treatment of Blacks and Jews. They all replied yes and said it comes from the top down. It is even taught in the Police Academy. He said that one police officer told him that he would rather deal with Blacks any day than with Jews. Because if a Black insulted him he could bust his head open and nothing would be done about it. While, on the other hand, if he was insulted by a Jew, he could not touch him.

Police officers told me of another practice that occurs in November and December, at which time the police turn their heads. During those months there are a rash of reported burglaries and thefts in the Hasidic community. Very few, if any, actually occur. It is done to gain reduction on the income tax. The police officers who are cognizant of this chicanery and refuse to go along with it are given harsh treatment within the police department. This is a known fact, and officers in the 66th Precinct in Borough Park Brooklyn will validate it, if their identities could be protected. Fear of the Hasidim permeates the police department. The belief is that, should officers stand up to

197

the Hasidim, they will not be protected.

The June 11, 1988, edition of the *Amsterdam News* carried this headline, "Are Police Afraid to Arrest Hasidic Jews in Brooklyn?" The reporter, Mr. J. Zamgba Browne, records the story of a 15-year-old honor student named Yarvilah Fulcher who was beaten by a 27-year-old Hasidic Jew named Avraham Greenberg, and the run around the family received from the police in their quest for justice. The irony of this case is that the Fulcher family, though African American, is Hasidic.

This incident is of particular interest because in this one act of violence is manifested four of the areas about which we have complained:

1) The violence of the Hasidim.
2) The racism of the Hasidim.
3) The double standard of the police department.
4) The double standard in the provision of ambulance service.

According to the *Amsterdam News* article, the victim's mother, Adinal Fulcher, said the police were undecided about what to do when they arrived at the scene of the assault, 1650 President Street, and discovered that Greenberg was involved. She said they were told by the cops that, after speaking privately to Greenberg, who was hiding out in his parent's apartment, they had phoned the precinct and the captain would be coming over.

After waiting for 30 minutes outside the Greenberg apartment and the Captain didn't show up, Mr. Fulcher decided to make a call to the precinct from an apartment next door. He was told, "There was nothing on the captain's schedule to indicate that he was on his way to the scene of the incident."

At this point, according to Mrs. Fulcher, a cop asked what they wanted done. Mr. Fulcher said they wanted Greenberg arrested. They also told the officer they had witnesses and if nothing was done there would be trouble in the community. *[Careful Mr. Fulcher, you are threatening Jews; you are try-*

*ing to start a riot.]* The sergeant then invited the Fulcher family and the Greenberg family to the precinct, "all the time the victim was in pain." The ambulance which they had called took about 45 minutes to arrive.

When they arrived at the precinct Mr. Fulcher asked again, "When would Greenberg be arrested?" The desk sergeant replied he would have to talk to the Captain. While the sergeant was away, Mrs. Fulcher said her husband started a conversation with some of the cops and he told them, "had I been the perpetrator, I would have been arrested without question." According to Mrs. Fulcher, one of the cops told them, "Look man, we cannot arrest a Hasidic Jew. The last officer who arrested one of them folks was immediately reassigned to the South Bronx." A cop then cited another incident involving a Hasidic Jew, in which a number of Hasidic Jews, enraged over something that had happened in their community marched on the precinct, destroyed a patrol car, and caused about $2,000 worth of damage inside the building, and nothing was done about it.

The victim's grandfather, William "Bill" Tate, Vice President of United Auto Workers (District Council 65) and Chairman of the Board of Restoration Corporation, expressed anger over what he called the "double standard of justice applied at the 71st Precinct." *[It's not just the 71st precinct, Bill, it's much bigger than that, (my observation).]* Mrs. Fulcher said,

> "I felt so wronged. I am a Jewish person and Greenberg only saw me as a Black person." But she said she is not surprised. "It happens to me a lot. They see me in the street and they treat me one way until they find out I am Jewish, then they treat me in a whole different way."

Mr. Fulcher complained it took the ambulance 45 minutes to arrive. That is typical of the double standard applied to the delivery of goods and services. All the time there was a private ambulance parked just a few blocks away, reserved only for Hasidic use. The last time an investigation was done, the ambulance was

199

supported by public funds.[5]

Mr. Greenberg's attitude toward Mrs. Fulcher was duplicated by Rabbi Abba Paltiel. On August 26, 1991, the racism of the Hasidim was conspicuously demonstrated before the startled T.V. viewers, host Jim Jensen, and guests when, on *The Sunday Edition* (Channel 2), Rabbi Paltiel refused to appear on camera with the Reverend Heron Sam, Rector of St. Marks Episcopal Church in Crown Heights. It does not take a genius to figure out that the continuing tensions and the occasional conflicts are the inevitable results in a community where there is such blatant contempt and racism.

## COMPOSITION OF COMMUNITY PLANNING BOARD 9

There is a disproportionate representation of Hasidim on Community Planning Board 9, which encompasses Crown Heights. Half of the members of the Board of Directors are appointed by Brooklyn Borough President Howard Golden. The other half are appointed by the City Council members representing the area, with the approval of the Borough President. Of the approximately 200,000 community residents, somewhere between 10 and 20% are Hasidim, yet the Hasidim make up 25% of the Board, and the Board's Chairperson is Rabbi Jacob Goldstein.

For years Dr. Vernal Cave, a long-time resident of Crown Heights, complained about the situation. In a letter written to Mr. Fletcher H. Graves, New York State Director of Community Relations Service, United States Department of Justice on June 28, 1978, Dr. Cave wrote:

High officials of New York City including then Mayor Abraham D. Beame, violated the civil rights of the Black citizens of Crown Heights when in forming districts for community boards in accordance with provisions of the New York City Charter as revised in 1975 it violated two of the three provisions it was legally obliged to obey. These provisions were as follows:

a) that the new districts conform to historical, geographic and identifiable communities.

b) that they facilitate efficient service delivery by city agencies, particularly by the Police Department and the Sanitation Department.

c) that they be compact and congruous and be within the population of 100,000 to 250,000.[6]

Dr. Cave went on to say that in redrawing the community district lines at least two of the three guidelines were violated.

Can you imagine an Italian, an Irish, or Jewish community in which African Americans make up only 10-20% of the population and yet exercise the same control and influence as the Hasidim in the 80-90% Black community of Crown Heights?

Surely, you will agree with me that no other community or people would allow such a situation to exist, and their fight against said situation would be applauded by all democracy loving people. Not so in Crown Heights. The struggle there is defined as anti-Semitic and this definition is accepted by the public at large because the majority population does not have the power, the wealth and/or the influence in power centers (i.e. media, politics, economics, etc.) to make their point of view heard and accepted.

## HASIDIM ON THE SCHOOL BOARD

In Crown Heights, two Hasidim sit on the school board. Certainly, it is their right to get elected to a seat on the school board. But if they have no children in the schools, why take the seats from parents who do have children in the schools? The approach of the Hasidim toward their Black neighbors calls to mind the old saying "what's mine is mine, and what's yours is mine," or to modify it, "What's mine is mine, what's yours we'll share."

201

## Manipulation of Public Funds

On the question of public funding for housing, anti-poverty programs, etc., in 1978 Carol Bellamy, then President of the City Council, did a report on Chevra Machazikei Hashcunah, Inc., and found numerous irregularities. Yet this report did not bring about any major changes. In fact, there was little or no public disclosure of the report. The Hasidim continued business as usual.

## Housing

On Crown and Albany Streets, there is a 51 unit housing development which was built with public funds. It is required that such units be allocated according to lottery. Public notice of availability must be placed in two newspapers. Requests for applications must then be submitted by interested parties. A date for selection is set and the names of the winners are announced.

In the case with the Crown and Albany development, the units were built with double sinks, an obvious accommodation to the Hasidim. Should public funds be used to support religious requirements? According to my information, announcements were placed in the *Jewish Press* and *Newsday* (Suffolk County section)—compare with what was done in Williamsburg in 1976. Also, it is said that the Hasidim sent in their applications in easily identifiable brown envelopes. All of this resulted in 90% of the units being allocated to the Hasidim. So in a community 80-90% Black, the system is manipulated so that Blacks get 10% of the new units—two sinks and all.

Across the years, the Hasidim have been accused of fire bombing, rent gouging, and intimidating their tenants ... anything to get property close to the synagogue. I cannot confirm that all the allegations are true, but the general rule is that if an allegation persists for years, and is held by many people, there is at least an element of truth in the allegation—in other words, where there is smoke, there is fire. The point is, most people in Crown Heights believe the allegation and, therefore, relate to the Hasidim based on the allegations.

There are two other points which give credence to the allegations. First, since they arrived in Crown Heights, the behavior of the Hasidim indicates that they will do anything to get their way. Second, their religious requirements, i.e. prohibitions on use of vehicles on Sabbath and holidays, make it mandatory that they live near their places of worship.

The Reverend Heron Sam, who has lived in Crown Heights for quite some time, discusses his problem with the Hasidim on the question of housing. In the August 31, 1991, edition of the *Amsterdam News*, Vinette Price wrote:

> A 50-year old resident of Crown Heights sat on his stoop Saturday talking with fellow Jamaicans and relating the problems he endured as a homeowner and neighbor to Orthodox Jews who have replaced Caribbean homeowners whom he said were "at the left and right" of him not so long ago.
>
> Intimidated and fearful of reprisal, he said he had been approached to sell his house with offers of cash, friendly persuasion and regular visits before "things started to get nasty."
>
> He said phone calls, harassment and provocation persist; but he [would] not give up the last of his homes that he purchased and rented out as a rooming quarter for new immigrants during the 1930's and '40's.
>
> "I am in my 20th year here as the spiritual leader of the largest predominately Black church in Crown Heights," said Rev. Canon Heron A. Sam, rector of St. Marks Episcopal church, taking time out of his chat with community residents to speak with AmNews.

In the September 7, 1991, edition of the *Amsterdam News*, in an article written by David Hatchett, there are more complaints about housing.

> A number of Black leaders in Crown Heights say that the area's Hasidic Jewish community has used its special access to municipal government to get opportunities to purchase city-owned buildings and other property at the expense of the

neighborhood's majority Black and Latino population

".... There are constant complaints that there have been many abandoned buildings in the community which have been rehabilitated and few of them have gone to black people," states Una Clarke, president of the Caribbean American Political Association and a candidate for City Council from the area.

"Under previous city administrations, there was a steering of housing toward the Hasidim," states Assemblyman Clarence Norman, whose district is centered in Crown Heights. "We do not know the exact mechanism, because we were not in the room, but we do know the result."

Of course city officials and Hasidic leaders deny this to be true. They claim it is all perception.

## STREET CLOSINGS

Another problem is the closing of streets on the Lubavitcher Sabbath and Holy Days, which inconveniences the rest of the community and creates a climate in which violent confrontation occurs not only between Hasidim and Blacks, but sometimes between Hasidim and Police, and sometimes between all the above parties.

For years, Dr. Rufus Nichols, who lives and works several doors from the Lubavitcher headquarters on Eastern Parkway, has had many confrontations with the Hasidim. In the October 17, 1991, edition of the *Daily News*, he complained that his patients, some of them pregnant, could not get to and from his office on the Hasidim's Sabbath and Holy Days. Even his wife was arrested as she sought to return home after shopping. The Hasidim do not deny taking over the streets. They say they do it for safety reasons. What other religion consistently takes over the street on their Sabbath and holidays, with the cooperation of the city, I might add? Also for many years Dr. Cave has complained about the street closings. In his same letter to Mr. Fletcher H. Graves, referenced above, Dr. Cave wrote,

At least one public street has for years been closed by sign and police presence on the Jewish sabbath. This discriminatory policy was not a decision of the local precinct but was on orders from City Hall. These closings also occur on special Hasidic days other than their Sabbath.

In fact, on Tuesday, September 17, 1991, while tensions were still high, there was a melee between the police and the Hasidim. The Hasidim took over a street, a woman and her children were surrounded. The Hasidim began to rock the car where the woman sat petrified. When the police arrived, they were attacked, and four officers were injured, police helmets and radios were taken. No Hasid was hurt or arrested, and there was no demand to get tough with the Hasidim. In fact, just the opposite. There appeared to be a cover-up. The public was not informed of the incident by the press until Thursday, September 19, 1991. And then only because Dominic Carter of WLIB was secretly informed about the incident and raised the question in a September 18, 1991 news conference with the Mayor Dinkins. The whole incident was downplayed.

In the October 26, 1991, edition of the *Amsterdam News*, Vinette Price reports on a "heated public meeting" between Black Crown Heights long time residents, most of them elderly, and police. They complained about the takeover of the streets by the Hasidim, among other things. Significantly, none of the terrible characters that some people like to "beat up on" or blame for all the problems in the city, and/or the disruption of the great harmony between Blacks and Jews was present, patently revealing that the problem is not "outsiders." Crown Heights residents have minds of their own. It is really an insult to say to Blacks in Crown Heights, "You cannot think for yourselves, you need someone else to tell you how you feel and what you should do."

The ultimate insult is the imposition of the passes to enter the block. Long time residents, including Dr. Nichols, and their guests have had to show identification to gain entrance to the block where their homes are—homes on which some are still paying mortgages. To any person of African ancestry, South Africa immediately comes to mind.

## Hostel for Eastern European Hasids

Another source of irritation is the presence of some kind of hostel on President Street. For years Blacks have complained that zoning laws and common decency prohibited a hostel on this block. This has been another complaint lodged by Dr. Vernal Cave. Again, in the letter to Mr. Graves, Dr. Cave wrote,

> On President Street between Kingston and New York Avenues are two of the most lovely residential blocks in the city. The Hasidic have purchased some of these houses. In some instances their alterations have violated zoning codes. Among others, we site a detached house which has no number on it now but is between 1377 and 1395 President Street which formerly held a raggedly looking sign, "Free Friends of Refugees of Eastern Europe." Construction work has been done in that house. Many, many people live in the house. The terrible appearance of the grounds outside are in striking contrast to the well- manicured lawns of the beautiful one family house— which are not in code violation—which are indeed utilized as residence[s] and which are in compliance with the zoning laws.

## Private Ambulance and Police Service

Another bone of contention was/is the ambulance and the police car parked in front of the Lubavitcher headquarters and the home of the Grand Rebbe, respectively. The car in front of the Grand Rebbe's home was to protect him from the Satmar in Williamsburg, at least that is what we were told. We complained bitterly that this was preferential treatment. The car was removed for awhile and then returned, and we were told the funding for the ambulance came from private money, which was not totally true ... part of the money came from the public. Of course, things remained the same.

There is another extraordinary practice which was terminated on November 4, 1991. Each year, on the Friday night before Chanukah, Hasidic VIPs would light a menorah in Manhattan and then would be given police escort to the heliport for a private helicopter ride back to Crown Heights in time for the beginning of the Jewish Sabbath.

Oddly enough, the two items about which we complained, the ambulance and the police car, were the two items involved in the tragic traffic incident which took Gavin Cato's life. Perhaps if corrective actions had taken place when we raised these issues earlier, maybe little Gavin would be alive today and you would not be distorting my words and defaming my character.

## ATTACK ON OTHER JEWS

Another important point, other Jews have themselves been subjected to the violence of the Hasidim, as they tried to force their orthodoxy on everybody. In the October 26, 1991, edition of the *Amsterdam News,* in an article written by Vinette Price, she quotes Dr. Cave:

> He had seen many of his Reform Jewish friends driven out of Crown Heights by strong-arm tactics employed by representatives of the Lubavitcher sect who demanded they close their businesses on their most profitable day simply because the group dictated their Sabbath be upheld by all Jews.
> "Jews, African Americans, Christians lived in harmony for years before the black suits and black hats moved in," he said. "They are intolerant ... about trampling the rights of others."

In the August 31, 1991, edition of the *Amsterdam News*, Publisher Bill Tatum discusses the tension among the various Jewish groups. He wrote:

> While most Blacks are not familiar with this, the two most prominent Lubavitcher adherents, the Hasids of Crown Heights and the Satmar of Williamsburg, are as much an enig-

ma to the Reform, general Orthodox and Conservative Jews as they are to us. They are, in fact rivals and enemies.

The reason for the police escort for the rebbe stemmed from the time when the members of the sect fought each other in what was described as a "blood feud."

Not a single spokesman for the organized Jews in this city can speak for the sect, nor do they have the kind of relationship with them that could result in a dialogue between Blacks and Jews. Thus the only leadership has come from those who are now falsely charged with inciting the young Black people to violence.

In the same August 31, 1991, edition of the *Amsterdam News*, J. Zamgba Browne wrote about, "Letters, Faxes from the Jewish Community..." One letter came from a Jewish resident of Crown Heights named Alicia Lacher. Mr. Browne wrote concerning her:

Mrs. Lacher also pointed out in her three page letter that Jews in Crown Heights and other parts of the city are fond of buying buildings from Blacks and then renting the apartments to other Jews.

"They wouldn't rent to Reformed or Conservative Jews unless they repent and go to the synagogue on Eastern Parkway," Mrs. Lacher stated in her handwritten letter.

## ARE HASIDIM CLASSIFIED AS MINORITIES?

It is believed that the Hasidim are defined as a minority comparable to African Americans, Hispanics, women, etc. Obviously this causes confusion and resentment. What African Americans want to know is, how does a religious group get to be defined as a minority? And what wheeling and dealing and power plays were involved in obtaining this special consideration?

## IMMIGRATION LAWS AND SERVICES

There have been complaints regarding immigration laws and

services. Crown Heights is 60-70% Caribbean. What angers and frustrates these residents are immigration laws that favor the Hasidim who seem to come and go as they please. Nobody seems to interfere with their movement, while, on the other hand, people from the Caribbean encounter great difficulties trying to stay in this country.

They argue that nobody should be treated any better than they, after all their forebears' labor and bodies laid the foundation for the wealth not only of America, but of white Western Civilization. And when the wealth and freedom enjoyed by white Americans were threatened, their forebears died defending them and what they themselves did not have.

Also even in the assistance provided to immigrant Hasidim reflects preferential treatment. The reason offered for favoritism is their classification as refugees. Eastern European Jews are considered refugees, and this enables them to be the beneficiaries of certain goods and services. Food stamps, housing, etc. awaits Jewish refugees when they arrive. But the same classification does not apply to Haitians. Haitians are turned back, dying in the sea by the hundreds, because they do not fit the criteria as political refugees. Now that the Eastern European countries have disintegrated or radically changed their policy, now allowing freedom of movement for Jews, it will be interesting to see how this will alter the present immigration arrangement with Eastern European Jews.

There are many other examples I could cite to show a double standard, the arrogance, and the utter disregard to which the Black commumry has been subjected. But I think that I have illustrated my point sufficiently for you to get the picture. Again, I do not remember the American Jewish Congress saying or doing anything during those times.

## APPEALS FALL ON DEAF EARS

During those days I appealed to everybody I could think of to intercede before it was too late. In June 1978, I even wrote to the President Jimmy Carter, but to no avail! We even persuaded the Executive Secretary of the Organization of African Unity to comment on the situation in Crown Heights. The Jews who are now creating hysteria, where were they? If they would have put half the energy into resolving the conflict many years ago as they have put into whipping up the present frenzy, the eruption in Crown Heights never would have occurred.

There has never been any outcry from the Jewish community at large when we have pointed out the violence, manipulation, and misuse of public funds by the Hasidim. I am convinced that the Hasidim have intimidated most Jews, just as they have intimidated the police department. So the only time we hear from the Jewish community at large is when the Black community is attempting to achieve justice and then what we hear is "anti-Semitism" and "stirring up trouble."

I have urged for years: Let's have a federal hearing or investigation or something to clear the air once and for all. The Hasidim claim that Blacks get preferential treatment, and they are the victims of Black anti-Semitism and violence. They too want federal intervention. So why is there delay? Blacks want it, the Hasidim want it, so let's have it now! Let us have a federal hearing on Crown Heights ... NOW!

## REFLECTIONS ON AFRICAN AMERICAN JEWISH RELATIONSHIPS

On a personal note, it is interesting to me that I have not heard or read [that] Jewish and/or White leaders and/or journalists who were at the Cato funeral have come to my defense or to the defense of truth. Not one of them has said "I was at the funeral, Reverend Daughtry didn't say what you are claiming he said." Nor did any prominent Jewish or White leaders denounce the march in front of my home or the malicious attacks by the press and other Jewish and White leaders. How strange indeed, since Black people are often called upon to denounce this or that Black leader or this or that statement some Black leader is alleged to have made.

On the other hand people of African ancestry who were at the funeral are quick to point out how the same white/Jewish journalists and leaders twist and distort the words and character of Black leaders to suit their interest.

There was a support rally on September 31, 1991, held at P.S. 167 in Brooklyn, organized by Samori Marksman, Chairperson of the Caribbean American Resource Center, where Jews, Whites, Latinos, Asians, African- and Caribbean-Americans came to my defense. There was also a supportive letter which appeared in the *Amsterdam News*, written by someone I believe is Jewish or White.[7]

Nor did prominent Black leadership rush to my defense. The influence of Jewish leadership is so dominant that when some Jewish leaders launch an attack, whether true or false, some Black leaders start running for the hills or join the attack. I have had the painful experience of being assailed with groundless allegations by some Jews, and then feeling a chill or distance from friends, some of whom are supposed to be strong Black leaders.

It is not the change in behavior and attitude that is disappointing. For any number of reasons, everybody is resented by somebody, or some religious group, or some political or civic organization. But one would expect one's friends to say, "I need this grant, or I have to keep my organization alive, or I want to win this election. I need Jewish support. They don't like you, so I am going to have to put some distance between us." It is this lack of candor, this pretense that everything is as it has always been, that is the disappointment.

Jewish leadership knows that once they slap an anti-Semitic label on someone, however groundless, it will create problems for that person. Knowing this, some Jews recklessly throw the stigma on anyone who questions their tactics, programs, policies, or priorities, etc. When President Bush, in an attempt to gain peace in the Middle East, withheld U.S. guarantees for Israeli loans for three months, he was called an anti-Semite by some Jews. Some years ago, even Governor Cuomo had to defend himself against attacks of anti-Semitism.

The book, *They Dare to Speak*, by Paul Findley (Lawrence Hill & Company, Westport, CT), records a list of prominent Americans who dared to question Jewish programs or policies or truthfulness etc., and the consequences of their actions as they came under furious assault by some Jews.

In this connection, lest I be misunderstood, it should be stated that Mayor David Dinkins is a known supporter of the Jewish causes, in fact some African Americans accuse him of leaning over backward to support Jews. In derision and humor they call him "Dinkinstein." But I can say, no matter how intense the smear campaign against me, I have never felt anything but brotherhood and goodwill toward me personally from the Mayor, and a commitment to decency and equality for all people, especially people of African ancestry.

One of the reasons for the love/hate relationship of Mayor Dinkins in some segments of the Black community emanate from a perception that Dinkins has allowed himself to be used by Jews. In spite of his unarguable support of Jewish issues, reciprocity has not been forthcoming. This provides yet another reason for the tension between Jews and Blacks. There is the perception that Jews have said they are our friends, but they are always using us to promote their own interests or they reap the greatest benefits from the relationship or they are not there when we need them.

If they were truly our friends, the reasoning goes, then more would be done toward our empowerment where they are capable of doing so. In true friendship, the essential quality is unconditional sharing, which results in mutual benefits. On the other hand an exploitative, manipulative relationship, masquerading as friendship, reduces one of the members in the relationship into a pawn to be used and even in the most munificent gesture, there is a hidden agenda for self-aggrandizement with little or no benefit to the other member in the relationship.

212

The influence of Jews over Black leadership is derived primarily from money, that is gifts to various Black enterprises, and political clout. Money is king even in its ability to influence elections. The threat to withhold money and votes can make politicos, both Black and White, do amazing flip-flops. Also, there are what might be called social contracts. That is to say support from the various institutions which they own or over which they have influence, assistance in career opportunities and advancement, opening doors to valuable contacts and social status, and support on various issues. I have made the point often, when I have sent out a call for help on some issues, the largest contingent to show up invariably would be Jews. I was made sensitive to this point by Percy Sutton, former Manhattan Borough President, who once told me that of all nationalities, excluding African Amencans, and religions, Jews would [make up] the greatest numbers in demonstrations, and would offer the greatest support on all issues. Especially in the South, did this make an impression on him.

And because of this support, Blacks are indebted to and/or substantially dependent on Jews. In its worst manifestation Blacks are reduced to spineless paupers; pathetic "yes" men and women, who are always running scared. They bark when Jewish leadership says bark, and they bite when Jewish leadership says bite. They are the modern counterparts to [the] "Uncle Toms and Aunt Tomisinas" who sang and danced when whites needed them to do so. They knew that if they didn't, they could not get old clothes, house cleaning and shoe shining jobs, and would incur the wrath of their white benefactors. While we understand that sometimes survival forces demeaning behavior, the best these persons can get from us is pity, not respect. It is amazing that when there is tension or conflict between Blacks and Jews and the usual Black-Jewish dialogue follows, these are the same people who, for the most part, are invited to participate.

Let me re-emphasize that I am not referring to all Jews. I know that there are Jews who deplore this situation. They have no respect for this master-slave relationship. They know that if you can "rent-a-Tom" for two bucks, someone else can "rent the same Tom" for three bucks. If they bite someone when you say bite for a price, they will bite you when someone else with a better price bids them to do so.

There have been, and are, countless Jews who are fair, who are driven by a sense of justice and compassion, who are prepared to lend assistance wherever they can, and who are prepared to participate, as equals, in the struggle for empowerment, human rights and self-determination for African people, indeed all people, with no strings attached, and without trying to create and/or sustain dependency. They know that when they help others, they help themselves. That is the best manifestation of Black-Jewish relations, and it is this kind of relationship we should preserve and expand.

Let there be no misunderstanding. Nobody ought to blame Jews for using whatever resources they have to advance their own interests. Nor should African people—or any people—demand or expect assistance from any other people. All people should strive for their own independence, but should not strive to live independently of other people. There must be cooperation and there must be coalitions, if there is going to be the kind of world most people desire. But coalition and cooperation imply [the] participation of equals or, at the least, each member carrying his or her own weight. Otherwise, there is always the potential that the stronger will exercise too much influence over the weaker. Then we have a situation comparable to what someone said prevailed between whites and Blacks in the 1940s. He said, "cooperation between Blacks and Whites usually ends up with Blacks cooing and Whites operating."

In addition to the practical wisdom, mutual cooperation for mutual benefit, there is the ethical question. There is a Biblical statement that says, "To whom much is given, much is expected." So there is a challenge for everyone; no people can escape the moral responsibility God, or the Universe, or Mother Nature has put upon them. To those who have not developed their own potential: "do for self." To those who have developed their potential: "Do for others." And to all: "Cooperate." Where this challenge is neglected, all will be the loser, and the world will never be the place it ought to be—paradise.

In my opinion, there are only several significant African-American organizations that have the independence to resist Jewish and White pressure to conform to their wishes: the Nation of Islam, the Black church, Secret Societies, Fraternities and Sororities. It should be said potential independence, for many of these leaders have bartered away this freedom for various reasons, i.e. programs, grants, acceptability, access, and political ambition. However, because the resources of the Black church are derived from Black people, it has a freedom that can be awesome. This explains one of the reasons that Black ministers have been in the vanguard of African peoples' freedom struggle.

There are Black politicos who represent all Black or nearly all Black constituencies, who have an independence in some sense comparable to the Black minister. But the very nature of politics, the ambition to move up higher, the imperative of compromise for accomplishment and, in the case of Black politicos, the absence of resources or the unwillingness of Black people to invest in electoral politics sufficiently to free Black politicos renders the Black elected officials vulnerable to outside pressures.

The frustration that dwells in the hearts of African people everywhere is that, for whatever reason, we have not been able to develop our economic, political, and academic potential. Hence, we tend to lean too much on, and, therefore, expect too much from, other people. However, the argument can be made that given four hundred years of unprecedented devastation, whatever African people have developed or whatever progress they have made, is truly miraculous. There does exist a welfare mentality in a large segment of the African community. We have to admit that there is a widespread dependency syndrome among African people in all classes and all places. And when help is not

215

rendered or is terminated, oftentimes it angers the would-be recipient, who then lashes out at the benefactor, or there follows an argument on who has done what for whom, all of which adds up to more tension.

*   *   *

Now to return to the American Jewish Congress, let me pose a question. Before you issued your resolutions, would it not have been more helpful to arrange a meeting with me and whomever else was concerned to ascertain what was happening in Crown Heights, what my role was, where I see things going, and what will make for peace? After all, I have had on-going relationships with some of the members of your organization.

We could have had a constructive dialogue, and then if you still wanted to call me anti-Semitic or accuse me of inflaming the crowd or exercising opportunistic leadership, at least you would have acknowledged the doctrine of fairness; before you convict, give the accused his or her day in court.

Now, one thing more, if you find that you have made a mistake regarding my role in Crown Heights, which you obviously have, are you going to publicly apologize? And are you going to give as much dissemination to the apology as you have done to the resolution? And would you be so kind as to send me a copy?

## NOTES

1.  Given the concern in Black-Jewish relationships, I have tried to identify Jews where possible. When I write "White and Jewish leaders and journalists," I am trying to single out the actions, right or wrong, of some Jews, and how their actions contributed to the tension or helped to diffuse it. Whether it is written clumsily or clearly, when I have occasion to refer to Jews, I by no means intend to include all Jews. In any event, Ed Koch makes this distinction at least when he corresponds with me, and I have heard other Jewish leaders make this same distinction.

2.  It is revealing, that although Mr. Goldman spent considerable time with me in preparation for a positive profile which appeared several years ago in *The New York Times*, on the issue of Crown Heights, although he wrote several articles, not once did he interview me during the period of August 19-August 26, 1991.

Mr. Jim Sleeper, in the November/December edition of the *Tikkun* (Vol 6, No. 6), joined the posse. While he does not point to anything I said or did, nevertheless he called me a "demagogue" and became libelous in his claim that I participated in a scam. Significantly, Mr. Sleeper is another one of those Dr. Jekyll/Mr. Hyde journalists with whom I have had extensive interviews on many subjects prior to Crown Heights. But when the eruption occurred in Crown Heights, no interviews. Why? It was as if they were on a crusade, motivated by their own malicious intent, or perhaps sent by others, and didn't want to be distracted by such things as decency, honesty, truth, and accuracy.

3.  I have been told that Councilman [Noach] Dear appeared on a Channel 13 [PBS] TV program and called me a clown. I know that on a Channel 9 (WOR TV) program, on which I appeared along with Attorney Colin Moore and Assemblyman Doug Hikind, the Assemblyman accused me of standing before Lubavitcher headquarters on Eastern Parkway and urging the crowd to throw rocks. This is, of course, a lie.

Senator Al D'Amato, the Italian [Republican] Senator from New York, whom everyone agrees will never win an award for ethics in politics, also decided to join in the posse. In a march in front of Gracie Mansion and in the media he launched a vitriolic attack on me. He called me a racist and wondered why the Mayor was taking me on the South Africa trip, although he did hope that the Mayor would stay in South Africa.

Now I cannot recall ever spending time in the Senator's presence or conferring with him about anything. So where does he get his information or misinformation about me?

Channel 7 (ABC T.V.) was one of the stations which carried Mr. D'Amato's attack. I called the station, seeking an opportunity to respond. A couple of lines from my statement, which I read over the telephone to a producer, were read that night on television. Ordinarily, when a person is attacked, the media contacts that person far a response. After all, the media thrives on conflict. Not so in my case, I had to argue for time to respond.

Also [the] Monday, September 16, 1991 edition of *Newsday* carried Mr. D'Amato's fulmination.

On the same radio program, D'Amato lashed out at the Rev. Herbert Daughtry, pastor of The House of the Lord Baptist Church in Brooklyn. Daughtry was among those invited on the South Africa trip. "What was he going to talk about?" D'Amato said. "He's a racist."

Although the reporter, Mr. George E. Jordan, claims I could not be reached for comment, I had held a news conference earlier in the day, and they have all my numbers.

4. When the outsiders marched by my home, I kept asking the media to challenge the marchers to cite one example of anything I said or did that inflamed the crowd or that was anti-Semitic.

In the Monday September 16, 1991 edition, *The Bergen Record* did just that. In the article "March: Protest in Teaneck," written by Vera Titunik, one of the leaders of the march was asked to cite one example of my use of offensive language to Jews.

> Daughtry, who leads a Brooklyn church, was singled out for "applauding" the recent racially charged riots in Crown Heights section of Brooklyn, said Michael Guzofsky, a Kahane Chai spokesman. However, Guzofsky would not cite any specific examples of offensive statements made by Daughtry.

The marchers later made reference to my [Cato] funeral statement, when asked what I had said or done that was offensive.

5. It is instructive that when Yankel Rosenbaum was attacked in Crown Heights, he was taken to Kings County Hospital. Later, it became public that doctors did not recognize the seriousness of his wounds, and so [they] did not provide proper medical attention. Consequently, Mr. Rosenbaum died in the hospital.

There was a furious outcry and demands for investigation. Practically all public officials joined in the call for action against Kings County Hospital.

Yet many people of African ancestry had been complaining, demonstrating, and holding press conferences about Kings County Hospital, trying to call attention to the inadequacies of the hospital and the need for immediate help. They cited instances of abuse, ill treatment and untimely death, but little, if anything, was done.

What kind of signal does it send the community, when the death of one Hasid can move a city and state to action, where years of complaints and God only knows how many unnecessary deaths could get no response.

6. Dr. Vernal Cave's June 28, 1978, letter to Mr. Fletcher H. Graves, New York State Director of Community Relations Services, United States Department of Justice, can be found in Daughtry personal files.

7. *New York Amsterdam News* (October 12, 1991), Letters to the Editor section.


*"In praise of Rev. Daughtry"*
Dear Editor,
It is unfortunate that rather than attack societal problems we seem to attack the messenger.

My experience has been that Rev. Herbert Daughtry is a human being filled with compassion, concern for serving others, is fair and exhibits intellectual as well as spiritual honesty.

Several meetings where tempers were out of hand and reason was needed, Rev. Daughtry brought that reason. No, I am neither a close friend nor have I been asked to write this letter.

I am someone who has been a beneficiary of Daughtry's openness and righteous orientation.

When the Rainbow Coalition needed to hammer out a joint statement to bring all Semites (Jews and Arabs) together, Daughtry was there.

When there was a need to bring African-Americans and Jews together, Daughtry was there.

We always talk about living on Monday what you hear taught on Saturday and Sunday. Daughtry does just that. Those who attack him fear the truth. Let his light shine.

In faith and fellowship,
Robert Deutchman

# Related Correspondence

## A Response to the Media

〜〜〜〜〜〜

The House of the Lord
Brooklyn, New York
January 6, 1992

Mr. Edward I. Koch
New York Post
210 South Street
New York, NY 10002

Dear Ed Koch:

In the beginning of 1990, we began to correspond, primarily on the question of anti-Semitism. At that time I drafted a letter to you. (This will explain why some of the references are dated. I did not want to change the substance of the letter to make it fit present realities.) I then decided that the exercise wasn't worth the time and energy.

But with the eruption in Crown Heights, the same old anti-

Semitic bugaboo raised its ugly head, so I decided to finalize the letter as I had originally intended.

In responding to you, I am writing for the record. The allegations that you have raised have been raised by others, and no matter how strenuously I deny or clarify the allegations, they are always brought up at opportunistic times to promote the interests of my accusers.

Surely, you are all drawing from the same file. I hope in your last letter you emptied the drawer. If not, please make public the rest of the materials; don't wait until it suits your political objective.

Finally, I am going to include our correspondence in my Crown Heights report, which I will be sending you presently.

Now as I indicated regarding Jitu [Weusi]: He is my friend. A principled struggler. A coalition builder. There are many people from all ethnic backgrounds who will concur with my assessment of him. But he is perfectly capable of defending himself, and I will leave that to him.

Again, I never said, "We will get the Jews..." and I never said my refutation did not appear in print. I did not think it was necessary to cite or produce evidence of my refutation. I thought when two persons of integrity are communicating and one categorically denies a statement and goes to great lengths to explain and clarify the misquote, it would be unnecessary to produce anything. The other would accept the denial. Pardon me, but I forgot for a moment with whom I was corresponding.

I am enclosing a couple of places where I denied the quote, the *Phoenix*, a Brooklyn paper, July 13, 1978 and *The New York Times*, June 23, 1978. Everywhere I had the opportunity I denied the quote. That means electronic as well as print media. My correspondence with the *Post* is surely on record at the *Post*. I told you the *Post* blamed the [Associated Press] and never printed my denial. I don't see why that should be hard to believe, particularly given the history of the *Post* vis-a-vis African Americans.

Regarding the other quotes attributed to me. "We stand in the shadow of Hasidim who symbolize our oppression. And the next time Hasidic terrorists touch one of our kids we are going to tear this community apart." Both of these quotes are correct. Although they were made in different places but on the same march and rally.

With respect to the first quote, "We stand in the shadow ...," we have a saying in our church: "Before I take it back, I will add to it." The Hasidim did symbolize our oppression for all the reasons I cited in my previous letter. When they came into the community, even other Jews fled as they were forced to obey the Hasidim orthodoxy. The Hasidic lifestyle did not lend itself to a pluralistic society. Their expansionist tendencies forced Black residents out of their homes and apartments.

Before your disastrous years as Mayor, a group of us sat with then Mayor Abe Beame trying to dissuade him from changing traditional community lines to give greater power to the Hasidim. Of course, he did not heed our pleas. Consequently lines were redrawn to enhance the interest of the Lubavitcher Hasidim. Across the years there have been documented instances of abuse and bias. On and on I could go citing examples of bias and abuse. I will state it a thousand times and shout it from the rooftops that the Hasidim of Crown Heights symbolized the oppression to which African people have been subjugated for hundreds of years. It seems that every people have oppressed and exploited us. By the way, it may be of interest to you that I have also criticized people of African ancestry for allowing it to happen to them. The fact is, I have often pointed to the Hasidim as an example of how to amass power and have urged our people to do likewise. To develop power as the Hasidim did, but not to misuse it the way they have.

Regarding the quote, "The next time the Hasidim ...," I took a calculated risk with that statement. There were thousands of angry people in the march and rally that day. Many really wanted to tear the community apart. There were others, in which category I stood, who opposed a violent reaction. There were heated internal arguments as to what to do. I could have easily walked away from the whole thing and left matters in the hands of those who preferred a violent option.

I gambled on making the most threatening statement I could make in the hope that it would satisfy the violent wing or, if not, at least win over those who were undecided. I knew the statement would be emphasized and misunderstood by those who did not know the internal dynamic. Well, it worked. There was no incidence of violence. We engaged in a lot of strong rhetoric, but no violence. Not a soul was attacked. Not a building was torn down. And, in fact, no one, not even you, can accuse me of advocating violence.

My language at times was necessarily strong. I say necessarily because, when a people have been abused, those who have accepted the mantle of leadership must express the anger, frustration, and resentment felt by said people. I am sure you know what I mean.

However, you cannot say that the Hasidim never used violence. As I cited in my previous letter, there are numerous instances of assaults, including [those] against police precincts. Remember the one in Borough Park to which you hastened to beg for calm. The Mayor of the City standing on the steps of a precinct literally destroyed, pleading with the culprits, only one of whom was arrested. And you are upset because I simply verbalized the feeling of thousands of abused people!

I do not recall saying "the Hasidim were a kind of KKK." But if I said it, I will stand by it. It does express the sentiment felt at that time. I think the Hasidim of Crown Heights, in their actions and attitudes, manifested all the hated characteristics of the KKK. Now whether or not that was adding to harmony was not my primary concern. I wanted everybody to know what kind of people the Hasidic were. They who were trying to convince the world that they were innocent, harmless, and God fearing. And I wanted the world to know you were protecting them, rather than being the Mayor of all the people.

Now you pose the question: If the Satmar Hasidim of Williamsburg, who recently suffered the murder of one of their distinguished Rabbis, were to say about Blacks or others minorities what I said about the Hasidim in Crown Heights, how would I feel? As always you miss the point. If a segment of Blacks who embrace a particular philosophy or religion consistently attacked the Satmar, and consistently clashed because of special needs of said Black group (we are not talking about the criminal element; all decent people condemn criminality irrespective of who the culprits are), I would have no problems with the Satmar issuing a threat in the strongest language possible to the said Black group—just as long as the threat was directed to the Black group and not to all Blacks.

My language was directed specifically to the Lubavitcher Hasidim of Crown Heights, not to all Jews. What the Hasidim did, with the help of people like yourself, was to inflate our conflict with them into one against all Jewish people and issues, further exacerbating the situation, for it enhanced the anger of those who felt wronged as they observed their legitimate grievance with one segment of Jewish people turn into a battle with all Jews.

Regarding another quote, which you took from the *Daily News*, "the Rev. Herbert Daughtry aligns his Black United Front with the PLO and vowed to fight Zionism ...." Again I ask should not fairness dictate that before newspaper quotes are disseminated as a "thus saith the Lord," the person quoted should be conferred with to ascertain the accuracy of the quote and the context in which the quote was made? Specifically, should this not be the rule for people who are frequently quoted by the media? One thing I think both of us will agree, we each have been misquoted by the press.

Now to [address] the quote: I did not align the Black United Front (BUF) with the PLO. The Black community was angry [about] the firing of Ambassador Andrew Young, which was contrived by members of the Jewish community, on what we thought were feeble and hypocritical charges. Once again, as a leader it was imperative that I provide an avenue of expression. The logical place was the Israeli Embassy.

When a demonstration occurs, all kinds of groups show up with all kinds of agendas. That is one of the risks of demonstrations; they attract everybody, and if there are not sufficient safeguards the rally and/or demonstration can be usurped. When we demonstrated at the Israeli Mission, there were various Arab groups that joined. In fact,as I remember it, there were more Arabs than African Americans. They had their own agenda and we had ours.

With respect to the quote about fighting "Zionism," I cannot remember the context, but it was true ... Zionism, which I understand to be a political ideology held by some Jews. Some Jews, not all, were blamed for Ambassador Young's dismissal.

It is true that when I wanted to criticize certain policies, programs, or actions by the Israeli government and some Jews, I did try to make a distinction in my criticism by pointing to members of the Jewish people who embrace a political philosophy called Zionism. It doesn't require much intelligence to see that. So why is criticism of Zionists, for a particular action, labeled as anti-Semitism?

"How much longer can this country carry Israel?" is another quote you attribute to me. In this connection let me address another inaccurate statement you attribute to me: "anti-Israel." I am not anti-Israel. I am, however, opposed, as are some Jews, to some of the policies of the Israeli government. I think the Israeli government's reaction to the West Bank uprising is the most recent example. I believe that Israeli support of South Africa is wrong. And please do not refer to African states doing business with South Africa. It is an unfair comparison. Some of these states are land-locked, making them economically dependent on South Africa. They really don't have too much choice. Moreover, it is the quality of the relationship that is most important. The Israelis are accused of trading in the most sophisticated weaponry.

My position is that Israel should exist within internationally recognized borders. But [there] should also be a Palestinian state. I am convinced that, with the support of the "Super Powers," this could work. I believe that one day Israel and Palestine will each have their own states and I even believe that they will live together in peace and mutual respect, prospering together.

I do not believe in eternal enemies. History teaches that today's adversaries are tomorrow's allies. We have but to remember the configuration of allies and enemies during World War II. Our enemies of that war are our friends today and our friends [then] are now our enemies.

A question that perplexes and disturbs me is why do human beings have to shed so much blood and wreak so much suffering before we change and do the right thing? I have just returned from the Namibian Independence Celebration. I was honored to be invited by the President, Mr. Sam Nujoma. As I sat in the stands I could not help but reflect on lives and property destroyed to bring that day to pass. It should have happened a long time ago. So much could have been saved. That is my conviction, and that is my position.

Now I come to the question of U.S. support for Israel. I believe that the one sided support for Israel makes for strained relationships with the Arab world, feeds Israel's leadership intransigence, make enemies of Palestinians, and erodes moral authority. Most of the world believe that the Palestinians have a right to their own state, and that the U.S. government has been unfair in its handling of the situation. And there is a constant drain on [the] economy of the U.S. as well as that of Israel.

Questions persist about how much longer this situation can exist. Surely you know that I am not the only one raising that question. Most people I know believe that this country's relations with Israel cannot continue in its present state.

It is not anti-Israel to believe that. In fact, I could argue the contrary. Those who want U.S. policy toward Israel to continue with more of the same are really arguing against the best interest of Israel. They are arguing for what cannot continue to exist. They are arguing against history, to say nothing of arguing a questionable moral position. They are, therefore, anti-Israel. I am opposed to Israeli policies of gun running for tyrants and dictatorships as in South America.

Another quote regarding Black racism, you make reference to my conversation with Ken Auletta. When you refer to Ken Auletta, it is difficult to respond. He is one of the most notorious out-of-context quoters I know. Auletta does not just take paragraphs or even sentences out of context, he takes words. He will take a couple of words, wrap them in quotation marks and set it where it suits his purpose. More than once, I have been victimized by his deceptive journalism, and I would never place any credibility on any quote he employs.

Let me give you an example, with which you should be familiar. Sometime ago, in my correspondence with you, he quoted me as say-

227

ing "Jewish savages." When in fact, I was referring to the thirty to fifty Hasidim who beat Victor Rhodes.

The exact quote was, "...who uncaged thirty to fifty of their savages." The way they viciously assaulted a 16-year-old lad named Victor Rhodes, savage wasn't even an appropriate description. I think the gang of 100 Satmar Hasidim in Williamsburg who beat William Pickney into a pulp were savages. I would say the same to Blacks, if they had done a similar thing. The Bible says "if your works are evil, you are of your father the devil." If you act savagely, you are a savage.

Returning to the quote to which you referred: On the occasion on which the quote was made, I was trying to explain to Mr. Auletta how I define racism. I believe racism is a tradition, a mind-set, a worldview, a value system, and the power to create institutions and systems which sustain the privileges of those positions. I don't think Blacks fit that definition. Ours is a history of inclusion, of fairness, of live and let live. That is probably one of the reasons for our predicament. We have been too generous. When Europe and everybody else came to Africa, they found a hospitable people eager to share. Well, the history is too well known to need repeating here. The point is, racism, as I define it, is not some Blacks screaming at White folks in a fit of anger or in retaliation. It is an ingrained legacy of superiority, backed up with power. Blacks do not fit in that category. Hence, Blacks, by my definition, are not racist.

You can agree or disagree with my definition. But at least you have a better understanding of why I find debatable the issue of Black racism. This again underscores the need to confer with the person who is being quoted, instead of being like a puppy who picks up an imitation of a bone and running up and down the streets boasting about what he has found.

Let me try to respond to another one of these incomplete quotes. "Anti-Semitism is no stranger among Blacks," he writes. From your writing, I know you believe this. "Blacks are anti-Semitic, no matter what B'nai B'rith says," you once wrote. And that is one of the reasons I am convinced of your bias.

228

Anti-Semitism, I understand, is to be against Semitic people. Although some Jews have monopolized this term, Jews are not the only Semitic people. Similar to racism, anti-Semitism carries with it a tradition, a mind set, etc. Based on that definition, I contend there is little or no Black anti-Semitism, that is, hatred of Jews because they are Jews. There is no aspect of Black life where Jews have not been welcomed, and oftentimes some Jews and others have taken advantage of this openness and accessibility. Politically, economically, academically, socially, and artistically, African people have been exploited by everybody, including some Jews. If there existed widespread anti-Semitism, how is it that Jews have always been welcomed among African people?

What people like yourself call anti-Semitism is often group conflict, the legitimate interests of groups colliding. What generally happens in these times of tension is that people like yourself rush in with emotional, unfounded charges of anti-Semitism. Thus the real issue becomes clouded, making it impossible to find a solution.

Ocean Hill-Brownsville was a classic example. What started out as an experiment to give more power to parent and community people became an ugly mess. When Rhody McCoy and the school board tried to transfer teachers thought to be incompetent—precisely what the present chancellor, Mr. Fernandez, has argued for and won—there was opposition from the teachers union, which felt threatened by the experiment. They began making allegations of anti-Semitism. There were charges and counter charges, picket signs, demonstrations and walk outs, all because people wanted to experiment on how best to teach their own children. Jews were welcomed before and were welcomed afterwards. In fact, some Jews suggested [the project] and experimented [with] the project.

What I think is extremely unfair is that when African people, who have endured unprecedented devastation at the hands of everybody, from time to time vent [their] rage, they must defend themselves against charges of anti-Semitism or racism in reverse.

That, to me, is the unkindest cut of all. The victim [is] enslaved, colonized, exploited, denied human rights and opportunities, battered

229

from a constant stream of abuse in unnumbered ways, sometimes blatant, sometimes subtle, robbed of land, religion, history, culture, and language for four hundred years. Then when some event or issue or people tightens the screws on the victim so that he/she can no longer keep quiet, but is constrained to challenge and criticize a given people or situation with words, the victim finds that he/she must defend himself or herself against the allegations of being anti- this people or [anti-] that people.

Presently, there is a conflict with some stores operated by people of Asian descent, and there are voices calling it anti-Asian. There are ugly things being said. But is it really anti-Asian? I think not. There is no history of anti-Asian sentiment in the Black community. Originally the stores operated without incident. Most of them still do and will continue to do so when the conflict is resolved.

What you have are some African Americans who, weary with the abuses to which some of the merchants have subjected African people, have decided to do something about it. We can agree or disagree with the tactics used. But to make it "anti-Asian" is to further exacerbate the situation, rendering a solution more difficult.

Group conflict and name calling do not necessarily mean racism or anti-Semitism—much more is required. Now, you may agree or disagree with my definitions, clarifications, and analogies. The only point I am making is that anti-Semitism, reverse racism and racism [are terms] not so simple and easy to apply.

It was this I tried to convey to Mr. Auletta in my conversation with him, standing in the crowded Council chambers, surrounded by well wishers, trying to acknowledge their greetings and converse with Mr. Auletta at the same time.

Again you quote Auletta, "Knees begin to buckle when Rev. Daughtry declares, 'we need to look into Jewish influence within the NAACP....'" Whose knees began to buckle? As long as African people have been struggling for human rights and self-determination, the question of who is controlling or influencing our affairs have been a constant debate. Reverend Henry Highland Garnett and Frederick Douglass argued this very question over 150 years ago regarding

230

William Lloyd Garrison and the abolitionist movement.

Every Black leader I know or read about publicly or privately expressed concern about being co-opted, controlled, or unduly influenced by others. The question has nothing to do with Jews per se, it could easily have been Irish or Italians if they were in the same place as Jews. And I think any self-respecting people would feel the same way, and there is nothing wrong with it.

I wonder how Jews would feel if African Americans had similar presence and influence in B'nai B'rith or the World Jewish Congress. I wonder how Auletta would feel if African Americans exerted enormous influence in Italian organizations. Certainly questions would be raised—and legitimately so.

All oppressed people must develop independent institutions, organizations, etc. It is necessary for their own sense of self-respect to say nothing of the need for ownership. Help should be welcomed. But with the understanding that the help is not to perpetuate dependency but to promote independence. Yes, even from the helper. And if the helper is truly trying to help, they will understand this principle. Anything short of help toward independence simply feeds an arrogant paternalism in one and a servile dependency in the other—a mutually demeaning situation.

Moreover, African Americans criticize each other more severely on this point than anybody else. Across the years, African Americans have had a kind of lover's quarrel with the NAACP. You would be shocked at some of the names African Americans have used with reference to the NAACP. It is our oldest and most cherished civil rights organization, and my criticism and anger is that after all these years it is still not independent. That is to say, it has never developed a way of making the people it claims to service support them entirely.

Quite frankly, if after a number of years the people I was servicing did not think enough of what I was doing to support the organization or church, I would quit. People have to learn to pay their own way. If the NAACP is working for Black people, Blacks ought to either sustain it or let it go out of business. Agree or disagree, but that is my conviction. It is not anti-anybody.

Now with respect to Bayard Rustin [organizer of the New York A. Philip Randolph Institute]. Bayard was a rather pathetic creature. I really felt sorry for him. During his last days he would come around, trying to get involved but was not welcomed.

What I said about him was true. He had no Black base, no Black constituency of consequence. He was rejected in the Black community for precisely the reasons I have stated. He supported interests contrary to Black interests. I believe he was being used and would be forgotten when he was no longer useful.

That is the hard reality in the struggle for power. People use and manipulate people, set people up as spokespersons and when these people are no longer useful they are pushed aside or forgotten. I am sure you have witnessed that in your political life and probably practiced some of it yourself.

I can name a number of leaders who fit that description today. No constituency, completely rejected in the Black community, but they are Black leaders. What they are in reality are puppets, servicing the interest of other people, for which they are usually paid in the form of grants, praise, and acceptance by puppeteers.

And let me emphasize, what I said about Bayard and other people is not just my view. I am reflecting the prevailing views of that community. I do regret, however, that I did over-generalize in my criticism of Bayard. I surely did not mean all Jews. I should have said "some Jewish leaders," for that is what I meant, and we know who those Jewish leaders were.

I am not sure if my criticism is helpful, but I know it [is] the truth. Here is another quote attributed to me. "The police have failed to meet the needs of the Black community because of Jewish domination." Frankly, I don't know what that means. If I said it, I need the context in which it was said. It doesn't make sense to me, so I will not respond to it.

You criticize me for holding you responsible for police abuse of power and the condition of New York, and go on to state the number of Blacks and Hispanics killed during the Dinkins Administration, and accuse me of not holding Mayor Dinkins and Commissioner

Brown responsible. Therefore, you reason, neither should you have been held responsible.

I disagree. We have a saying: "like priest, like people." Leadership influences the people it leads. I have pastored the same church for thirty-one years. I accept responsibility for the priorities, values, ethics, and ethos of my church.

You were Mayor for twelve years. Your influence is stamped upon this City. Therefore, you have to accept the responsibility for a city that is polarized, tense, falling apart and teetering on bankruptcy. During your years in office you were consistently belligerent, pugnacious, and vindictive. You were always on the low road, always trying to pick a fight, setting one group against another, always cantankerous and mean-spirited. You were never healing, reconciling, forgiving—no statesmanship at all. And so you cannot escape culpability. You cannot scapegoat your sins away. You bequeathed an enormous deficit, not only in fiscal matters, but in human relations. Dinkins and Brown have had to deal with your legacy. If Dinkins leaves this City in the same condition in which you left it, I will be the first to criticize him.

Finally, in your pathological need to be infallible and reduce people to servility, you grossly misunderstood my hypothetical question about the extension of forgiveness, to my seeking forgiveness of Jews and Whites. Interestingly enough, you make a distinction between Jews and Whites. People have been known to be called anti-Semitic for doing such a thing.

I am not seeking forgiveness from Jews or anybody. I have thirty-one years of dedicated service to my credit, I am respected, and in some instances honored, by different people including Jews, not only in New York, not only in the U.S., but in different parts of the world.

I was simply posing a hypothetical question to you because of your unwillingness to see that you, as much as or more than anyone, need forgiveness. If Herb Daughtry, Jitu Weusi, Ed Koch, or anyone else says or does something wrong to someone ... should they be forgiven at some point? Should Ed Koch be forgiven for all the misery, hatred, and divisiveness he caused while Mayor?

In the thirty-one years of struggle, I have said and done things I wish I could alter. I am a public servant not a perfect servant. But that does not mean I am now seeking forgiveness from someone. My work speaks for itself.

Sincerely,
Reverend Herbert Daughtry
National Presiding Minister

●　●　●

August 28, 1991

The Editors
The New York Times
229 West 43rd Street
New York, NY 10036

Dear Editors:
Your article in the Weekend Review—The Region—"As Blacks Clash with Hasidic Jews in Crown Heights, Who's in Control?" by Ari L. Goldman, dated Sunday, August 25, 1991, ostensibly refers to local residents in Crown Heights calling me a demagogue and also states that I stirred up the crowd and then departed.

First of all, nobody spent more time in Crown Heights than I. In the late afternoon and through most of the night from Tuesday, August 20, 1991, through Thursday, August 22, 1991, I walked the streets. I prevented confrontations between the police and youths, and I talked to young people regarding the expressions of their rage in constructive ways. Only once did I make a public statement; this was Thursday, August 22, 1991, on President Street and Utica Avenue. At that time I was asked to do so. My utterance lasted for about two minutes. I urged people to come away from the sidewalk, where a confrontation was brewing into the middle of the street. My importunities lasted for about two minutes.

Sincerely,
Rev. Herbert Daughtry
National Presiding Minister

•  •  •

2 October 1991

Max Frankel, Executive Editor
The New York Times
229 West 43 St
New York, NY 10036

Dear Mr. Frankel:

Your article entitled "In Teaneck, Jewish Group Marches Past Jeffries Home," written by Robert D. McFadden, manifested some of the most reckless, irresponsible, shoddy journalism that I have witnessed in a long time. There are four points of criticism I would like to make:

1) Over a picture of marchers there is the caption, "Militant Jews March Past New Jersey Homes of Controversial Blacks." To whom am I controversial? Aren't you taking the words and actions of my enemies to describe me? Is a person controversial because other people disagree with him or her? The President of the United States has many critics, yet we do not refer to him as the controversial Mr. Bush. The point is, to refer to somebody as controversial automatically labels him or her. And since controversy carries a negative connotation, the label is disparaging.

2) In the article itself, Mr. McFadden refers to me as a "Black Pastor of a Brooklyn Church who has invoked inner-city racial issues for years." It is true that I have raised racial issues, but my struggle for justice has been far more comprehensive. I have raised questions relative to American foreign policy. I have supported the Irish struggle in Belfast. I have supported candidates of various religious and national backgrounds for local, state and national office. I have been involved in the issues related to workers rights, homelessness, bias-related violence, and the struggle for African liberation.

Mr. McFadden's reference, put in the context of his entire article, conveys the message that I stir up racial problems in the inner city, then run off to suburbia.

3) Mr. McFadden gives not only the town in which I live but also my house number and street address. I cannot ever recall, and I

236

have talked with other people [who] neither can recall when *The New York Times* printed the address of a person, particularly a person who is being attacked or whose home is subject to a march or demonstration. The most recent example is District Attorney Charles Hynes' home in Breezy Point. When the Rev. Al Sharpton marched in front of his home, his address was not given. I must say that not only was *The New York Times* guilty of this irresponsible and reckless journalism, but other so-called White media, which forces the question, Why? To me, Mr. McFadden and *The New York Times* were saying, "Here is where this controversial troublemaker lives; go get him."

It might be of interest to you that if your intention was to make me a target, to some extent you have succeeded. Hate mail; which prior to the march was never sent to my home, is a daily ritual. Vulgar and threatening letters, which had never before been read or seen by my wife and/or children, are now a daily experience. While I do not put the sole responsibility upon *The New York Times* but surely you must bear a large share of the responsibility.

4) *The New York Times* committed another act of irresponsible journalism. It did not give me an opportunity to state my position or defend myself. The paper was more concerned with what my accusers had to say. At 11 am on the morning of the march I called a press conference. *The New York Times* did not send a reporter, they did send a photographer, Mr. Chester Higgins. And as far as I know no one from *The New York Times* attempted to contact me after the march. It seemed to me that fair journalism would have dictated that:

A. I would have been given a chance to respond to any allegations made against me, and

B. That those who were making allegations would be challenged to validate their accusations. *The New York Times* did neither.

Had you been at the press conference, or contacted me, you would have heard me state that I defy anybody to state one word I uttered or one act on my part which could be interpreted as inflammatory or anti-Semitic.

Honesty [constrains] me to say that my respect for *The New York Times* has decreased considerably in the last several months. This I

237

say from personal experience. This is now the third letter that I have had to write because of misquotes and misrepresentation.

Significantly, I wrote you to on August 28, relative to an article written by Ira Goldman, in which an unnamed source (again somebody is quoted, criticizing me, without my having the opportunity to respond) accuses me of stirring up strife and running away.

Also, on August 19, I had to correct a misquote in a speech I made at Bethany Baptist Church.

I would hope the Editors of *The New York Times* would put an end to this kind of sloppy, irresponsible, reckless journalism.

Sincerely,
Rev. Herbert D. Daughtry
cc:Jack Rosenthal, Editorial Page Editor
Gerald Boyd, Metropolitan Editor

•  •  •

October 9, 1991

Anthony Marro, Editor
New York Newsday
2 Park Avenue
New York, New York 10016

Dear Mr. Marro:

Your article in the Monday September 16, 1991 edition, "Two Jewish Groups Protest Black Anti-Semites" was unfair and irresponsible.

First of all, I think it is questionable journalism to use the words of one's adversaries, although in quotations marks, as a headline to an article.

Second, nowhere in the article do I respond. Although, I had a press conference at 11:00 am, at least 2 hours prior to the start of the march, to state my position.

So any outsider group, significantly the media did not emphasize outsiders as it does when the outsiders are Black, can make wild allegations against a prominent clergyman respected by people of various religious and national backgrounds and the *Newsday* does not challenge the outsiders to substantiate their allegations nor give the targeted persons an opportunity to respond.

A third point worth making, all of the media made a point of showing my home. Some even went to the highly unusual length of recording the address and street name. It was as if they were saying, "Here is where he lives, go get him."

It has been a long time since I have seen such irresponsible, reckless and biased journalism.

Sincerely,
Rev. Herbert D. Daughtry, Sr.
National Presiding Minister
cc: James S. Toedtman, New York Managing Editor

•   •   •

239

October 9, 1991

Peter S. Kalikow, Publisher
New York Post
210 South Street
New York, New York 10002

Dear Mr. Kalikow:

In the article titled "FURIOUS SHARPTON VOWS NO MORE PROTESTS," printed in the Monday, August 26, 1991 edition, you state,

> " Colin Moore and C. Vernon Mason are complete and total sellouts" said Maddox. "How they could abandon a cause and not work to get their young men out of jail and to help us achieve our aims is just unbelievable." "You heard the man," said Daughtry. "Where is Moore? Where is Mason? Maybe they don't want justice anymore."

This is one of the most incredible examples of a reporter hearing his own thoughts that I have ever seen. Mr. McDarrah does not misquote me, or take my words out of context, he makes up his own words. I never said a word! [During] the conversation to which Mr. McDarrah is alluding, I never said a word! I have to believe that Mr. McDarrah wanted to create hostility [between] Mr. Mason, Mr. Moore, and myself. He did not succeed!

I know that this response is late, but better late than never!

Sincerely,
Rev. Herbert Daughtry, Sr.
National Presiding Minister
cc: Jerry Nachman, Editor

•   •   •

October 18, 1991

Peter S. Kalikow, Publisher
New York Post

Dear Mr. Kalikow:

In your Monday, September 23, 1991 editorial, "Where Are the 'Activists'?"—with picture and all—you mention a Garth Briscoe who was allegedly killed by two brothers. Then you take off in a typical *New York Post* tirade about Black leaders not touching this incident, because they can't use it to stir up hatred of Jews, Asians, Italians. You continue by pointing out how Black people are always killing each other.

Since I was among those Black leaders mentioned, let me first say I knew nothing about the case of Mr. Briscoe. But, had I known I still could not guarantee my involvement.

Second, since you ask, "Where were the 'activists'?," allow me space to tell you where I was, by giving you a glimpse of some of my organizational affiliations and activities.

I am the National Presiding Minister of The House of the Lord Pentecostal Churches, which is the highest office in our church. I have held this position, which entails local and national responsibilities, for close to thirty (30) years.

In addition to serving on a number of local and national boards and committees. I also serve as the Chairperson of the African American Clergy and Elected Officials of Brooklyn, which consists of almost all African American elected officials and a substantial number of clergy. I am also the Chairperson of the Association of Brooklyn Clergy for Community Development (ABCCD). ABCCD is engaged in providing new and renovated housing development, scatter-site programs for people with AIDS, and an experimental, residential program for mentally handicapped children.

Also, I am founder and President of "MAN To man," a big brother/little brother program to help African American males, ages of 13 to 18, who live in female headed, single parent households. Additionally, I am the founder and President of the African Peoples'

241

Christian Organization (APCO) [which] attempts to: (1) bring a Christian ethic to the struggle for human rights and self-determination, (2) provide a forum for scholarly research in African history, particularly as it relates to religion, and (3) support economic independence through the establishment of various enterprises. Finally, in addition to all of this, I have a wife, four children, and a grandson.

Everyday, all day, my office receives requests for assistance from all kinds of people (most of whom are not members of my church or any of my organizations), for all kinds of reasons. It is physically impossible for me to deal with all of them. So here and there, my staff and I select the persons, groups, or issues which have the greatest need.

Occasionally, I am thrust into a situation as in Crown Heights. I went to express my sympathy and support to the Cato family and found myself drawn deeper and deeper into the Crown Heights caldron.

Some of the things that I respond to attract public attention; most of them do not. I might ask, where is the press which basks in sensationalism—your paper the head of the pack—when I am quietly answering the many needs and responsibilities of my calling? Probably looking for sex, violence, and scandal stories, in an attempt to increase sales and extract yourself from bankruptcy.

I recall your interest in the Randolph Evans Memorial Scholarship Fund when you thought there were some improprieties. But when you discovered that for 12 years we had been helping needy students with scholarships and counseling, you lost interest.

The point is, I do not look for issues or people to help. They look for me. If I do not respond, I am criticized by the persons or group seeking help, and if occasionally I do respond, I am then criticized by persons like yourself.

*IF* there were no bigotry, *IF* the goods and services were equally distributed, *IF* the media, especially your irresponsible, reckless, racist pamphlet were more responsible, fair, and factual, *IF* the city bureaucracy [were] more humane and responsive, *IF* the police service [were] more courteous and competent, and moreover, *IF* racism were eradicated, *THEN* I could devote myself entirely to my pastoral duties.

A couple of years ago I gave public notice that I was resigning from the so-called activist life. I informed the public that after over thirty years of struggling as an activist, I now wanted to give more time to my church work, do some writing and act as a kind of elder statesman. This public notice has not, however, stopped the calls for assistance.

As for urging mourners to throw stones at the synagogue, I heard no one urge such an act.

Regarding the Korean grocer, a delegation of clergy and I were the first to go to the store—again invited to do so. We warned the grocer, whom we found to be arrogant and feisty, then we left. Although I believe that the grocer was/is guilty of assault. The only reason I did not organize a boycott was that my schedule was already full. Let me emphasize, I participated in no demonstration.

Moreover, the boycott against the two stores was confined to those two stores. It was not against all Koreans, as evidenced by the fact that other Korean stores in the same neighborhood were flourishing.

Significantly, the same people, your "paper" being the ringleader, who expanded the boycott against two stores into a Blacks against Koreans conflict (and you are still doing it), expanded a local conflict between Blacks and the Hasidim—a conflict which has been in existence for nearly twenty years—into a Blacks against the Jews, thus enlarging and inflaming the conflict.

I shall never forget that you tried to fuel the Korean/Black tension, by linking an altercation between Black youths and Vietnamese to the boycott of the two Korean stores.

As far as my role in Crown Heights, I challenge you to cite one word or act that I said or did in Crown Heights that can be interpreted as inflammatory or anti-Semitic.

Sincerely,
Rev. Herbert D. Daughtry, Sr.
National Presiding Minister
cc:Jerry Nachman, Editor

•   •   •

November 18, 1991

Eric Breindal
New York Post

Dear Mr. Breindal:

Your Tuesday, October 3, 1991 article, "Identifying Genuine Black Leaders," you wrote: "the fact that Herbert Daughtry warned of more violence against Jews—'I want to predict the same thing for Williamsburg'—doesn't disqualify him...." again reveals the incorrigible addiction to distortion and misrepresentation as it relates to people of African ancestry, which characterizes most of the *New York Post* journalists.

First, a point I find interesting, the Goldstein article in the *Village Voice* which you criticize didn't mention me. Yet in your distorted article you brought me into it. Why?

More importantly, one of the direct references to me in your article is inarguably negative in tone. The subtle attempt to make it appear that I am threatening all Jews obviously exacerbates an already tense situation and makes me the "boogie man," "the anti-Semite," or "the riot inciter." Let me emphasize that my appeal for quick action referred to Williamsburg specifically, not to Jews in general.

With regard to your saying, I "warned of more violence against Jews," it is very important to note that when I ask people to cite one example where I said or did anything that can be honestly interpreted as inflaming the crowd or as anti-Semitic, the only thing they point to is my statement at the Cato funeral, where I pleaded for quick action to prevent violence. And to my knowledge the only ones who have done that are Lila Weymouth, *Nightwatch*, (September 4, 1991), David Evanier, *New Republic*, (October 14, 1991), Eric Breindal, *New York Post*, (October 3, 1991), Robert W. Laird, *Daily News*, (August 29, 1991). Mr. Laird is not sure if what I said was meant as a threat, although he admits it was "helpful counsel." Mr. Ari L. Goldman, *New York Times*, (August 31, 1991), Councilman Noach Dear, Assemblyman Doug Hikind, and the outside agitators who marched in front of my home on September 15, 1991—surely an interesting collection of bedfellows. This really says that they cannot cite an example of an offensive word or action; they therefore have to make up something to fit into their sinister designs.

Here are my exact words from the transcript of the funeral, and while it may be lengthy I feel it necessary to include the context in which the statement was made.

> Well, I know I have been long on the history and I know some will criticize me but I don't want to see more of these occasions. I've been around a long time. Lord knows I don't want to see it happen again. We have got to rise to the occasion. And if it happens again, and it will happen again if we can't read the signs of the times and move swiftly and do something meaningful. If we can seize the moment, face the truth, confess our sins, our failures and weaknesses and commit ourselves to right the wrongs, to heal the rifts, to bridge the distance that separates us; if we can lay hold on the events of this day and allow them to serve the interests of justice and fairness; if we can take the tension of these days and not diffuse it but use it, then little Gavin [Cato] would not have died in vain.

> The Chinese character, you know, for crisis, I'm told, [also means] opportunity and danger. We have the opportunity to do the right thing. To end the abuse of police power. To end the double standard, the preferential treatment. Let justice be even handed. Let there be an equitable distribution of goods and services. Put the young people to work. Let's turn this midnight into morning. It is dangerous, yes, it is dangerous if we don't do something about it. If we let the events just drift and drift we will be back here very soon and there may be more fire next time. That was just a taste of what awaits on the horizon and the next time it might not be just Crown Heights. Look to Williamsburg. I want to predict that the same ingredients that brought the explosion here to Crown Heights now exists in Williamsburg. Let us move. Let's do something now. Don't wait until it explodes.

Also let me include another statement that I made at the beginning of the speech.

I want to reflect on the injustice and failures of bygone years. It's a thankless task, but I think I have earned the right. I do so not to inflame, but to educate and to appeal for change. Someone has said, "those who ignore the lessons of history are doomed to repeat its mistakes." Let us not ignore the lessons of history. Across the years we have had enough killings and destructions, abuses, conflicts, and injustice in this community.

Clearly, these are statements pleading for action to circumvent violence. Only a grossly biased mind could interpret my statements as threatening Jews, urging violence, justifying violence, or exalting in violence. I hate violence against anyone, and I try to prevent it. One of the ways to prevent it is to correct conditions which can produce the unwanted event.

Significantly, Bob Herbert, an African American writer for the *New York Daily News*, who was at the funeral has a completely different version of what I said. In the *Daily News*, August 27, 1991 he writes,

The most sensible comments at the funeral were made by the Rev. Herbert Daughtry. Way back in the 70's, Daughtry was marching against the double standard that applied on the one hand to the Hasidim in Crown Heights and on the other to the African American and Caribbean people in the neighborhood. Also in Williamsburg.

"We warned that the seeds of discord if ignored, would reap a bitter harvest," Daughtry said yesterday. The tensions between blacks and Jews in Crown Heights and Williamsburg were not secret.

They were written about in every newspaper and covered on television, but still the double standard prevailed.

Daughtry mentioned the notorious occasion in which a police precinct was put under siege by the Hasidim, and he wondered aloud what would happen if a New York City police station was ever overrun by a mob of blacks.

"I warned that there was going to come an eruption," Daughtry said, "that people were not going to take this." But no one listened.

"If we let events drift and drift and drift, we'll be back here again," he said. He urged whomever was willing to listen to do something now. "Don't wait until it explodes."

Let me convey to you what I perceive to be the ingredients in Williamsburg to which I was referring. Once there was the struggle around the public schools. The Satmar wanted to set up dividing walls in the schools. After an intense struggle, this effort was rejected. On the matter of housing, although they are the minority, they want the lion's share of the housing; the issue is in litigation brought by the Latino leaders. Again there was intense struggle. There have been attacks on police officers; Ganson Chambers and Hector Arisa. Mr. Arisa complained about the double standard and was transferred. There was the destruction of the 90th Precinct, Police Officers were hurt, but no Hasid was arrested or hurt.

A similar thing was done in Crown Heights in 1977 and also in Borough Park. Hasidim have destroyed Police Precincts, injured Police Officers and nothing happened to them. The slightest violation or apparent violation of the law by Blacks and Latinos results in beatings, jail, and sometimes death. Also in Williamsburg there have been persistent complaints of the Satmar Patrol attacking innocent citizens. In 1989, a young man named Pickney was beaten by some say 100 Satmar Hasidim, similar to the beating of Victor Rhodes, a 16-year-old Black youth, who was beaten by 30-50 members of the Lubavitch Hasidim.

In two separate meetings, I implored Mr. Andrew Maloney, U.S. Attorney for the Eastern District of New York, to investigate not only the attack on Pickney, but also the Satmar community. I tried to persuade him that they were a very powerful group who were in collusion with the city government and other powerful elements. They had used their power in violent, discriminatory, and oppressive ways. I reminded him that, in the South, when this was done by hate groups like the KKK, the federal government would intercede. Of course, nothing ever happened. Mr. Pickney will never return to normalcy. His father, some months later died of cancer. I am sure his condition was exacerbated by the savage attack which left his son unconscious. No Hasidim was ever arrested.

Finally, why didn't you inform the public that I walked the streets day and night trying to prevent violence? It is recorded in Peter Noel's article in the September 3, 1991 edition of the *Village Voice* and also the article in the August 23, 1991 edition of *New York Newsday*. Mr. Noel and others were on the scene and saw with their own eyes what I said and did in Crown Heights.

However, I know that this request is an exercise in futility. I am certain that you are not going to be fair and honest, even if God screamed in your ears. For the image of my quietly and honestly trying to prevent violence, urging constructive channels for discontent, bringing people together to find solutions, and appealing for swift and meaningful change does not fit into the concerted scheme to defame and discredit carried on by some of the journalists at the *New York Post* and [its] few cohorts and, therefore, you have tried to create another image.

Sincerely,
Rev. Herbert Daughtry
National Presiding Minister

Cc:Peter S. Kalikow, Publisher, *New York Post*
Jerry Nachman, Editor, *New York Post*
James P. Willse, Editor in Chief, *Daily News*
Robert W. Laird, *Daily News*
Bob Herbert, *Daily News*
Thomas Raftery, *Daily News*
Andrea Kannapell, *Daily News*
Max Frankel. Executive Editor, *New York Times*
Ari L. Goldman, *New York Times*
James S. Toedtman, *Newsday*
Jonathan Z. Larsen, Editor in Chief, *The Village Voice*
Richard Goldstein, *The Village Voice*

Peter Noel, *The Village Voice*
David Evanier, *The New Republic*
Martin Peretz, Editor in Chief and Chairman, *The New Republic*
Lanie Webb, *Nightwatch*
Lila Weymouth, *Nightwatch*
William Lynch, Deputy Mayor City of New York
Mr. David Hall, Editor, *Bergen Record*
Vera Titunik, *Bergen Record*

•   •   •

December 23, 1991

Mr. Martin Peretz
Chairman & Editor-in-Chief
The New Republic
1220 19th Street, NW
Washington, DC 20036

Dear Mr. Peretz:

In the October 14, 1991 edition of *The New Republic*, the article by Jonathan Rieder, entitled "Crown of Thorns" is so steeped in bias, inaccuracies, and hearsay that one has to wonder how a reputable magazine would print it. In addition to the distortions and misrepresentations, there is an attempt to implement the old "divide and conquer' tactic. Mr. Rieder made several references to what he perceives as the divisiveness within the African American community. I cannot help but feel that he passionately hopes that what he writes is what exists.

With regard to myself he writes:

Many prominent Caribbean leaders affirmed the healing of Hasidic-black dialogue. One of them, in sharp turnabout, decried the Rev. Herbert Daughtry's critique of "grinning and skinning" at Carnival as disrespecting Caribbean people.

"Many prominent Caribbean leaders affirmed the healing of Hasidic-black dialogue." How he would love that to be true. Healing?

249

What healing? This process has happened before, with the community returning back to business as usual in a few months. It is my opinion, unfortunately, the same thing will happen again this time.

Admittedly, there were some misunderstandings related to the quote attributed to me, which by the way was taken directly from the September 7, 1991 edition of the *Amsterdam News*. No one in the Caribbean community including the *Carib News* conferred with me about the quote. When I spoke to the editor of the *Carib News*, and some of the Caribbean leaders the misunderstanding was cleared up.

If the matter interested you enough, and if you were fair, you would have reported my response which appeared in the *Carib News* (October 2, 1991), instead of picking out the line that suited your purpose and leaving it there.

The only point I was emphasizing was these parades, public displays of harmony, verbal declarations of desire for peace and goodwill really don't mean anything. We have all been that route before. The real issue is, is there going to be an adjustment to the double standard? And if so, when? And what can be done immediately as a good faith gesture? It is obvious I could not have been "critiquing" the carnival itself. For I was there, as I have been almost every year since its inception.

Then Mr. Rieder calls me "a scourge of Crown Heights and Williamsburg Hasidim." Yet I have never physically attacked or threatened anyone, or called for violence. Rather, it is the members of the Hasidim of Crown Heights and Williamsburg [who] have been the "scourge" of their own communities. They have attacked men, women, children, news people, and police officers. They have literally destroyed police precincts. Their acts of violence, intimidation, and manipulation are documented and publicly known. So who is the "scourge?"

However, if by "scourge" you mean that for nearly twenty years I have consistently pointed out the violence, racism, and hypocrisy of the Hasidim, and the double standard they enjoy, then I am guilty. And no matter how many lies and distortions you and your cohorts write, or how maliciously you attempt to defame my character I will not cease crying out against the oppression, exploitation, and violence perpetrated by the Hasidic people against people of African ancestry—indeed, all people in these communities—even against other Jews; Hasidic violence and intimidation have not been confined to Blacks, but everybody has been victimized.

Mr. Rieder also quoted me from the WLIB radio program. He wrote:

> On WLIB recently Daughtry, a scourge of Crown Heights and Williamsburg Hasidim, conceded that the problem was not the Jews, "What is it with us? We need to take a long hard look at ... our own lethargy, our disillusionment with the system." The Lubavitchers are practicing ethnic power in a form that black power advocates would be happy to achieve.

It is interesting that I quickly became credible when I criticized Black people. If Mr. Rieder would have engaged in a little honest research, he would have found that I have always been critical of my people.

For example, in 1976, the community planning board district lines were redrawn (some say illegally) to empower the Hasidim. Obviously Black people were furious at this incident of favoritism, I added my voice to the chorus of denunciation of the Hasidim and others, including city officials, who participated in the power grab. But in a sermon I preached Sunday, December 26, 1976, entitled "The Agony of Powerlessness," I criticized Blacks and Hasidim.

In *The New York Times* (December 28, 1976), Mr. Francis X. Clines in his column quotes me:

> "I said that the Hasidim had demonstrated real power-power that they actualized, but that black power advocates could only conceptualize and verbalize these last 10 years and that we needed to learn some things from the Hasidim," the minister said. "Power is not a statement over the news media; it has to do with organizing people."

I have been consistent in criticizing everybody, African Americans, Jews, Latino, etc. The difference is that when you criticize some Jews,

251

you are labeled by some Jews as anti-Semitic.

You could have also stated that when I was asked on the same radio station, WLIB, August 27, 1991, if I believed that Jews and Blacks could work together, I responded affirmatively—although I thought it would be more difficult with the Hasidim. I said, "I am addicted to hope, and I know if we are going to make this world a better place we have to work with other people." This has been my consistent theme, my life's work. It should be noted I said that amid much ridicule. Many in the Black community have become so disillusioned with coalitions that any talk of working with other people is met with rejection.

What I have said to others I say to you. Would to God you and others who have subjected me to this sustained, malicious vilification put as much time into research, truth, and accuracy as you have put into misinformation and distortion of persons and events.

Sincerely,
Rev. Herbert D. Daughtry
National Presiding Minister
cc: Mr. Jonathan Rieder

• • •

December 24, 1991

Mr. Martin Peretz
Chairman and Editor-in-Chief
The New Republic

Dear Mr. Peretz:

In the October 14, 1991 edition of *The New Republic* magazine, Mr. David Evanier writes, "the Rev. Herbert Daughtry called for more violence: 'I want to predict the same thing in Williamsburg' (another Hasidic community in Brooklyn)." I am not sure if Mr. Evanier was at the funeral of Gavin Cato. And if he was, he must have been wearing the most defective heating device known to humankind.

Here are my exact words, taken from the transcript of the funeral, and while it may be lengthy, I feel it necessary to include the context in which the statement was made.

Well, I know I have been long on the history and I know some will criticize me but I don't want to see more of these occasions. I've been around a long rime. Lord knows I don't want ro see it happen again. We have got to rise to the occasion. And if it happens again, and ir will happen again if we can't read the signs of the times and move swiftly and do something meaningful. If we can seize the moment, face the truth, confess our sins, our failures and weaknesses and commit ourselves to fight the wrongs, to heal the rifts, to bridge the distance that separates us; if we can lay hold on the events of this day and bend them to serve the interest of justice and fairness; If we can take the tension of these days and not diffuse it but use it, then lit-de Gavin [Cato] would nor have died in vain.

The Chinese character ... for crisis, I'm told, [also means] opportunity and danger. We have the opportunity to do the fight thing. To end the abuse of police power. To end the double standard, the preferential treatment. Let justice be even-handed. Let there be an equitable distribution of goods and services. Put the young people to work. Let's turn this midnight into morning. It is dangerous, yes, it is dangerous, if we don't do something about it. If we let the events just drift and drift we will be back here very soon, and it may be fire next time. That was just a taste to what awaits on the horizon, and the next me it might not be just Crown Heights. Look to Williamsburg. I want to predict that the same ingredients that brought the explosion here to Crown Heights now exist in Williamsburg. Let's move. Let's do something now. Don't wait until it explodes.

Also let me include another statement that I made at the beginning of the speech.

I want to reflect on the injustices and failures of bygone years—it's a thankless task, but I think 1 have earned the right. I do so not to inflame but to educate and to appeal for change. Someone has said, "Those who ignore the lessons of history are doomed ro repeat its mistakes." Let us not ignore the lessons of history. Across the years we have had enough killings and destructions, abuses, conflicts and injustice in this community.

It is obvious that I was appealing for change before it was too late. To interpret the statement otherwise, can only mean that Mr. Evanier came to the funeral—if, in fact, he was there—with preconceived ideas, or he is badly misinformed, or he is a part of a concerted scheme to defame my character. Bob Herbert of the *Daily News* was at the funeral and wrote in his August 27, 1991, column:

The most sensible comments at the funeral were made by the Rev. Herbert Daughtry. Way back in the 70s, Daughtry was marching against the double standard that applied on the one hand to the Hasidim in Crown Heights and on the other to the African American and Caribbean people in the neighborhood. Also in Williamsburg.

"We warned that the seeds of discord if ignored, would reap a bitter harvest," Daughtry said yesterday. The tensions between blacks and Jews in Crown Heights and Williamsburg were not secret. They were written about in every newspaper and covered on television, but still the double standard prevailed.

Daughtry mentioned the notorious occasion in which a police precinct was put under siege by the Hasidim, and he wondered aloud what would happen if a New York City police station was ever overrun by a mob of blacks.

"I warned that there was going to come an eruption," Daughtry said, "that people were not going to take this."

" But no one listened."

" If we let events drift and drift and drift, we'll be back here again," he said. He urged whomever was willing to listen to do something now. "Don't wait until it explodes."

In the light of the above misquote, do you not think it would be appropriate for you to offer an apology?

Sincerely,
Rev. Herbert D. Daughtry
National Presiding Minister
cc:Mr. David Evanier
Mr. Bob Herbert, Daily News

•  •  •

January 8, 1992

Tikkun
5100 Leona
Oakland, CA

Dear Editors:

In his petulant, unwarranted, reckless, and infantile excoriation of people of African ancestry, Mr. [Jim] Sleeper manifests a supercilious pedantism and arrogance that is, at once, amusing and irritating. In our naivete, we thought that White and Jewish experts on African people had died out or, at least had become more knowledgeable, truthful, accurate, and respectful. But we slept on Sleeper.

Mr. Sleeper criticizes people of African ancestry for [the way] they acted toward other Blacks on issues ranging from Tawana Brawley to Dr. Leonard Jeffries to Crown Heights to the Korean Boycotts.

Needless to say all these issues created disagreements and tension within the Black community. Black people struggled with themselves on what constituted truth and appropriate response, all in the context of rising racism, escalating poverty, internal violence, ravishing disease, widespread drug abuse, bias related violence, and internal differences on everything from sports to politics.

The Tawana Brawley case almost tore the Black community apart. From beginning to end, there were continuing, heated arguments, threats, and charges of collusion with the police. Some wounds are still not healed.

Mr. Sleeper and his ilk added to our woes by trying to coerce and cajole Black people into adopting words and actions that were critical of other Black people. In some instances, there were arrogant demands that denunciations be issued even before the statements and/or actions of the accused person/persons had been analyzed.

However, it is satisfying that Sleeper can find only a few Blacks to commend. Mr. Sleeper and his ilk always can find, must find, a few leaders of African ancestry to ordain. God help those leaders. For they whom the Sleepers ordain, are rejected by their own people. It is better to be blasted by the devil than to be blessed by him.

What Sleeper and his ilk want is to dictate tactics, time tables, targets, and issues that Black people should adopt among themselves in their struggle for human rights and self-determination. In other words, bark when they say bark and bite when they say bite. But for those of us who vigorously reject the paternalism or colonialism of Sleeper and his ilk, our reactions fluctuate between amusement and anger.

So Sleeper threatens us, with the obnoxious gall of a spoiled brat throwing temper tantrums and hurling wild threats. Mr. Sleeper warns us that if we do not behave ourselves and do what he and his ilk want us to do, we are going to find ourselves isolated. Already, he pontificates in his smug arrogance and ignorance, we have alienated feminists, Asians, Jews, and Whites.

As one who has been active on many issues with many different kinds of people, I have seen and participated in many multi-national, multi-religious coalitions. One of the most recent was around the St. John's University sexual abuse case. That issue brought together representatives from various religious faiths, gays, lesbians, feminists, Asians, Jews, Whites, and people of African ancestry. I do not remember seeing Mr. Sleeper or reading anything he wrote on the case.

On a more personal note, Mr. Sleeper labeled me a demagogue in relation to Crown Heights. Yet he fails to mention anything I said or did. The reason is quite simple: there is nothing I did or said that Mr. Sleeper or anyone else can point to that was either anti-Semitic or inflammatory. In addition, Mr. Sleeper makes the libelous allegation that I participated in scams. Again, he does not single out one instance where this occurred. I criticize not only Mr. Sleeper for this reckless, irresponsible, and libelous piece of journalism, but also the editors who allowed it to happen.

It must be noted that Mr. Sleeper received a grant to support his research. It is amazing what one will write when money is on the table. Those who funded this effort should demand their money back.

Sincerely,
Rev. Herbert Daughtry National Presiding Minister
co: Jim Sleeper, *New York Newsday*

•   •   •

January 8, 1992

Mr. Max Frankel, Executive Editor
The New York Times

Dear Mr. Frankel:

Well, here I am again, with another complaint. This time from Johannesburg, South Africa, from where Mr. Todd Purdum has written an article entitled, "Dinkins in South Africa, It's Not Quite Clock Work," *New York Times*, Thursday, November 14, 1991. I found the whole article to be negative and concerned only with minutia.

Here in the midst of history-making events, indescribable poverty, superlative courage, significant meetings with Black and White South African leadership, and visits to pediatric clinics and the memorial for massacred Black South Africans, Mr. Purdum elects to major in minors. He writes about who snubs the Mayor, not who honors the Mayor. The number and work of security officers.

Especially regarding myself does this blatant negativism and this hatchet job become apparent. First, the description of me as a "fiery Pastor" is a questionable adjective. Inarguably, the adjective employed to describe a person depends upon how that person is perceived and what image of that person the writer wants to project. Mr. Purdum could have used another adjective: prominent, influential, thoughtful, etc. Mr. Purdum could have referred to me as the prominent or influential Brooklyn minister who has pastored the same church for over thirty years. He could have said, *The Rev. Herbert Daughtry, the veteran pastor, who for almost thirty years, has been in the forefront of African liberation struggles in general and South Africa in particular. It was at his church that Mrs. Winnie Mandela made her first public address in the USA.*

Second, the reference to me positioning myself for photo opportunities with the Mayor is totally distorted. On the day of our arrival, Tuesday, November 12, 1991, we visited the Baragwanath Hospital. As the Mayor was going into the clinic, Deputy Mayor Bill Lynch motioned for Dr. Betty Shabazz and [me] to follow the Mayor. A little later he told us to stay close. I thought it was the thing to do, after all, I am a Pastor. Should not the Mayor have close to him a clergy person, and a long-time friend? How does that become positioning for photos? It could have been written another way. Mr. Purdum could have pointed out that I was close to the Mayor because he was in a hospital. He could have mentioned that the children sang a religious song, and I joined in. NBC's Carol Jenkins immediately picked up the connection.

We also visited the house where there had been a killing; I, as a clergy person, was present then as well. There were several other times when I spent time with the Mayor, away from the press and everybody else. For example, on Wednesday, November 13, 1991, only the Mayor, Mr. Lynch, and I visited Mr. Oliver Tambo, President of the African National Congress (ANC).

Mr. Purdum could have said, *close to the Mayor was his long-time friend, the Rev. Herbert Daughtry. Several years ago, when the Rev. Herbert Daughtry coordinated the demonstrations at the South African Consulate, where the two men were among the first to be arrested.* He could have said, *The Rev. Herbert Daughtry, was very close to the Mayor, assisting him in distributing gifts at the clinic and in the village. He helped to coordinate the Mayor's movements and constantly offered advice.*

Moreover, after the first day I was no longer near the Mayor. By the time of Mr. Purdum's article, the emphasis of the trip had shifted to education, housing, and business which required other persons to be near the Mayor. That is so elemental, a protocol understood by everyone who is remotely associated with this process. I cannot believe Mr. Purdum was not aware that this is what was happening.

Third, the reference to pool shooting taken by itself is innocent enough. But put in the context of suspicion, it conveys the impression that I was doing something furtive, when, in fact, it was done before the entire delegation. I even invited the Mayor to join us. It could have been emphasized that pool shooting was a way of connecting with the people at another level. Mr. Purdum could have said, *The Rev. Herbert Daughtry, always trying to relate to people, whatever their station in life, picked up a pool stick and invited all to participate.*

It should be emphasized that at the restaurant, where I was seen at the pool table, a very important meeting took place. During this meeting a detailed account was given of the history and present situation in Soweto. While the press was barred from the meeting, there was plenty of opportunity to question Mr. Dinkins afterwards, as many of the press did. Mr. Purdum chose not to mention the meeting or any of the important discussion which took place. It was for a few minutes before and after the meeting, in a room adjoining where the Mayor met with many civic leaders from Soweto that I paused to play around at the pool table.

More importantly, why was it even necessary to mention pool shooting? Of all the issues which the Mayor was addressing, how pool shooting ranks high enough to gain entry into *The New York Times* escapes logic. Except, of course, that Mr. Purdum wanted to project an image of a fiery, media seeking, pool room hustler whom the Mayor brought along on this trip, which characterization not only disparages me but also the Mayor.

My point is this: It was up to Mr. Purdum or somebody to put a positive or negative interpretation on the Mayor, the trip, and my presence and activities. Mr. Purdum or somebody clearly chose the negative. Why?

I contend that no person of African ancestry would have written that kind of article. [For an African American view on the South Africa trip, see Earl Caldwell's article, *Daily News*, December 13, 1991.] That is why we say all American institutions are infected with the disease of racism. Whatever relates to people of African ancestry in particular, and the so-called Third World in general, is seen and interpreted through the eyes of [the] white male, religion, history, tradition, world view, value system, political and economic interest. By the way, this myopic and biased perspective is what we hope a "curriculum of inclusion" will help to correct.

When I put Mr. Purdum's article along side the recent spate of malicious, inaccurate, distorted, and negative articles written by others, I cannot be blamed if I believe that there is a concerted scheme to discredit and disparage me. Coincidence is too far-fetched an explanation, and the writers are too suspect to be trusted.

Sincerely,
Rev. Herbert Daughtry
National Presiding Minister
cc: Mr. Todd Purdum

• • •

January 21, 1992

Mr. Peter S. Kalikow, Publisher
New York Post

Dear Mr. Kalikow:
    In the January 11, 1992 edition of the *New York Post,* in an article entitled "When the Crime Is White on Black," you wrote:

> One member of the group was the Rev. Herbert Daughtry, whose distinguished contribution to inter-racial harmony after the anti-Jewish riots in Crown Heights last summer consisted of "predicting" that Hasidic Jews of Williamsburg would be the victims "next time."

Obviously you were not at the Cato funeral, where the speech from which you picked a word and sentence to suit your purpose was made. Or perhaps, you were there but had on ear plugs, or you were asleep, or you are just plain biased, or you have consciously or unconsciously joined the smear posse.
    Since I have already responded to the smear crusaders in many places, I will respond to you with a letter I wrote to your fellow journalist at the *New York Post*, Mr. Eric Breindal.
    Sincerely,
    Rev. Herbert Daughtry
    National Presiding Minister
    cc:Jerry Nachman, Editor
    Mr. Scott McConnell

# Crown Heights Post Script:
# David Dinkins

The 1993 defeat of David Dinkins for a second term as New York's first Black mayor, was one devastating result of the Crown Heights episode. Dinkins was blamed for the continued violence and rioting in Crown Heights, specifically for not applying greater police action. In fact, the Mayor was accused of restraining the police in the community.

There were two coded messages communicated in the accusation: *Dinkins deliberately handcuffed the police because the rioters were Black*. Therefore, *this Black mayor must be removed*.

One of the reasons Dinkins had been elected in the first place was to keep Blacks in check; to ease the racial tensions which had reached the boiling point. During the election year of 1989, when a Black youth, Yusef Hawkins, was killed in Bensonhurst by a gang of Whites, the city was in turmoil. If Dinkins could not keep things cool, he was of no use.

## KOREAN BOYCOTT

Added to the tensions of Crown Heights, was the Black boycott of two Korean stores. In one case, a Haitian woman accused a Korean merchant of assaulting her. I was called at my church to investigate the matter. At the time I was in a meeting with clergy. I asked them to accompany me to the store, and they readily agreed to do so. When we arrived, we asked the merchant to give his version of the story. After hearing both sides, I came to the conclusion that the woman's accusation was true, at least in part.

We decided to issue a stern warning to the merchant and leave it at that. It wasn't an easy decision to make, not only because we believed the woman, but because the merchant's attitude was so obnoxious we had to restrain one of the minsters as he argued with him.

Since my schedule was heavy, I had neither the time nor the energy necessary to organize a boycott. Others, however, were so incensed they initiated a boycott along with a militant demonstration. Calling themselves the December 12 Movement—after the date of their involvement in the Tawana Brawley case[1]—the group was led by Robert "Sonny" Carson (aka Abubedika) and Viola Plummer, both long-time activists. They continued the boycott until the merchant closed his store.

Again Dinkins was accused of restraining the police because the boycotters were Black. These two incidents—Crown Heights and the Korean store boycotts—gave Dinkins' enemies enough fodder for their cannon, and the cannon fired away, massively and mercilessly, shooting Dinkins down. Given even the most cursory examination of the two incidents, one can easily discern hatred, deception, and chicanery, and racism.

## REALPOLITIK

In the days following the Crown Heights rioting, most of the press and even the Hasidim applauded Dinkins for his handling of events there.

In the West Indian Day parade (the largest in the city), which takes place on Labor Day, Dinkins and Black leaders marched for the first time with Hasidic leaders in a show of unity. But something shattered this harmony; what was it?

Lemrick Nelson, a Black youth accused of participating in the killing of a rabbinical student, Yankel Rosenbaum, was acquitted. This infuriated the Hasidic leadership, who in turn began to inflame the situation again, regurgitating all the explosive rhetoric and using their considerable influence to reopen old wounds and revive the fears and suspicions of the Jewish community, and swaying public opinion at large.

People who only a few months earlier had applauded Dinkins were now criticizing him. There was no difference in Dinkins' behavior—from the laudatory days to the castigating days—to warrant such an incredible flip-flop. Of course, tied into this reaction of hatred and racism was politics. It was, after all, an election year.

Caving in to the pressure was New York Governor Mario Cuomo, a friend of the Hasidim. Cuomo had only lukewarm support for Dinkins all along, and many Black leaders had come to believe that Cuomo was prepared to throw Dinkins overboard, or, at the very least, was not prepared to risk his own election for Dinkins. There were ominous hints that the gubernatorial race would not be an easy one for Cuomo. So as the Governor surveyed the scene, seeing the incumbent Black mayor (who had won by only a few percentage points over a Jewish mayor, Koch, in the last election) embroiled in heated debate with White, Jewish, and Asian groups, his support dwindling among traditional liberal supporters, Cuomo decided to back away from Dinkins. In addition, he *knew* (or thought he knew) he had the Black vote already locked up. Moreover, this time Dinkins would be running against an Italian candidate, Rudolph Giuliani. It is reasonable to conclude that Cuomo was under enormous pressure from the Italian community to support Giuliani (though a Republican) or to do nothing to hinder his success.

Cuomo's unenthusiastic and clearly ambivalent support for Dinkins should have had no effect, for after all, Cuomo's popularity was waning too. But Cuomo went on to show his *true colors*. A few days before the election, he issued a report highly critical of Dinkins' handling of Crown Heights. Then he tried to convince Dinkins supporters that this wasn't going to really hurt Dinkins; rather it would bolster him with the voters. One wit commented, "the Governor is peeing in our face, which is awful enough; but now he wants us to believe it's rain."

Realizing that the highly critical report would generate a great deal of resentment in the Black community, the Governor's office called Black leaders to a briefing at Manhattan's World Trade Center before the report was to be released. Interesting! If Cuomo honestly believed that the report would help, why the briefing? But the larger question was, why did Cuomo find it necessary to issue his report just a few days before the election? Its release could have waited a few months, a few weeks, or even a few days.

The Governor's contradictory action and statements made it crystal clear; either he was against Dinkins, or he wasn't going to help him.

In the end, Rudolph Giuliani won the election. Or is it that Dinkins lost it? For despite all the shenanigans, the outcome was in the hands of people of African ancestry. On Election night, after a hard day of campaigning, I went to the Dinkins headquarters. I asked Bill Lynch, Dinkins' campaign manager, for an honest assessment of our chances. His reply was, "It's in our hands. If we vote our potential, we win."

Unfortunately, tragically, the enthusiasm for Dinkins was not what it had been. While there were some Jews and Whites saying that Dinkins showed too much favoritism towards Blacks, Black were saying that Dinkins was showing too much support for Jews and Whites. Some Blacks even call him Dinkinstein. Although this allegation cannot be supported by his record, many Black people felt that Dinkins wasn't doing enough for the community.

There had been twelve years of the Koch administration's policies against Blacks and the poor. And Dinkins had only won the 1989 election by four percentage points. Even under normal conditions, neither Dinkins nor anyone else would have been able to meet the high, though unrealistic, expectations of Black voters at that time. Factor in ubiquitous racism, and years of deep suspicion and alienation emerge. So by and large, Blacks stayed home, the 1993 turnout in no way matching that of the previous election in 1989. In 1993 Dinkins received 380,000 Black votes compared to the 501,000 he won in 1989, a difference of 121,000. Guiliani won the 1993 election by just 45,000 votes.

Then, in 1994, it was Cuomo's turn. The Black community that Cuomo thought he had in his pocket didn't show up; at least, not as expected. The gubernatorial election brought an upset victory to little-known upstate politician, George Pataki. There was a kind of poetic justice in Cuomo's defeat. His loss was directly influenced by the disaffection by the people whose leader he had forsaken.

During that gubernatorial campaign, Cuomo received a most unusual endorsement. Guess who came to dinner? The Republican Mayor of New York, Rudolph Giuliani. That settled it. If some had merely surmised that Cuomo had made a deal with Giuliani, and had rejected Dinkins on that basis, this endorsement confirmed it. The tragedy is that the defeat of both Dinkins and Cuomo was a set-back for Black people. Mario Cuomo, with all his faults was a better advocate for Blacks than George Pataki.

## CONCLUSION

As stated earlier, another incident that dramatically influenced the 1989 mayoral race was the Korean store boycott. Somehow the boycott of one store came to be cast as a boycott against all Korean stores. According to some press accounts, and in White leadership circles, Blacks were against all Koreans and, by extension, against all Asians.

The fact of the matter is that Blacks organized a boycott against two Korean stores: the main one, where the Haitian woman was assaulted, and a store across the street (said to be owned by the same family). All other Korean stores flourished as they always had. Moreover, no matter how vigorously or eloquently we presented the facts (i.e., that the boycotts of these particular stores were isolated events), no matter how conspicuously or compelling the facts stood out for themselves, those who wanted to believe the contrary couldn't or wouldn't be moved. The reasons, for most of them, were power and racism.

While the boycott was in progress, there was an altercation between Vietnamese and Black youths in the same neighborhood. Some media and White leaders immediately linked that incident to the Korean boycott. I visited both the hospitalized Vietnamese and one of the Black youths. Neither one knew anything about a Korean boycott. Their dispute was personal, completely separate from anything political. Even when it was shown beyond a shadow of a doubt that there was no connection, the same aforementioned crowd refused to acknowledge their error.

The same crowd making the charge of Blacks against Asians had been making the charge of Blacks against Jews. The same journalists and White leaders who historically had shown little concern for the community-based issues of Asians and Jews, especially of the Hasidim, were now their leading advocates - against Blacks, of course, for whom they were even less concerned.

Clearly it was not their love of Jews and Asians that drove them, nor their desire for justice or peace. Rather, it was their love of power. They had their eyes on the mayor's office. And the distorted spectacles of Crown Heights and the Korean boycott gave them a powerful platform on which they could achieve that goal.

I cannot conclude this chapter without reflecting for a moment on the lust for power; the lengths people will go to achieve it, in this case, by racism or by promoting self-interests. The period under discussion was one of the most tension filled in New York's history. The citizenry was almost literally sitting on a powder keg. That self-seeking people played with lighted matches was dangerous, irresponsible, even suicidal. And that is precisely what some of the White and Jewish media and leadership did at that time. They did so by deliberate distortion and magnification of the issues and by pitting a people against one another, using lies, misrepresentation, and exaggeration, thus creating and sustaining an incendiary climate. The people, fed with constant dose of lies regarding each other, have not recovered and may never be able to do so. And for what reason? For racism, yes, but primarily for power. Had it not been an election year, these issues would never have grown to the magnitude they did.

## NOTES

1. Tawana Brawley, a 16-year-old, claimed she was raped and abducted by six white men in Wappinger Falls, New York, in November 1987.

# Appendix A

BLACK UNITED FRONT INITIATIVES
ORGANIZATIONS, PROGRAMS, AND EVENTS
EMANATED FROM OR INFLUENCED
BY THE BLACK UNITED FRONT (BUF)

## ORGANIZATIONS

**Black Veterans for Social Justice (BVSJ) - April 1978**
Founded and led by Job Mashiriki, BVSJ became one of the most viable organizations in the country, not only for its many programs for vets, but also for its stance on social, political, and economic issues.

**Coalition for Economic Fairness - November 1978**
The Coalition, for a time, sponsored the Randy Evans Scholarship Awards Luncheon.

**Career Opportunities for Brooklyn Youth (COBY) - 1979**
COBY was founded by Francesco Cantarella, consultant for Abraham & Strauss, with the assistance of Charles Innis,

Brooklyn Union Gas; Bruce Wittner, Con Edison; and Edward Richardson, IBM. They created a youth job training and placement program, locating over eight thousand positions.

**Coalition for Quality Education - 1979**
This Coalition succeeded in restoring African/Asian study material in elementary schools; from kindergarten through sixth grade.

**Project Youth Employ - June 1979**
The Project was organized to locate jobs, especially during the summer, for Black youths. Adeyemi Bandele, who had been International Affairs Coordinator for BUF and NBUF was the project's director.

**Black Coalition for a New City Government - 1981**
This citywide coalition organized Blacks for greater political effectiveness.

**African Peoples Christian Organization (APCO) - 1983**
The APCO charter was to synthesize the struggle for human rights, and self-determination, and cultural and historical awareness in the context of biblical Christianity. Charles Barron, who was appointed Secretary-General, had also been chair of the Harlem chapter of BUF. Later, Barron founded and became President and Chief Executive Officer of his own training and educational organization, Dynamics of Leadership. APCO is presently led by LeRoy Applin, one of the unsung heroes of our movement.

**Michael Stewart Justice Committee - 1983**
This committee was organized to seek justice for Michael Stewart, a Black man killed by the police. Eventually, the family won a law suit (including damages) against the NYPD.

## Eleanor Bumpurs Justice Committee - 1984
This committee was organized to seek justice for Eleanor Bumpurs, a grandmother killed by the police. Eventually, the family won a law suit (including damages) against the NYPD.

## Michael Griffith Justice Committee - 1986
This committee was organized to seek justice for Michael Griffith, who—along with stepfather, Cedric Sandiford, and cousin—was attacked in Howard Beach, Queens, by a gang Whites wielding bats and sticks. Griffith was killed in the process.

## Sisters Against South African Apartheid (SASAA) - 1986
SASAA, chaired by Dr. Karen Daughtry, created a six-point moral and material support program, providing substantial assistance in the struggle against Apartheid. Karen Daughtry, along with Julie Belafonte, chaired the women's division of the Mandela Welcome Committee. In particular, they planned and coordinated Winnie Mandela's itinerary during Nelson Mandela's first trip to New York in June 1990. Winnie Mandela made her first public statement at The House of the Lord Church, and the Mandela's daughter, Zenani, made her first public statement there.

## ACTIVITIES
### July 16, 1978
Over 5000 rallied and marched in Brooklyn to protest police and Hasidic violence.

### August 8, 1978
Hundreds rallied at City Hall in New York to confront President Jimmy Carter on human rights issues.

**September 28, 1978**
Thousands marched to City Hall to protest the policies of Mayor Ed Koch. Ten demands were posted at City Hall.

**November 6, 1978**
Thousands marched to Wall Street to focus attention on police brutality and on the economic plight on Black New Yorkers, particularly Black youth.

**December 11, 1978**
To highlight the genocidal conditions of Blacks, hundreds rallied at United Nations, presenting at 700-page document as validation. The lead organizations in the preparation of the document were (1) the Commission of Racial Justice of the United Church of Christ, Dr. Charles Cobb, Executive Director; and (2) the National Alliance Against Racism and Political Repression, Charlene Mitchell. Attorney Lenox Hines represented both groups.

**June 14, 1979**
Mobilization rally in Brooklyn in memory of Arthur Miller, who was killed by police on June 14, 1978.

**February 1981**
NBUF organized the National Hearing on Racist Violence in twenty-five cities. In New York, hearings were held at Hunter College. (See Herbert Daughtry's speech before the hearing: "Racist Violence, a National Phenomenon.")[1]

**April 4, 1981**
NBUF sponsored a national march against racist violence in cities across America.

## May 3, 1981
An estimated one hundred thousand people participated in an anti-war rally at the Pentagon. (See Herbert Daughtry's speech delivered at the march: "Struggling Against Madness.")[2]

## August 15, 1981
New York BUF celebrated its third anniversary with a rally in Albee Square, Brooklyn, New York.

## March 27, 1982
Over fifty thousand attended an anti-war rally in Washington Park, Washington, D.C. (See Herbert Daughtry speech delivered at rally: "What's Going On.")[3]

## June 12, 1982
Disarmament rallies and march: The rally began at the United Nations, then proceeded to Central Park, where another rally culminated the day's events; over one million attendees from across the globe, representing the widest national, political, and class backgrounds. This remains the largest rally ever held in New York City. (See Herbert Daughtry's speeches at the United Nations and in Central Park.)[4]

## July 22–25, 1982
Third NBUF Convention, Brown High School, Atlanta, Georgia.

## August 28, 1982
NBUF participated in "I Have A Dream Celebration," Dr. Martin Luther King Memorial Plaza, Atlanta, Georgia. (See Herbert Daughtry speech delivered at celebration: "It Will Take More Than A Dream.")[5]

**July, 1983**
Fourth NBUF Convention, Portland, Oregon.

**July and September 1983**
Two congressional hearings on police brutality: BUF was instrumental in bringing a subcommittee of the Judiciary Committee of the U.S. House of Representatives chaired by Congressman John Conyers, to New York in order to conduct hearings on police brutality. (See Library of Congress for BUF presentation.)

**July 19—22, 1984**
Fifth NBUF Convention, Chicago, Illinois.

**July 20—23, 1985**
Sixth NBUF Convention, Houston, Texas.

## POLITICAL CONVENTIONS

**July 20, 1978**
First BUF political convention, Masonic Temple, Brooklyn, New York: The delegates were elected to choose the slate for the September 1978 statewide election.

**September 8, 1978**
Rally for political unity within the Black community to support BUF-endorsed candidates.

**December 1979**
Black Agenda Convention developed an agenda that all candidates would endorse in order to gain community support; held at the Sumner Avenue Armory in Brooklyn, New York.

**February 1980**
Ratification of the Black political agenda Convention; held at Boys and Girls High School, Brooklyn, New York.

**Spring, 1982**
The House of the Lord Church hosted a convention to determine who would run against Fred Richmond in the 14th CD. All the candidates, that is, Rev. Sam Austin, State Senator Vander Beatty, Bernard Gifford, and Simeon Golar, all graciously agreed to accept the convention's decision, and Gifford was elected.

**September 1983**
On September 6, 1983, all of New York's most significant Black leaders gathered at The House of the Lord, in Brooklyn, to help Jesse Jackson decide whether he should run for President of the United States. BUF played an influential role in Jackson's decision, organizing to gain credibility for Rev. Jackson among the Pan-Africanists, nationalists, grass roots, radical, and revolutionary peoples and movements as well as reaching out to other segments in the Black community.

## INTERNATIONAL INVOLVEMENTS
During the summer of 1977, The House of the Lord Church spearheaded a fund-raising effort for the Patriotic Front in Southern Rhodesia (Zimbabwe). We succeeded in raising $5000 which we presented to Joshua Nkomo, President of Zimbabwe African Peoples Union (ZAPU) at the church in August 1977. In the context of limited time (several months) and resources and grass-roots focus, it was indeed a generous effort. Nkomo continues to the present to express his gratitude. While this was a church-sponsored event, it had significance for BUF's future involvement in international affairs.

## SUPPORT FOR SOUTHERN AFRICA FREEDOM STRUGGLES

Countless rallies, marches, demonstrations, boycotts, speeches, and fund raisers in support of the Southern African Freedom Struggles which included:

**Angola**—fight against Jonas Sivimbi and South African forces. Southern Rhodesia (now Zimbabwe) —the major rally against then Prime Minister Ian Smith's visit to the United States.

**Namibia**—major rallies and fund raisers in support of South West African People's Organization (SWAPO).

**South Africa**—In 1984 Congressman Walter Fauntroy, Randall Robinson, Executive Director or TransAfrica, and Dr. Mary Frances Berry were arrested at the South African Mission in Washington, D.C., while they were protesting against conditions in South Africa. This set off a nationwide jail going movement. Some of the most prestigious personalities in America were arrested, and BUF was part of the leadership that gave direction to the New York effort. Charles Barron coordinated the jail going activities. Other major efforts include:

- Free Mandela—a major program that called for 1000 men to organize and attend a rally at the United Nations for Mandela's birthday/Father's Day, June 15, 1985; thousands participated.
- I was a member of Mayor Dinkins' delegation that visited South Africa in 1992.
- Rev. Jesse Jackson, Bishop Emerson Moore, and I had an audience with Pope John Paul II and with the Archbishop of Canterbury to discuss more pressure on South African government;
- Annual Soweto and Sharpeville programs.

All of the nations we have supported have since gained their independence; save Angola, which was already independent, but needed assistance against insurgents. (See Herbert Daughtry's book, *All You Need to Know About South Africa*.)

## SUPPORT FOR HAITI, CUBA, GRENADA, EL SALVADOR, NICARAGUA, AND IRISH CATHOLIC BELFAST

Countless rallies, demonstrations, marches, boycotts, and speeches in support of Haitian freedom, Cuba, New Jewel Movement in Grenada, FSLM in Nicaragua, FDR and the FMLN in El Salvador, and Irish Catholics in Belfast. (See film: *"The Black and The Green,"* St. Clair Bourne, Producer/Director, which documents BUF's visit to Belfast.)[6]

## SPEECHES, LECTURES, SERMONS, ETC

There were countless speeches, lectures, sermons, forums, seminars, workshops in schools, in seminaries (including some of the most prestigious), in houses of worship, at community-based organizations, and at major conventions, conferences, and anniversaries.

On two occasions, I addressed the political subcommittee of the United Nations (See Herbert Daughtry speeches at the United Nations.)[7] There were numerous trips abroad to speak or participate in rallies, conferences, conventions, and anniversaries. The countries visited included: Bermuda, Cuba, England, France, Grenada, German Democratic Republic (East Germany), India, Indonesia, Iraq, Jamaica, Kenya, Libya, Namibia, Nicaragua, Italy, Singapore, South Africa, Trinidad, and Vietnam.

\* \* \*

Additional information on BUF and NBUF available through The House the Lord Church, 415 Atlantic Avenue, Brooklyn, New York 11217; telephone: 718.596.1991; fax: 718.625.3410. See also:

## BOOKLETS

- "Seize the Future" (two speeches by Rev. Herbert Daughtry)
- "What's Going On" (three speeches by Rev. Herbert Daughtry)
- *Pictorial History of New York Black United Front*
- *The Front Page* (official newspaper of BUF)
- *International Report* (the official organ of the International Affairs section of NBUF)
- *The Sermon* (a film produced by Bob Knight)
- 1980 Calendar (with pictures and important dates indicated)
- Posters and flyers announcing important events

## NOTES

1. Herbert Daughtry, speeches are available from Daughtry's personal files.
2. *Ibid.*
3. *Ibid.*
4. *Ibid.*
5. *Ibid.*
6. For information on *"The Black and The Green,"* contact: First Run Features, 143 Waverly Place, New York, NY, 10003, telephone: 212-243-0600.
7. Speeches are available from Daughtry's personal files.

# Appendix B

## THE BLACK AGENDA

### THE POLICE

1. As a result of the unnecessary deaths of Randolph Evans and Arthur Miller, we demand the following:

a. [That] all police officers at the scene of Arthur Miller's death be suspended immediately and remain suspended until a thorough investigation of the murder be expedited and the killer or killers be brought to justice;

b. [That] three black psychiatrists be appointed to examine all police officers involved;

c. [That] the entire investigation, including psychiatrists' findings, be made public;

d. [That] a screening board be set up to evaluate the files of policemen about to begin assignment in all Black communities; and that the Black United Front be part of the selection process.

2. We demand a full-scale investigation into the 71st Precinct's preferential treatment of the Hasidic community and

a. That all discriminatory practices toward the Black community be stopped;

b.   That immediate changes in the staffing pattern be altered to represent 50 percent Black and Hispanic policemen.

3.   Model Precinct for the community:

a.   That the 77th Precinct be made into a model precinct;

b.   That there be a screening test for all officers entering the police force.

The Randolph Evans killing has established that the present system of selection of police officers is sufficiently defective in screening officers to permit a police officer to become psychotic for fifteen minutes, during which period he may kill innocent citizens. Therefore, we demand a total review of the New York City Police Department not only to eliminate psychotic and disturbed officers, but also to correct racial imbalance, to eradicate corruption, alcoholism, and drug addiction and to develop a law enforcement agency that will truly be a force for peace and order for all.

## HASIDIM

4.  Police Car

Equal protection under the law is supposedly a tenet of our society. Therefore, we demand that the twenty-four hour a day, seven days a week [patrol car] in front of the residence of the Rebbe Menachem Schneerson be removed immediately.

5.  Ambulance

That the ambulance be moved from its assigned place and be placed between Kingston and Albany Avenues and made available for all to use. That there be an investigation into the land takeover and abuse.

6.  Tax Exemption

There is widespread exemption from real estate and sale taxes on religious groups. Therefore, we demand that tax exemption based on religious grounds in Crown Heights be thoroughly reviewed to assure that only bona fide religious institutions receive these exemptions.

7.  Enforcement of House and Zoning Codes

Within Crown Heights are some of the finest residential areas in the city. We have noted, with recent migration, some deterioration in these areas. Therefore, we demand that there be enforcement of all housing and zoning regulations in Crown Heights.

8.  Street Closings

The street belongs to all the people. Therefore, we demand that the practice of regularly closing off service roads on the Jewish Sabbath and other special Hasidic days be stopped immediately.

There has not been equitable distribution of programs and services. We further demand review, reorganization, and continual monitoring of all city, state, and federally funded programs and services allocated to Brooklyn to ensure the proper distribution and use of such funds.

## THE MAYOR

9.  We demand that the Mayor of the City of New York take the initiative to have the Board of Estimates reverse the violation of both the spirit and the letter of the law; namely the violation of the provisions of the New York City Charter, as revised in 1975, and reunite the Crown Heights community by erasing the irrelevant line at Eastern Parkway and make Crown Heights wholly Crown Heights again.

10. The Albany Housing, a low-rent housing complex, is a part of Crown Heights. Furthermore, the Crown Heights Community Board in no way reflects the composition of the area it purports to service. Therefore, we demand if the Crown Heights Community Corporation is to be recertified for funding, that those funds not be allocated until and unless the lines are redrawn to include the Albany Houses and until a full, open, appropriately announced and conducted election of new members has been held.

# BIBLIOGRAPHY

Levine, Naomi, with Richard Cohen. *Ocean Hill-Brownsville: A Case History of Schools in Crisis,* New York: Popular Library, 1969.

Lilienthal, Alfred, M. *The Zionist Connection: What Price Peace?* New York: Dodd. Mead & Company, 1978

Siegel, Martin. *Amen: Confessions of a Rebel Rabbi, The Diary of Rabbi Martin Siegel,* Greenwich, CT: Fawcett, 1970.

Stevens, Richard P., and Abdelwahab M. Elmessiri. *Israel and South Africa: The Progression of a Relationship,* New Brunswick, NJ: North American, Inc., 1977.

# Index

South Africa, 69-70, 142-146, 206,
217, 226, 258, 260, 278-279,
285
Sumner Avenue Armory, 33, 276
Sutton, Percy, 49, 89, 122, 213

Torsney, Robert, 27, 29, 62, 65
Town Hall Meetings, 71, 73, 75, 77,
79, 81
Trager, David, 29, 67
Turner, V. Simpson, 80-82

Uhuru Sasa Shule, 35
United Federation of Teachers, also
UFT, 19-20, 22, 61
United Nations, also UN, 5, 68-69,
70, 102, 137, 139, 141-142,
147, 274-275, 278-279
United States Justice Department,
63, 200, 218

Vann, Al, also Albert Vann, 25, 27,

30, 33, 51, 77, 83-84, 86, 117-
120, 122
Varick Memorial, 84

Walker, Dave, also David Walker,
32, 174
Weusi, Jitu, 25, 27, 30-31, 34-35,
72, 222, 233
Wilkins, Roy, 41
Williamsburg, 62, 120, 183-188,
190-192, 202, 206, 224, 228,
244-247, 250-251, 253-255,
261
WLIB, 70, 90, 102, 172, 205, 251-
252
Worrill, Conrad, 35
WWRL, 49, 90

Young Andrew, also Andy Young,
141-142, 147, 225